Why Am I

(The Science of Sanatan Dharma)

By Udaylal Pai

Cover designed by Adhrika Pai

Copyright © by Udaylal Pai
All Rights Reserved. No part of this book may be reproduced or utilized in any form or by any means, electronic or mechanical, including photocopying, recording, or by any information storage and retrieval system, without permission in writing from the author.

"May all the beings everywhere be centered in happiness and joy, free from suffering; May peace and harmony prevail everywhere!"
- A typical Vedic Hindu prayer which espouses the universal wellness that forms the basis of Santan Dharma

Thank You!!!

Aiswarya Lakshmi
Devadas Kamath
Sahana Madhyastha
Sruthi Rajeesh

CONTENTS

Chapter - 1
Am I a HINDU? /1

Chapter – 2
Do You Believe in GOD? /9

Chapter - 3
The Immoral Hinduism /12

Chapter - 4
Incredible Ancient Hindu Temples /22

Chapter- 5
Are Hindu Temples Anti-Sanatan Dharma? /30

Chapter - 6
Gods - The Good, the Bad and the Ugly /41

Chapter - 7
Who Created the Universe? Is There a Creator? /51

Chapter - 8
We Hindus Have 330 Million+ Gods, Seriously! /61

Chapter - 9
Is Single God Theory Ridiculous? /71

Chapter - 10
Do Hindu Gods Eat food? /77

Chapter - 11
Stone is God, but God is Not Stone! /84

Chapter - 12
Are Puranas Real? /93

Chapter - 13
Anytime Hindu! /101

Chapter - 14
Dharma, Religion and my Muslim Friend /112

Chapter - 15
Why Should You Question Hindu Rituals? /120

Chapter - 16
Are You Superstitious? /130

Chapter - 17
Snake Worship and Idiotic Superstitions /137

Chapter - 18
The Clear and Present Danger for Hinduism! /146

Chapter - 19
Hindu Economics /153

Chapter - 20
Do You Believe In Caste? /163

Chapter - 21
Hindus Don't Respect Women! /172

Chapter - 22
Misquoting all Scriptures /180

Chapter - 23
The Truth about Sati Practice /183

Chapter - 24
Is Wearing a Bindhi Relevant Today? /189

Chapter - 25
Hindu Hypocrisy over Sex and Chastity /197

Chapter - 26
Souls, Soul mates and Other Funny Things /206

Chapter - 27
Are you a Sinner? /214

Chapter - 28
Ridiculous Spirituality, Useless Knowledge /223

Chapter - 29
Why Am I NOT Spiritual? /229

Chapter - 30
When Human Becomes Powerful than God /237

Chapter - 31
Why Am I NOT afraid of GOD? /242

Chapter - 32
Offshore Spiritual Harvesting Industry /250

Chapter - 33
Konkani Lullaby and a Tragic Goan History /260

Chapter - 34
Global Warming - The Curse of Indian Pagans? /269

Chapter - 35
The Gurudom - Easy Way to make Money? /278

Chapter - 36
Hindutva Politics /287

Chapter - 37
Is the Word "Hindu" of Foreign Origin? /295

Chapter - 38
Yoga is Not Secular. It's Part of Hindu Dharma /301

Chapter - 39
Does Hinduism Prohibit Love Marriage? /311

Chapter - 40
Marriage Compatibility /320

Chapter - 41
Is Horoscope Match Necessary for Marriages? /326

Chapter - 42
Hinduism and Child Marriage /335

Chapter - 43
Gotra System in Hinduism /341

Chapter - 44
Brahmins - Victims are penalized! /347

Chapter - 45
What's Brahmam? Is it scientific? /356

Chapter - 46
Hinduism Vs. Sanatan Dharma /365

Chapter - 47
Hinduism = Humanity /372

Chapter - 1

Am I a HINDU?

On the 23rd of April 2004, I was flying from John F. Kennedy International Airport, New York City to San Francisco to attend a press meeting at Monterey, California.

An American girl was sitting right beside me, near the window.

It would indeed be a long journey – nearly seven hours!

I was surprised to see the young girl reading a Bible, which is unusual for young Americans! (Later, I came to know that September 11, 2001 terrorist attack on USA had changed the mind-set of many American citizens. Many people suddenly turned religious, it seems.)

After some time, she smiled and we introduced ourselves to each other. I told her that I am from India.

Instantaneously, the girl enquired, "What's your faith?"

"What?" I asked as I didn't understand the question.

"I mean, what's your religion? Are you a Christian or a Muslim?" she elaborated her question.

"No!" I replied, "I am neither Christian nor Muslim."

With a perplexed look, she questioned, "Then who are you…?"

"I am a Hindu", I said.

She gazed at me as if seeing a caged animal. She could not understand what I was talking about.

A common man in Europe or US knows about Christianity and Islam, as they are the leading religions of the world today. But, this was not the case about Hinduism.

I explained to her, "I am born to a Hindu father and Hindu mother. Therefore, I am a Hindu by birth".

"Who is your prophet?" she asked.

"We don't have a prophet," I replied.

Keenly she enquired, "What's your Holy Book then?"

"We don't have a single Holy Book, but we have hundreds and thousands of philosophical texts and sacred scriptures," I replied.

She persisted, "Oh, come on…at least tell me, who is your God?"

"What do you mean by that?" I asked.

"Like we have Christ, Jews have Yahweh and Muslims have Allah – don't you have a God?" she asked wondering.

I thought for a moment. Muslims and Christians believe in one God (that too a Male God) who created the world and takes an interest in the humans who inhabit it. Her mind seemed to be conditioned with that concept.

According to her (or anybody who doesn't understand Hinduism) view, a religion needs to have one Prophet, one Holy book and one God. The mind is so conditioned and rigidly narrowed down to such a notion that anything else is not acceptable. I understood her perception and concept about faith.

You can't compare Hinduism with any of the present leading religions where you must believe in one concept of God. Other religions are known because they have been propagated.

Hinduism is 'Self-Manifested' and does not need propagation. Neither do we register our birth in any temple or religious institution, nor create records in religious institutions for marriages.

I tried to explain to her: "You can believe in one God and be a Hindu. You may believe in multiple deities and still be a Hindu. What's more – you may not believe in God at all, still you can be a Hindu. An atheist can also be a Hindu."

This sounded crazy to her. She couldn't imagine a religion so unorganized, still surviving for thousands of years.

"I don't understand…but it seems very interesting. Are you religious?" she probed further.

"How can I explain to this American?" I pondered.

I said, "I do not go to temple regularly. I do not perform any regular rituals regularly. I have learned some of the rituals in my younger days. I still enjoy doing it sometimes."

"Enjoy? Are you not afraid of God?" she asked.

I smilingly replied, "No - I am not afraid of God. God is a friend. Nobody has compelled me to perform these rituals regularly."

She thought for a while and then asked, "Have you ever thought of converting to any other religion?"

I said, "Why should I get converted to any religion, as I am not bounded by any rigid commandments. Hinduism does not bind you but frees you to seek answers yourself.

I continued, "Even if I challenge some of the rituals and faith in Hinduism, nobody can change me from Hindu Dharma.

Because, being a Hindu allows me to think independently and objectively, without conditioning… I remain a Hindu never by force or fear, but by choice and freedom."

I further explained that Hinduism is not a religion, though it has a set of beliefs and practices. Unlike Christianity or Islam, it is not founded by any one person or does not have an organized controlling body like the Church or the Order, I added. There is no institution or supreme authority.

"So, you don't believe in God?" she asked as if wanting everything in black and white.

I clarified "I didn't say that. I do not discard the divine reality. Our scriptures – Sruthis, Smrithis, Veda, Upanishads and Gitas (sacred texts comprising the central canon of Hinduism) – say God might be there or he might not be there.

But many of us pray to that supreme abstract authority called 'Para Brahma' in Sanskrit. You can call it cosmic consciousness or the force or universal energy whatever."

"Why don't you believe in one personal God?" she wanted to know.

I clarified, "We do have some concepts of Gods, and most of them are abstract and not a personal God."

"The concept or notion of a personal God, hiding behind the clouds of secrecy, telling us irrational stories through few men whom he sends as messengers, demanding us to worship him or punish us, does not make sense. I don't think that God is as silly as an autocratic emperor who wants others to respect him or fear him," I added.

I told her that such notions are just fancies of less educated human imagination and fallacies, adding that a major chunk of ethnic religious practitioners in Hinduism also believe in personal Gods, though it is not mandatory that a Hindu should believe. Lot of people prays like you, I said.

The entry level Hinduism has over-whelming superstitions too. The philosophical side of it negates all superstitions. Hinduism derives from Sanatan Dharma which is developed upon logical and rational thinking.

"Good that you agree God might exist. You said that you also pray. What is your prayer then?" She enquired.

I replied in Sanskrit, "Loka Samastha Sukino Bhavantu. Om Shanti, Shanti, Shanti."

She laughed and said, "Funny, what does it mean?"

I translated, "May all the beings in all the worlds be happy. Om Peace, Peace, Peace. We pray like that because we believe in Vasudhaiva Kutumbakam"

"What was that again?"

"It means the world is one family"

"Hmm…It is very interesting. I want to learn more about this religion. It appears so democratic, broad-minded and free…," she exclaimed.

I described, "Hinduism is too broad and vast to be called as a religion. Yes, you may consider it as a religion if you want - a religion of the individual, for the individual and by the individual with its roots in the Vedas that was created some 7000 years ago. It is all about an individual approaching a personal God in an individual way according to his temperament and inner evolution – it is as simple as that."

"How does anybody convert to Hinduism?" she asked.

I patiently told her "Nobody can convert you to Hinduism, because, as I said, it is not a religion per say, but a set of beliefs and practices. For identity sake, you can call it as a religion – but it is not exclusive one, it is an inclusive religion for entire humanity.

There is no single authority or organization either to accept it or to reject it or to oppose it on behalf of Hinduism."

I told her – if you look for meaning in life, don't look for it in religions; don't go from one cult to another or from one guru to the next.

For a real seeker, I told her, the Bible itself gives guidelines when it says "Kingdom of God is within you." I reminded her of Christ's teaching about the love that we have for each other. That is where you can find the meaning of life.

Loving every creation of the existence is absolute and real. 'Isavasyam idam sarvam' (God is present or inhabits everywhere) – nothing exists separate from God, because God is present everywhere. Respect every living being and non-living things as God. That's what Hinduism teaches you.

Hinduism is a loose form of 'Sanatan Dharma', the eternal order by the existence. It is based on the practice of Dharma, the code of life. The word Dharma includes duties, responsibility and privilege. The most important aspect of Sanatan Dharma is being truthful to oneself.

Hinduism has no monopoly on ideas. It is open to all. Hindus believe in one God (not a personal one) expressed in different forms or multiple Gods.

God is regarded as a timeless and formless entity. A person is free to choose any God and worship Gods in any forms.

Ancestors of today's Hindus said there are many paths to seek eternal truth.

And this truth is open to anyone who seeks them.

However, at a later stage many people or sections have been trying to make this as a narrow organized religion like the others. They are either superstitious or people who have turned into fanatics. It was British who classified "Hinduism" as a religion to represent non-Semitic believers in Indian sub-continent and then promoted it that way.

I said: "Religions have become MLM (multi-level-marketing) industries with an agenda of expanding the market share by conversion. The biggest business in today's world is Spirituality. Today's Hinduism is no exception…"

I am a Hindu because it doesn't condition my mind with any faith system. Hinduism has no fixed dogma to give us. However, it covers all. This freedom has allowed me to see it for what it is, instead of glossing over only the better aspects and turning blind eye to what is unfavorable for its image.

Chapter – 2

Do You Believe in GOD?

"Do you believe in GOD?" a Western atheist friend once asked me.

"Your question to me is incomplete, irrelevant and unessential..." I said.

"Why is it incomplete?"

"There are many concepts and beliefs about GOD. So, first, you have to explain your concept of GOD and then ask the question - Do you believe in 'this' concept of God?"

"I believe in NO-GOD..."he said, "but how come the question is irrelevant?"

"I don't have to subscribe to any belief, that's why. You already have a set belief. Belief has nothing to do with truth. And, whether you believe in it or not, TRUTH doesn't change..."

"But why is it unessential?"

"For, I am a practicing Hindu. The idea of believing in God is alien to us. Our ancestors and scriptures did not teach us to believe or disbelieve. We are asked to seek truth and experience the GOD..."

"In Sanatan Dharma, nobody teaches us to believe in god. The word 'belief' comes from a root lies — which means to wish or to desire. When you say, "I believe in god" it indicates a no-trust statement like "I wish I have wings to fly"...When you say "I believe God is omnipresent" you really mean to say, "I wish there was a god who is omnipresent"

"Many people who follow religions say that everything about GOD is explained in their Holy books"

"All Holy books provide you the concepts of the writers who wrote it. Those are just beliefs..."

"So you don't believe in beliefs..."

"Belief=belief, not truth. Belief has nothing to do with truth...It doesn't help you to experience the real"

"How can we experience the God?"

"Once, a salt doll tried to measure the depth of the ocean. "What are you" asked the salt doll. "Come in and see" replied the Ocean with a smile. The salt doll waded in. The doll started dissolving in the water. The further it went; the more it dissolved. Before the last bit dissolved the doll exclaimed in ecstasy, "Now I realized what I am". Though, it didn't understand what the ocean is, it realized what the "I" is. So, you can realize what you are, the limitations of you before dissolving into GOD"

"Why can't a believer or non-believer in GOD experience it?" he asked.

"As I said, any belief is based on a concept. Concepts are limited by the boundaries of mind. The concept conditions the believer's mind. The conditioned-mind (ego or 'I') would always want to justify, judge, substantiate, analyze or interpret the set of beliefs and images that he/she has, rather than experiencing the real experience." I said.

If a person frees from the conditioning and earnestly searches like the salt doll, he/she can experience the beauty and love of GOD." I added.

Belief and non-belief condition one's enquiry, so does incomplete knowledge and verbalized experience do.

So does the imagination and thinking of the unreal future. Hence only perception of truth may be possible in the present, with full awareness of the mind and no interference from the conditioning of any sort.

A believer can never be a truth seeker. For him/her, the truth (as per belief) is already given in the respective Holy Book and not supposed to think beyond that.

Hindu is a born truth seeker. This is not possible in any other faith system because their concept of truth is already provided in their Holy books as final thing - all you can go is follow it as the final words of God!

The force is within you and outside you, everywhere. You do not have to believe the force or energy, just as you don't have to believe the sun.

Chapter - 3

The Immoral Hinduism

Last week, a pastor of a Christian congregation invited me to participate in a group discussion related to 'Ghar Wapsi' (meaning "Home Coming", a series of re-conversion exercises organized by various right wing Indian Hindu organizations).

My good friend, Jacob, who is an atheist, was also with me at that time.

The pastor said, "My cousin in USA has forwarded me your article "Am I a Hindu?" that explains the liberal and secular values of Hinduism. I am impressed, that's why I wanted you to come and share your opinion in our meeting."

"Thank you. But I am sorry, my karma (duty) is writing. I neither go for speech nor participate in any organized movements..." I explained my inability.

"Hmmm...People like you should come to the front and protect minority religions," he said.

"For what? How's it going to benefit me, my country, my world or the human race?" I asked.

He said "You know our religion professes morality and love. Our brother religion Islam talks about peace. So we have higher moral ground than Hinduism which doesn't have any code of morality or commandments."

"Yes pastor, your religions TALK about high morality, whereas Sanatan Dharma doesn't have such rules and regulations," I admitted.

He beamed. He may have expected me to defend my religion the way they do.

Excitedly he said, "Hinduism teaches immoral stories like a female having multiple husbands, a male having thousands of wives...it doesn't preach any morality at all."

"Your views appear right. I am the robbery in the robber, says Krishna (most popular Hindu God) in the Bhagavad Gita (Gita is a sacred scripture. There are 39 Gitas. Bhagavad Gita is most popular)."

"Oh, is it, I didn't know that," Jacob said.

"Shiva (Another great Hindu God) says in the YajurVeda-Taitreeya samhita (YajurVeda is one among four Vedas or "knowledge". Taittiriya Samhita is a part of YajurVeda) that he is 'Stenanam pathy' (leader of the thieves) and 'Thaskaranam pathy' (leader of the highway robbers)." I said.

The pastor couldn't conceal his excitement. "This is it...this is it...Uday, we need people like you who can bring out such immoral views in Hinduism...You are a person who knows Hindu scriptures and all its flaws. You should join us to fight against these fundamentalist right wing Hindus," he announced.

"Pastor, but there is a small problem," I conceded.

Reassuringly he said, "Any problem can be solved."

"I don't think so. I am an ardent devotee of Hindu Gods including Krishna and Shiva," I told him.

"Shame on you" the colour of his face changed, then, in a moment he said: "but relax, I can help you to come out of this nonsense devotion."

"But, tell me pastor, the religions founded upon high moral teaching have murdered or massacred millions of people all around the world (including India) who refused to get converted."Jacob paused.

"The Goa Inquisition by Francis Xavier is the most tragic example..."Jacob reminded the pastor.

"But I don't think there had been any single incident of a 'no-morals' Hindus killing even a single person for the sake of converting" I said.

"There are criminals in all religions," Pastor said as justification.

Responding to Pastor I said, "True, but when somebody kills in the NAME of religion, when terrorists are vouching by Holy books, when they claim killing is done for the religion and to get heaven as promised in their 'Holy Books', it is a clear warning: There are sickening fundamental flaws in religions professing such morality."

Defensively the pastor said, "That's not true. We teach everybody to love and spread peace with high standards of morality."

Suddenly Jacob asked: "Then what about the teachers themselves? Just check your own official records. In USA alone, the Roman Catholic Church paid billions of US dollars to settle cases of child sexual abuse by priests.

The proponents of "strict moral standards" – a many of Catholic dioceses have declared bankruptcy due to sex abuse cases. It's in the USA alone. And you are teaching me about morality."

He didn't have any answers.

I smiled at pastor and said, "But brother, your views are correct. As you said, Hinduism doesn't have moral codes. Still, Hindus are more tolerant and peaceful community ever lived in the earth. They have broader universal views and can contain all. Do you know why?"

"Why?" both of them asked simulataneously.

I explained, "Our religion teaches only about Dharma which is different from morality."

"Morality is a superficial and an easy-to-follow concept written for village communities (like shepherds, desert dwellers etc.) during the time of writing those Holy books."

"I really don't understand what you mean by the word Dharma," he sounded confused.

"If I call you a liar, you will get angry. You will feel hurt and may even slap me, right?" I asked.

"Yes, of course anybody would get angry. Because I am not a liar," the pastor said.

"If you are not a liar, then why should it disturb you? Why should it hurt you?" I asked in return.

"Hmmm," he seemed to be thinking.

"And if it is true, that is - if you are a liar - then I have just made a statement of fact...why should it disturb you? Why should it hurt you then?" I asked again.

"That's human nature Uday," he gave a general answer.

I said, "No, pastor. In that case, I should have got angry when you talked ill about my religion, the way you people get hurt. No... That's not the case. When you are being called a liar, you are hurt, because, there is something within you that creates a disturbance and it is not from the outside."

He gave me a blank look. I continued: "Why are you disturbed? Close your eyes and think about it. Go deeper. You may find out deep within, you tend to lie. But ever since you are born, everybody around you said: 'you should not lie'. That's immoral. So, you want to be good, you want to hear others saying: 'good boy'. You want to be in the "good books" of others. You are scared that lying is an immoral sin and you will be punished by God." I gave him a moment to think.

"So, you ignore the fact that you are a liar. You have suppressed your tendency to lie, in your subconscious mind. So, when somebody calls you a liar, you feel like you are being found out. You are being revealed. You are being uncovered. You are naked in the public...you don't want to show others that you are a liar. You feel emotionally insecure."

"That's psychology," he said.

I went on, "Your morality codes never address such a basic nature. You just create guilt and fear in people, telling them irrational stories on morality and punishments.

Thus, you create an emotional insecurity among followers and public, which you can cash in on later, in the name of salvation."

I told him, "But my ancestors, the founders of Sanatan Dharma said that 'if you are a liar, go ahead and lie'. That's the basic difference between your Semitic ideas and our Sanatan Dharma".

Morality is NOT Dharma. If your innate nature is to lie, go ahead and lie. But you should do it without guilt or regret. If your innate nature is to rob, go ahead and rob. But, it should be for the sake of robbing, not for the greed of money. That's what we call dedicated Karma.

There was a highway robber named Ratnakara who had been looting people passing through his jungle. He was doing it as his Dharma as he was not conditioned with your kind of concepts on morality.

He was so passionate and devoted to his Karma that he became Sage Valmiki who wrote the first and most beautiful epic in the world – the Ramayana. (Ramayana is the oldest epic in the world and considered as first poem (Adi-kavya) ever written.)

A robber can turn into great sage, that's the beauty of Hindu Dharma. There was a righteous butcher, who performed his Dharma properly. He wrote the Vyadha Gita (a sacred text) which taught philosophy to the Brahmins!" (Brahmins = those who were in the profession of teaching)

"We also have saints...," pastor said.

Nodding his head Jacob said, "I know you promote saints and build Churches in their names to create wealth."

Pastor's face turned red with anger

"You can't compare our sages who prayed for the well-being of the entire universe (Loka Samastha Sukhino Bhavathu) with the so-called saints who only marketed your religion." I told him. Comparison is the only way that he can understand. "We address even atheists as sages."

Jacob smiled.

I told him, "And the stories you quote about morality are from Puranas (stories of ancient times or a class of Sanskrit sacred writings on Hindu mythology and folklore), not from any of our authentic Sanskrit Vedic scriptures."

"We have thousands of Vedic scriptures that form the foundation of our Dharma. The Puranas are just stories created to explain some of those Vedic concepts. But what about your ONLY authentic scripture, the Holy book itself? If I quote mistakes in the Holy book itself, can you tolerate it?" I asked.

"What?" he asked with a perplexed look. Suddenly Jacob asked, "To begin with, pastor, take Genesis - The first creations of your God - Adam and Eve had only three sons (Cain, Abel, and Seth), but no daughters. Then, how did the world get populated?"

He smiled at us and said: "There was no other female on the earth. The only woman was Eve, their mother. So how did their next generations evolve? Isn't it immoral?"

The Pastor didn't have any answers.

Jacob continued: "Recently, your Pope, Francis, declared that the Genesis account of creation is NOT true. It shakes the foundation on which your religion has been built. This is an era of knowledge. Tomorrow the Pope will be forced to say that the Holy Book is filled with such irrational stories."

Jacob is a hardcore atheist. He won't waste any chances to attack religions.

I told Pastor: "I mean all Holy books have blunders and errors in it. I know that there are good things in your Holy book, and I respect it for that. But, you are spreading lies to expand religious base. For instance, you claim that St. THomams came to India and built Churches for himself. Then your people have built hundreds of churches for him. But, the Pope says Thomas had never come to India."

He didn't say anything. I told him, "Please try to see the teachings of Jesus Christ 'Love thy neighbour' in a larger canvas. Aren't Hindus your neighbours? Didn't they provide you shelter and land to build churches? You are doing total injustice to naive Indians to convert them."

"Pastor, why can't your moral preachers set right your own world - Rome, a country ill-famed for extreme sexual perversions and immoral night lives of vulgarity?" suddenly Jacob asked.

"There are good things and bad things in every religion," he said put forwarding the common statement about any religion that people say in general.

I said, "That exactly is my point. If you agree with that, how can you claim your religion is superior?"

"And there is one more reason for us Hindus not to follow any moral codes or commandments in your Holy books," I added.

"What's it?" He asked.

I replied, "Christians are taught that they are originally sinners and only through moral codes and through Jesus Christ one can attain salvation, right?"

He agreed.

I said, "But we are taught that everything in this world is pure as everything is divine. Hence, we can never be sinners, we are divine. We are being told to just do our good karma in a non-violent way."

"You are wrong," he murmured. But he didn't say anything further.

I told, "I am a practicing Hindu - it is not by compulsion, but by choice. Nobody promised me heaven to be a Hindu. And I don't believe in heaven or hell."

I added: "I always have a choice to leave my Dharma and nobody would prevent me from doing it. I have the freedom to think without any conditioning of a brain-washed mind. This choice and freedom make me a Hindu. I even have freedom to criticize Hinduism or make fun of our Gods. You never had such a choice - you are bound by your religion with much strings attached to it, which you can't break - that's the difference between you and me."

"Uday and Pastor, we all really learn morality from our parents, not from the religion. Morality is an individual pride, not something to be imbibed through fear of God. Morality should come from inherent strength and courage, and not from fear and weakness," Jacob said.

"But this is exactly what Sanatan Dharma teaches us," I said.

"Nikrishta vasthu, Utkrishta drishti," said our ancestors. That means, see the divine in even the dirtiest object. This is where Sanatan Dharma differs from other ways of lives.

If you look at any texts in Hindu Dharma, nowhere it is being even mentioned that one should follow any dogma or commandment to be a Hindu. All 'ism' were took birth mostly due to personal and political motives.

Many think that it is the freedom in Hinduism that makes it the weakest of all religion, but it is the same weakness that gives its unbreakable strength. Despite consistent and brutal attack from everywhere for the last 5000 years, this Dharma survives!

Religion is organized system which is different from Sanatan Dharma's self-organized system. A religion is based on membership; Dharma doesn't have such thing as membership.

Chapter - 4

Incredible Ancient Hindu Temples

My American friend, Ved Bell, asked me why was it that some South Indian Hindu temples didn't allow him to go in. He married to a Nepali Hindu woman and they follow Hinduism. Now that many African blacks, Caucasians, Chinese and people from other races follow Sanatan Dharma, Hindu temples need to rethink about a few conservative rules.

First, let's check some amazing facts about our Temples.

Most of the temples have huge, fort like gigantic boundary walls around them, whereas most of the palaces (built before 1000AD) in India never had a huge fort around them! In fact, royal palaces in other countries had huge protective forts and walls around them. In India, it was the other way around - that was a confusing mystery for me till recently.

I had an opportunity to see a few old documents of land (property records) in Kerala, the southern state of India.

It was ASTONISHING - I found most of the old records (prepared in brass plates) say the land is "pandaram vaha" (in Malayalam Pandaram=Bhandaram=Hundi; Vaha = belongs to) That is, the entire land was belonged to the deity in the nearby temple.

The King was just a Dasa (servant) of the deity.

Padmanabhaswamy Temple in Thiruvananthapuram (Trivandrum), Kerala State was in news recently after a Vault was open to find hidden treasure worth more than one trillion dollar.

The King of that county was known as "Padmanabha Dasa" (=servant of Padmanabha). And the temple was built for Sri Padmanabha (another name of Hindu God Vishnu).

My dear Tamil brothers and sisters are you familiar with the terminology, "Adiyen, Ramanuja Dasan" (Me, servant of Ramanuja)?

The old manuscripts preserved by temple authorities in the state of Karnataka elaborate the purpose, functions and activities of temples. The Kings only function is to act as guardian/protectorate of his subjects by collecting tax 1/6 to 1/12 of the produce and put it in treasury.

According to Indian civil law, even now, deities in all temples are treated as perpetual minors. And the king (instead of King, it is now managed by temple trust) is just a karyakar = servant, not owner.

In all other countries like the West and Middle East, Kings and royal families really "owned" the country. Barring some exceptions, in India, the land belonged to the deity. People of the country can build houses or do farming. The private property ownership was unheard in India.

Hence, the ancient Indian system of governance (in which temples played major role) cannot be compared with that of the West and Middle East where Kings were autocrats.

And, please, please, don't go by Indian 'official' history texts that are taught in schools and colleges which were written by die-hard fans of invaders.

When pirates and looters from the Middle East and Europeans came to India, the then Hindu kings in this country thought that they were "Athithi" (Guests). According to Hindu culture, Atithi Devo Bhava (the guest is equivalent to God). A guest is considered as "Deva" (God).

Hindu Kings provided them with food, shelter, free land and money to build Churches and Mosques along with freedom to worship. Anybody can check old documents - the land for Churches and Mosques were donated by Hindu Kings. (I have never heard anything otherwise happening anywhere in the world! Will Saudi Arabia or the Vatican give a small piece of land to build a Hindu temple?)

Ancient temples are known as Devalaya (abode or house of God) and are not a place for prayers. You may go to an old temple; the sanctum sanctorum itself is very small and dark. Hardly, two or three people can stand in front of it.

Temples never had a prayer hall like that in Churches or Mosque which are 'Prarthanalaya' (house for prayer). Of course, there were Mandap = pillared outdoor hall for performing arts and public rituals in temples.

That means temples had some other purpose.

Ancients say that temples were built as powerhouses of energy - a sort of battery. Every ritual, prayer, ceremonies were only secondary to be in a temple but the main thing is to be in the field of consecrated energy.

I don't know how they did it, but I have read somewhere that even individual karmic energy can be stored and retrieved in temple. But we lost all those ancient wisdoms on energy contact and we are left only with rituals or we have become overly ritualistic, without understanding the real significance of temples.

Another fact is that temples were store house of enormous treasures too. This explains gigantic fort around the temple.

Padmanabhaswamy Temple of Thiruvananthapuram and Tirupati Balaji Temple in Andhra Pradesh are examples of that. The wealth accumulated in the temples was used purely for Dharmic (righteous) deeds and education in Vedas.

The priest, mostly a poor Brahmin, in the temple would get one or two meals a day, that's all. There were Choultries (inns or lodges) and rest houses associated with those temples that provided food and shelter for the poor and needy.

Everything was done based on the concept "Sarvam Sri Krishnarpanam Astu" (Everything I offer to Krishna or the divine). Everybody in the kingdom followed the Dharmic way of life - the symbolic center of this system was the Temple.

That was our ancient economic system – our Dharma was based on sharing and caring.

Our ancestors built huge store houses of energy, wisdom (libraries and universities) and physical wealth associated with the temple premises for generations to come.

The ancient politico-economic system was developed based on a concept known as 'Madhukara Vritti' (The job of a honey bee).

Honey bees take nectar from the flowers to its hive and converts into honey. The honeybee doesn't exploit the flower. It helps flowers to bloom and populate. It saves honey for future and for future generations. It's a selfless activity considering ecology, environment and future generation. It is helpful to the entire world, not just few.

Similarly, Hindus worked hard and stored everything as a treasure for coming generations. Temples were the highest seat of marvelous architecture, sculptures, arts and science. And that's when the ancient world called, 'Glory that was India.'

The Dark Age began with the arrival of the brutal, religiously fanatic, barbaric invaders and pirates who attacked, looted and destroyed the temple-economy.

According to independent historians, more than hundred thousand Hindu temples (the likes of Somanatha temple) were destroyed by those demonic invaders and nearly 75 million Hindus were killed (who preferred death to giving up their Dharma) during the process.

The entire temple-system was thus perished. They burned away all our ancient universities and libraries. Nalanda University, Bihar, was a world renowned varsity (427 AD- 1197 AD) with access to many scriptures which were destroyed, too.

While our ancestors gave importance to education, arts, music, health, environment and nature, the barbaric invaders did not build even one school, library or hospital.

All they made was to build palaces and gardens for their enjoyment, tombs to perpetuate their memory and forts for their security. Lots of beautiful temples were destroyed and converted into tombs too - one example that many historians quote is the famous Taj Mahal!

Naturally, those ordinary, peace-loving Hindus around the temple-system became very scared and insecure; hence they tried protecting the remaining temples. They are given to believe that non-Hindus may destroy their temples, which were epicenter of their culture.

A temple priest once told me: "We do not allow the non-Hindus because of the fear of getting looted and destroyed and not because we hate or object their religion"

An ardent follower of sanatan Dharma like me would not blame any other religions for this downfall. We could have preserved whatever remained after the Independence. But, alas, the cunning, pimping Hindu politicians failed the remaining temple-system.

Indian politicians have arrogantly taken over the right to manage the richest temples in India.

For the most part, the temples and its wealth are transferred arbitrarily by the government for "secular", non-Hindu purposes.

The most damaging side-effect of this is lack of resources for maintenance and upkeep of temples, leading to irreparable damage to many medieval and ancient structures. I have personally seen and experienced this - go and see the status of huge temples in Tamil Nadu.

In short, the non- Hindus were not allowed because of the fear of getting looted and destroyed and not because Hindus hate or object other religion.

But Hindus are now feeling insecure and scared, not because of Muslims or any other religions, but because of so-called "Hindu Secular Politicians" (all political parties included) who are worse and more crooked than the brutal and barbaric invaders.

My friend, Rajendra Adhikari a Nepali residing in the USA wrote to me: "My father once told me that those who built different temples in Nepal in the past left a Tamra Patra (Declaration on a copper plate) or Shila Patra (Declaration on a stone). It was mentioned there that anybody utilizing the property or assets of the Temples will be born as a worm in the latrine for 7 consecutive rebirths, in Sanskrit.

It was a sort of fashion in those days to build big or small temples for the sake of Sanatan Dharma, rather than hand over the savings to the sons or daughters.

But today we have a politically backed mafia in Nepal too plundering the assets and land holdings of those sacred Temples."

From Gandhara (today's Afghanistan) to Suvarnabhumi (Indo-Chinese peninsula up to Philippines), people were following Sanatan Dharma, hence ancient temples can be found in those areas.

Ancient temples or its ruin can be found in Vietnam, Cambodia, Indochina, Langkasuka, Malay Peninsula, Sumatra, Java, Bali, and parts of the Philippine archipelago. There were temples in Azerbaijan and Saudi Arabia too. Angkor Wat, in Cambodia is the largest Hindu temple in the world.

The religious fanatics destroyed thousands of beautiful temples in Pakistan, Afghanistan, Bangladesh, Indonesia and Malaysia. Otherwise, a great, peaceful and harmonious civilization would have survived in the whole of Asia.

Chapter- 5
Are Hindu Temples Anti-Sanatan Dharma?

Harindran Nair and his friend came to visit me after reading my article on 'Ancient Hindu temples - Some incredible facts' (see above).

They represented an angry young Hindus who want to form sort of association to protect Hindus and Temples in India. Existing Hindu organizations have gone soft, they say. So they wanted to be extreme right wing Hindus – an impossible task as Hindus cannot be extremists.

"Hari - what's it that you want to save - Sanatan Dharma, Hinduism, Temples or Hindus?" I asked.

"Brother, our temples have been the center point of Hinduism and all Hindus for thousands of years, so we have to consolidate all Hindus under each temple..."

"Hmmm - I have confusion here. You said all Hindus."

"Yes - everybody - all castes..." he said, "because we are the only people who consider this land as Punyabhoomi (sacred land). For all others it is just a piece of real estate."

"Hari, have you heard of Mahatma Gandhi's Vaikom temple entry Satyagraha (nonviolent or civil resistance) and subsequent the historic Temple Entry Proclamation signed by Maharajah of Travancore on November 12, 1936?"

"Yes"

"Till then, lower caste Hindus were not allowed inside the temples. That means, nearly 70 % of population was not allowed to go inside ancient temples.

Are they not Hindus? And, what about those atheists and Nastiks (people who do not believe in God)? They are also Hindus. So, how can temples represent all Hindus?"

Their face became red. "Don't you go to temple? Are you not supporting temples? Don't you know its significance? There are various scientific reasons and facts behind going to temples. All modern scientists proclaim the science behind temple construction..."

"Hari, I go to temple, all temples - that's our tradition. I love it. But I don't need any scientific backing to follow my tradition of going to temple. I don't need neo-modernists approval for my temple visit. Even if it is termed as superstition, I will continue going to temple..."

"Then why are you not in favour of consolidation of Hindus under temples?"

"Your idea is just opposite to Sanatan Dharma and you are imitating Semitic ideas, that's why"

"I don't understand...."

"Simply put, Sanatan Dharma is all about following of Shodasha Samskaras (16 rituals or sacraments) and duties performed according to the system of Varnashrama

(There are four Varna (social divisions based on profession and four ashrams (stages in life) Both together known as Varna-Ashrama) . The temple visit is NOT mandatory anywhere"

On the contrary, in Semitic religions you MUST go to Church or Mosques and your life thus get bonded to those institutionalized religion...Your birth, marriage and death are related to those institutions.

For us, it is just the other way around. If somebody is born or died in your family house, you are not allowed to enter the temple for 7-14 days depending upon the Varna (profession) that you follow.

Today, people imitate Semitic ideas and even conduct marriages in temples. Our ancestors maintained marriage as was a family-community function. All relatives and friends get together in the bride's house and prepare for marriage. Today, temples allow marriages inside the premises, as this would fetch extra revenue.

As I said earlier, Temples = Devalaya (God's abode); Mosqes and Churches = prathanalaya (place for prayer). Semitic God's abodes are prayer halls. Hindu temples were never ever made for prayers. Only one or two priest can hardly enter sanctum sanctorum (Garbha Griha). Temple is NOT a prayer hall.

Hindu scriptures say that those who wanted to please any God, went to forest or mountains for Dhyana (profound, abstract meditation) or Tapas (a practice often involves solitude to attain liberation, salvation) or penance and NOT to temple.

They believed that the God would make appearance and grant them boon after the practice.

Take for instance any Vedic rituals (Havan, Yajna, Homamm, Pooja or Yagam) to please the God, we don't keep God's idol there. When you perform a Homamm for Ganapathi (a Hindu God), you invoke (Avahanam) the divine powers that removes obstacles.

And after the Pooja (the act of worship) we do disperse (Visarjan) that power. There was no temple Pooja in any of our traditional Vedic ceremonies - be it Upanayana (sacred thread ceremony of Hindus) or wedding or house warming, whatever. In short, temple had less or no relevance in Sanatan Dharma.

Our Dharma sees divinity in each and every thing in this universe. The entire universe is indwelt, enveloped, covered by the Supreme Being (Ishaavaasyam idam sarvam). God is not confined in a temple.

"Then why are temples for? Why did you say you are temple follower?"

"Temple is known as Kshetra. Kshetra literally means any "field, area, tract of land". Here it means a field or sphere of action."

"Ok"

"Bharat Kshetra means the divine field named Bharat (India). Kuru Kshetra is the field where Mahabharata War was fought. India was divided into many Kshetras - Jagannatha kshetra (Odisha), Bhaskara kshetra (Karnataka), Parasurama kshetra (Keralam), Sri Rama kshetra (Tamil Nadu), Sreenivasa kshetra (Andhra Pradesh), Mumbadevi Kshetra (Maharashtra), Vanga (Bongo) Kshetra (West Bengal) etc."

"Oh...I didn't know that..."

"Please try to learn facts before making sweeping statement about temples and Dharma. Our ancestors lived peacefully in villages observing Varnashrama Dharma. You can't and never will find such perfect system of way of life for human beings in this universe. Those who really learnt about social sciences would easily understand that."

The ancients didn't want to consolidate all powers into few people with vested interest. Hence they created social system based on professions and established the concept of Grama Devatha (Village Deity) in each village.

They said the village belonging to Grama Devatha. (This system was later destroyed by the British by introducing private property ownership.

But even today, under constitutional laws legally entire land surrounding the temple belongs to the deity - The deity is a juristic perpetual minor)

The land and its contents were belonged to the Grama Devatha who was the presiding deity or guardian deity (patron deity) in Hindu villages, towns and cities.

The villagers lived in total surrender to the deity and did their respective jobs without any expectations (Nishkama Karma).

There was no exploitation or selfishness. The village king was considered as the servant of the deity.

The best of first agriculture produce would be submitted to the deity. Today, I have seen people buy the smallest, cheapest coconut to break in the Ganapathi temple. They also put soiled currency notes in Bhandara (treasure vessel)

The entire wealth of the village was stored in the temple as gems, jewelry etc. for future generations to live and learn. (Later, these temples were became the soft target for brutal invaders from the Middle East).

According to ancient travellers to India, they were all living happily, peacefully and healthy (Remember the average life-span during Vedic times was 120years!). So, there could be NO social system that can be better than this.

During the period of Krishnadevaraya regime – a typical secular Hindu Kingdom - in India, gems were openly sold in heaps, on the roadside. So, you can imagine how much rich our ancestors were.

"That means the main purpose of temples was different..."

"Yes - its purpose was totally different. It was not for prayer and worship the way we do it now. Do you know the significance of idols of those deities?"

"Yes, I know, it was concentrated energy center and radiate energy to the devotees" Hari's friend said.

"I cannot comment on such energies as today's science cannot prove the existence of such energies. But those idols were most powerful, but for different reasons...Those were not just idols!"

"What?"

"Those idols (Vigraham) of the deities were made up of unique and sacred combination of Panchaloham (five metals), Sapthaloham (Seven metals) and Navapashanam (an amalgam of nine poisons). All of them have unbelievable medicinal values! In some places, they had used very special stones (Sila) like Anjana, Saligrama, Dvararvati etc make idols."

For instance, the idol of the Muruga in Palani and idol of Ayyappa in Sabarimala were made up of Navapashanam. When they perform Abhisheka (ritual of pouring) on the idol with milk or ghee, the outcome would be rare Ayurveda combination of specialty medicine.

And I remember a priest saying, during full moon day (Pournami), the Navapashanam idols would sweat as if it is a human! (In 1950 a mysterious fire broke to destroy the Sabarimala temple and the original idol is vanished. Nobody knows who stole the idol.)

"So whenever you hear that temple celebrates its Puna Prathista (Idol- re-installation) - be it known to you that the actual, rate sacred idol is going abroad and new marble and granite statue will take its place."

"Oh God!" he was excited.

"Hari, what can you do to protect those ancient temples? You people always help building new concrete structure with marble statue in it which has no relevance to Sanatan Dharma."

"We didn't know this much details..." Hari said.

According to independent historians thousands of such temples are destroyed by invaders and evangelists to steal wealth and sacred idols.

"Why majority of people were not allowed inside the temple?" his friend asked.

"Temples didn't have any space inside to contain the public - it was not a public prayer hall. In most of the olden temples the priests were from the profession known as Brahmins. There are thousands of temples were you can see non-Brahmin priests too. Even among Brahmins, only less than one percent of Brahmins were allowed inside the Garba Griha – those Brahmins who had specialized in temple rituals."

"Oh, I thought all Brahmins were priests," he said.

"No – very few Brahmins are priests. And only poorest Brahmins would go for Pooja till 1970s. Why? The only remuneration for a temple priest was (mostly) just one time food.

So, only the person who perform everyday Pooja and the king who kept the entire treasure inside the temple were among those few who need to go inside. Others had no business there..."

Are you admitted to all buildings in your locality without permission? No. So, why do you single out temples? There used to be huge ground outside the temple where everybody can play and celebrate festivals.

Some temples had Mandap (pillar hall) for art performance and Vedic or other skills learning - those who were doing it also can go in. Just like any ideologies or concepts, this system may have mis-used by people with vested interests.

"So, you mean to say there is no energy or miracles inside the temple?" his friend repeated the question.

Many people claim there are mysterious powers in these temples. Others say, it has some sort of positive energy - I don't know about both. But I also can make true claim of miracles that happened in life by performing Poojas in a temple - I can vouch it as it is my personal experience.

But individual experiences are not an empirical evidence for science. A more plausible explanation would be that temple provides psychological security.

However, such mysterious power or energies (if exists) come with huge responsibility.

The priest should perform all rituals and customs based on the sacred scriptures, for which he needs to have purity of body, mind and self, Sattvik (a serene, harmonious, balanced mind or attitude) in nature and keep the quality of karma.

But today most of the priests are greedy and exploitative. The chief priest of a famous temple went on record admitting to the High Court of Kerala that he doesn't even know Sanskrit!

It is said: 'Archakasya prabhavena sila bhavathi sankara, Archakasya aprabhavena siva bhavati sila' (Even a stone becomes God by dedicated rituals done by a priest. And by improper rituals, even the God itself will become a stone)

The enemies of Sanatan Dharma are traders and illegal brokers - those who built new temples or convert temples into cut-throat business centers.

They have already kicked the Gods out of the temple. There is a mafia group consists of politicians, priests, traders and astrologers to run temples.

"Do you want to consolidate Hindus under those crooks?" I asked him.

He didn't have any answer.

The only way to protect our temple culture is to create awareness among the public (irrespective of caste and religions) regarding the importance of Sanatan Dharma and Grama Devathas. Let the powerful Grama Devathas be back. Let out land be a heaven and Punya Bhoomi.

God is omnipresent. So, it is not necessary that one need to go to temple to offer prayers.

What you practice in your daily life (your Dharma) at your home and the places you dwell is the prime important aspect.

Most of the Hindus light lamp at home in front of the image of his/her favourite deity as a spiritual practice. Temples were religious places where one would visit occasionally, annually - when one gets time and occasion.

The temple culture and today's kind-of-a-Bhakti is relatively new to Hindu Dharma. Unfortunately, today, Hinduism is merely temple worship, just similar to monotheistic Semitic religions (preaches on faith to a personal God).

And today's temple is run like some business!

Why Am I a Hindu?

Chapter - 6

Gods - The Good, the Bad and the Ugly

Sometime ago, a Russian Bishop called Krishna "Satan". Many Christians say Hindus are devil worshipers. Many Muslims say Hindu Gods are animals and Hindus are infidels. Atheists would call Indian Gods primitive. Rationalists say that Hindu Gods are physically handicapped or have extra limbs.

In their perspective, they are all telling truth. The picture of Kali (A Hindu Goddess) appears horrible for a modern westerner. Krishna, Vishnu, Shiv are dark-skinned or black guys.

Many Hindu Gods are ugly looking and can be put under a group of physically challenged ones. Some have extra hands, double or triple heads, tails etc. Naturally Hindu Gods appear funny, ugly, bad or horrific to the modern world.

"Look at Jesus Christ - he looks so handsome, tall, trimmed beard, blue-eyed, a Caucasian or Westerner. Like a good-looking Hollywood star," an agnostic told me in comparison to.

These comparisons usually make Hindus unhappy, upset and angry.

I get such questions related to Hindu Gods and Puranas (Stories of ancient times). "Uday sir, your Rama didn't take care of his wife. He has left her in forest to die while she was pregnant."

Or "Krishna had thousands of wives." or "Kunti had pre-marital affair and had a child!" or

"The funniest part is 33 crores (330 million) Gods! The heaven should implement population control, or it would burst..."

Or "Uday, all Gods are carrying weapons. (And still you Hindus talk about non-violence) The Puranas or stories of ancient times are about wars and killings!"

Many devoted Hindus feel ashamed when others question such stories. They find it difficult to explain.

Disclaimer first: I am not an expert or authentic interpreter of Puranas. There are 18 Maha Puranas (Great Puranas) and 18 Upa Puranas (Minor Puranas) with hundreds of thousands of stories in it. Yes, I had spent nearly 15 years on Puranas. Initially it appeared interesting, during my school days. I lost interest when I reached college.

But I was compelled to go back to Puranas once again for my job - the assignment of translating Amar Chitra Katha (picture story books) and for writing manuscript of 'the Hindu book of Gods (out of print now) for a short period of 5 years. Now, it has been more than 25 years since I touched Puranas.

According to my understanding, we cannot compare Puranas with Holy books of any other religions. The current Bible was written some 1500-2000 years ago, to address a community consists mostly shepherds.

Quran was written in 1400 years ago, to address a community consists of desert dwellers.

Puranas were written 3000-5000 years ago, for a village community lived in Indian sub-continent.

Bible and Quran taught those primitive communities a better disciplined and morally right way of life. Through those books, they were taught rules and regulations or commandments that are claimed to be divinely ordained.

Those books tell you to be good, fight with evil and lead a God-fearing life. This has become the base foundation of today's civilized society.

On the contrary, Puranas (literally means "ancient, old) are mostly stories, it doesn't talk much about something that we believe to be the morally right according to today's context or life style, which is largely (99%) influenced by those Semitic religions.

Puranas tend to exaggerate. For instance, it says Krishna lifted Govardhana Hill by the little finger of his left hand.

A sane man cannot believe it. (Yes, I agree, all Holy books also exaggerate - The first miracle Jesus Christ performs is changing water into wine at a marriage feast in Cana. Or Allah, who created the heavens and the earth in six days, and is firmly established on the throne (of authority), regulating and governing all things.)

The authors of Puranas or Holy books wanted to communicate that Gods are not like us. They are very powerful - kind of Superman or Spiderman. So, it is normal to praise the super-human powers of Gods in such scriptures.

Purana is not history. But there are stories about historical characters too. For instance, Krishna and Rama were historical characters. Puranas have lots of exaggerated stories about them.

Puranas contain many factual errors and contradictions. According to Puranas, there are 24 incarnations (avatar) of Vishnu. Ten avatars are popular among them.

The purpose of Vishnu's fifth Avatar, Vamana was to teach a lesson to Mahabali who ruled Kerala. But the people in Kerala believe that the state was created by the Avatar number 6 - Parasurama!!!

Airavata is a mythological white elephant who carries the Hindu God Indra (The Puranic Indra is different from the Vedic deity Indra).

Indra's tusker Airavata was responsible for the churning of the ocean of Milk in order to obtain Amrita which will guarantee immortality.

But then it says: Airavata appeared only while churning of the Sea of Milk. The first object to emerge as a result of the churning was the moon (Chandra). But it is an apparent contradiction with Chandra earlier being described as the sage Arti's son.

So, you can find many contradictions and inconsistencies in Purana stories. Those are not authentic Hindu scriptures like Vedic literature.

Holy books also have much more blunders and errors.

If you fix an international award for factual and scientific errors on a yearly basis, you don't have any scope to win that award for first 1000 years - it will straight away go only to those Holy books!

The factual mistakes, inconsistencies and irrational stories are common to all those old writings, be it Holy books or Puranas.

The question was about good, bad and ugly Gods. Is it about external appearance?

Jesus Christ was of Asiatic origin, not a Caucasian or Westerner - many studies suggest. Till 13th century the paintings were depicted a bald, dark-complexioned and short Jesus. The average male at that time was 5'1" and weighed 110 pounds.

Today's Jesus is often described and pictured as a tall, white, handsome trimmed bearded guy with long hair. And even black Africans, brown Indians and yellow Chinese have silently accepted this new white Westerner as Jesus Christ.

Isn't it discrimination based on colour and race?

In Puranas, same God may have different attributes. People can also interpret even the same single God in different ways based on each one's convictions.

For instance, if you think Allah is an exclusive Islamic God, you are mistaken.

Allah is the God for Arabic-speakers of all religions (Christians, Jews and other sects), because in Arabic, Allah=God.

Those religions fight over whose concept of Allah is right.

There were self-styled prophets like Musaylimah, Sajah, Tulayha, Sayyad and Aswad Ansi during Muhammad's time. All of them interpreted Allah in their own view points.

Since Prophet Muhammad was the most powerful, all other prophets were called fakes and killed or destroyed. So, who interprets what, also matters a lot.

The pictures of Krishna and Rama are imagination of the artists, but mostly based on the poetic description in Puranas. (As you can see, photography was not invented during those times. And no artists have ever seen those Gods.)

In short, you cannot judge, analyze or comment on Gods in Puranas based on today's context and viewpoints.

Purana stories are not like movies and novels of good vs bad Or God vs Satan. In Hinduism, even Gods are subject to Karmic principle. Nobody is above Karmic law. Gods also get punishments and rewards.

Hence, today's Semitic-style concept of the "perfect God" does not apply here in Puranas.

The socio-cultural-economic situation was totally different. And you cannot compare things happened 5000 years ago with today's life style.

If you don't know about Dharma (duty to the nature) and Karma (deed), Puranas and Hindu Gods would look ridiculous. You won't get the sweet and powerful messages in Puranas.

It would be like eating banana peels and throwing banana away.

Dharma has nothing to do with Right or wrong and good or bad (as depicted in Holy books). What was good for Adolf Hitler was bad for Jews. Had Hitler won the world war, we would have treated him like God after studying history written for him.

In kindergarten and pre-primary schools, you are being taught how to pee, basic etiquette and morality. You tell them stories of good guys Vs. bad guys. The people who followed Dharma were far more evolved, superior than the kindergarten kids.

The wars and fights in Puranas were against Adharma. Puranas are not bed-time kids' stories like God vs Satan. Wars were fought not for forceful conversion or establishing supremacy of a religion like that happened during crusades or barbaric invasions. Yes - Hindu Gods carry weapon. But it is not for violence, but to protect non-violence.

Can you show me one single instant in the entire Puranas where a God used the weapon for his/her personal gain or increase his market share?

As a King, it was Rama's Dharma to take care of his Country. He was not like today's "DEMOCRATIC" rulers who live with luxury, comforts or pleasure.

As a son, his Dharma was to follow father's words, so he went to forest. He sacrificed his life for the Dharma and not for personal pleasure. He wanted to see every citizen in his country safe, happy and contented. He was forced to leave love of his life (wife) for his country.

Today, can you even dream of such rulers? And you judge Rama's deeds with your petty conditioned mind. For me, Rama is Maryada Purushottama (The Perfect Man) and I love and worship him for that. See the difference in perception.

After a war, when all men are dead, what will you do with thousands of widows? Leave them without any income, livelihood and protection? Krishna said: "I will take care all of you just like I take care of my wife..."

In today's context, the self-centered rulers have multiple affairs and mistresses all around. So you naturally guessed that Krishna was like them – a huge mistake!

What about Kunti's story? I think every girl in this country should read Mahabharata to know more about Kunti. What will happen in a society (imagine a society 5000 years ago) if a young princess fallen for momentary pleasure and give birth to a child without father?

The image of struggle, harassment and miseries that Kunti and her son Karna faced is enough for a girl (even in modern context) not to repeat such blunders.

(I have discussed about almost all questions regarding Rama, Krishna and mythological character in other manuscripts in which you will get satisfying answers)

All the stories, symbols and myths are so strong. It will create an ever-lasting impression in your brain, indirectly influencing you.

The Sanatan Dharma divides all attributes and characteristics (Gunas) into three - Rajasic (passion and desire), Sattvic (Purity) and Tamasic (dullness or inertia).

Every living and non-living things have all these gunas in various proportions.

Ravana was son of a Brahmin, master of 64 arts, great ruler and a good fighter. But he has done an Adharma, so he became Asura (Adharmic).

Rama was just a human being. But he followed his Dharma. He was Sattvik. So, he is God.

Krishna (dark skinned) Dwaip-ayana (island born) or Bhagwan Ved Vyas, was considered as an avatar of Vishnu. He classified the four Vedas, wrote 18 Puranas, Brahma Sutras, and uttered the Mahabharata which Ganesh (Ganapathi) penned down.

All ancient scriptures around the world put together cannot reach to the volume of his work. Such was his incredible skills! But he didn't picture himself as all-time-good guy.

Instead, he portrayed himself as a dark ugly looking hermit with rough body and hair matted. People could faint at the first sight of him.

He called himself, "Kanina" (illegitimate son). He didn't say he was 6 feet tall, fair, eight-pack body, handsome, fair, blue-eyed God.

He didn't threaten us through his books demanding us to worship him or any Gods. Or convert people to his cult by brutal force.

His Dharma was writing and he was dedicated to his Karma. His truthfulness, honesty and magnanimity prove that he is divine!

Puranas say that there are 33 crore (330 million) Gods. So, you can choose a God from them, if you want to – depending upon your taste and nature. You also can choose a method of worship.

The cosmic consciousness or divine or Brahmam will manifest in that God the way you want. You can also worship other Gods whichever way you want.

If you don't worship God, that too is welcome. After all, the Karma decides your destiny, not the Gods.

"Just as all the water that fall from the sky inescapably reach the sea, all salutations to all the Gods reach only Keshav (the cosmic consciousness or Brahmam)" (Aakashath Pathitham Thoyam Yatha Gachathi Sagaram Sarvadeva Namaskaram Keshavm Prathi Gachathi) - This could anytime be the real truthful message from the cosmos.

So, it is up to you to find out which Gods are the good, the bad and the ugly based on clear study and analysis. Please do not go by market hype and publicity.

Chapter - 7

Who Created the Universe? Is There a Creator?

So, you have curled up on the couch yesterday afternoon after the midday meal for a short nap. Suddenly a sound from the window disturbed your nap.

"Who is it?" you jump up asking aloud as your brain sensed some clear and present danger.

It was just the window door snapped by wind. Probably you knew it was. Still your brain wouldn't ask "What's it". It would ask "Who is it" That's the default setting of our brain.

Your three-year-old kid hits his head on the table. He starts crying.

Suddenly you or others in the house would mockingly beat the "table uncle" with loud shouts like "Tmar" or "Disshyum" - then suddenly the child stops crying.

How can a child understand there is "somebody" behind the table or the table is somebody that makes the child stop crying? That's the cognitive stance of human brain.

When a child refuses to eat, mothers would say – Eat this, otherwise some 'demon' (as in the local myth or legends like 'Khandakarna' or 'Tintdakarala') will come now and take away all your food.

Suddenly the kid would start eating, though he doesn't understand whom you are talking about.

The basic operating system of Homo sapiens' can see a person behind it - it is a cognitive functioning.

When you order Pizza, you know there is pizza-maker. There is a maker for "Paani-poori" or "Idly-Vada". There is a maker of your furniture or jewelry or anything that you have or see around. For everything, there is a maker or creator.

Our limited brain is conditioned with the idea that there is someone behind everything. We always seek an agent for everything. It began when human beings evolved from primates.

The psychological trait in question is "if you hear a twig snap in the forest, some sentient force is probably behind it".

This trait helps to prevent the primate from being murdered or eaten as food. This agent detection is the inclination for animals and humans to presume the purposeful intervention of a sentient or intelligent agent in situations that may or may not involve one.

The scientific term for this is "Hyperactive (or Hypersensitive) Agency Detection Device" or HADD. This hypothetical trait remains in modern humans. So, even if the snapping was caused by the wind, modern humans are still inclined to attribute the sound to a sentient agent.

When cavemen saw the rain, they thought somebody is pouring water down from the sky. That agent - the creator of the rain - was called "rain God". Thus, the maker or creator - Gods - evolved in each and everything - thunder, wind, fire, Sky Mountain, river, ocean etc.

This agent detection or HADD is the "foundation for human belief in God".

However initially there were small-time local Gods. Some people called it Pagan beliefs or Polytheism. Such local beliefs may be considered as retail Gods.

Then a couple of thousands of years ago, a new trend developed - just like giant corporate monopolies kill small time traders: The whole sale God! It was a giant killer app that changed the world.

The new concept of whole sale single God as creator has killed many retail Gods.

People started claiming themselves as Messenger of God, Prophet, Son of God (Since those communities were male chauvinistic, daughter of God didn't seem to appear) God-men, Avatars, Enlightened Masters etc.

Instead of retail Gods for everything, they did a hard selling of the idea of a whole sale God - the maker or creator of this universe. This stems out of the cavemen's cognitive stance - agency seeking.

To support the claim, they appeal to the following evidence: "a knife cannot cut itself". A "Paani Poori" cannot come to existence by itself.

There MUST be a person behind everything. "If there is an intelligent creation, there should be an intelligent creator..." This is a typical HADD thinking.

Thanks to HADD, 70% of human beings in the earth subscribed this "creator story" as the ultimate truth within last 2500 years, though such stories cannot even qualify to be a bedtime story for kids.

The creation story says: The Earth formed before the Sun. Earth is 6,000 years old (Fact: Earth is 4.6 billion years old). When God created earth, it was empty full of darkness.

And God said, "Let there be light," and there was light. God saw that the light was good, and He separated the light from the darkness. God called the light "day," and the darkness he called "night."

And there was evening, and there was morning—the first day - the story goes like this....

If you ask a very simple question, "Who created this creator?" there is no answer.

Nobody should ask such question. And some of them would answer like this: "Are you dare questioning the creator!? It's a sin. You should be God-fearing and worship this exclusive God or else you will be roasted in the hell after death!"

If there is an intelligent creator, what's the material with which he created the world? If the material is other than God, then who created that material?

"The creator created the world from nothingness..." they would say.

If something can come from 'Nothing' then could you please define the 'Nothing'? Can 'Nothing' exist?

Why Am I a Hindu?

If yes, what are its properties? If there can only have been a 'Nothing' - then how can your God exist? No answers.

It's okay to have faith in such stories. Kids worship superman and Spiderman. The problem arises when you insist your faith is truth. That's sickness. It creates violence in this world.

Our ancestors in India - sages or scientists - couldn't make such funny stories as they were aware of this HADD.

Our ancestors were not like cavemen who lived elsewhere outside this land. They were enlightened and evolved to awareness some 7000 years ago itself.

While the proponents of the creator story claimed that the earth is flat till AD1700s, our ancestors knew Earth as Bhugol (Bhugol Sastra= science of the globe earth) 7000 years ago.

'Cakracasah parinaham prthivya' (Rig Veda 1.33.8) means, people who reside on the surface of earth circumference.

'Madhye samantandasya bhugolo vyomni tisthati' (Surya Siddhanta. 12.32), meaning, in the midst of universe (Brahmamda), the spherical earth stands firm in the space. 7000 years ago, our ancestors said earth was spherically shaped.

But we cannot mock the Semitic story of creation that was supposedly happened 4000 years back. The biggest number known in that part of the world was 3999 (MMMCMXCIX). They didn't know how to count numbers beyond that.

Meanwhile, our ancestors said the life span of Brahma = 311.04 trillion years.

And one day of Brahma = 4.32 billion years (almost the age of earth as per science). Who was Brahma?

Many Hindus consider Brahma, a mythological God, as a creator. That's not true. He is considered as 'ancestor', not creator. Brahma was posturized as a creative force (not as the whole creator of the universe).

Brahma is not to be confused with Brahmam (cosmos). For the starters (who are still in the realm of HADD) ancient Hindus developed a Trimurti (three forms) which is a concept that was represented by Brahma, Vishnu, and Shiva whose duties were overseeing the creation, sustenance and destruction respectively of this cyclical universe.

Puranas are mythology stories. But, the writers of Puranas were evolved humans. So, even in such stories you can find some logic and rational thinking. They didn't commit blunders like projecting Brahma as the wholesale creator God.

As a matter of fact, Hindus do NOT worship this creator! (In case you want to picture him as a creator). There is hardly any temple for him.

He is not a superman creator as depicted in other stories.

And Brahma didn't create anything from Nothingness!

There were Panchabhootas (Five Basic Elements - prithvi or earth, apas or water, tejas or fire, vayu or air and akasha or ether) with which he can initiate any creation.

Brahma (Prajapati) is considered as the son of God. He is self-born out of a lotus flower which grew from the navel of Vishnu (or Keshav, representative of Brahmam), signifying the umbilical code of connection with the cosmos. You can interpret it as a story as well as the symbolism to reveal the eternal - that everything and everybody is connected.

Now let's try this question. Is there a creator? Who created universe?

Instead of spreading non-sense stories of creation and creator, our ancestors said, "We don't know much about creation. Creation is an unimaginable complex universal phenomenon.

The miniscule human brain with its insignificant existence on a small planet like Earth, just cannot comprehend the true form about the creation and sustenance of the universe with thousands of galaxies, millions of solar systems, trillions of planets, countless of life forms, etc."

Our ancestors went beyond God Brahma and all whole-sale creator Gods. They said the cosmos springs into view simultaneously with the seer and that there is no detailed process of creation.

This is known as 'yugapat-srishti' (instantaneous creation). It is quite similar to the creations in dream where the experiencer springs up simultaneously with the objects of experience...

"If there is a creator, then the creation should be an extension or aspect of him/her/it. The creator or whatever expands Himself outwardly, like a web woven by a spider...."

As the spider sends forth and draws in its thread, as plants grow on the earth, as hair grows on the head and the body of a living man- so does everything in the universe arise. (Mandukya Upanishad).

This universe thus came from Brahmam. It is sustained by Brahmam. It will eventually be withdrawn into Brahmam. (These three processes are represented by Trimurti or trinity God concept).

After a period of rest or repose in Brahmam, the universe will emerge again from Brahmam, exist and be withdrawn again into Brahmam. These cycles of creation, preservation and dissolution of the universe is an everlasting, continuous process.

Hence, Brahmam (the force) is everywhere in the universe. Brahmam exists in everything. There is nothing in the universe which is not God! That's why our ancestors said: Aham brahmasmi (I am Brahmam or I am Divine) and Ayam Atma Brahma (I am this Self -Atman - that is Brahmam).

In Bhagavad Gita, Krishna (who realized that he is Brahmam) says, "As the mighty wind blowing everywhere exist always in space, so do all being exist in me (Brahmam)." The entire world and all objects exist in space. Space supports everything.

He further says: "On me the entire universe is strung like jewels on a string." In a pearl necklace, each pearl may be different but the same string holds it together.

Similarly, Brahmam is the common factor in everything, though everything appears unique.

The Katha Upanishad explains this with the following example, "Just as the sun which helps all eyes to see is not affected by defects of the eye or external objects, so God dwells in the heart of all beings but is not affected by the defects on any being."

So, questions like "Is there a creator?" or "Who created the universe" do not hold any merits. Just because you put a question mark, it doesn't make a valid question.

It's like asking ridiculous questions like "Does moon get diarrhea?" Or "Does Australia feel shy?" Nobody can answer you. Why does universe need a creator? And why there should be a "who", why can't there be a "what"?

When you say "I believe in a creator" that just means you have faith in a Semitic story. We should respect all beliefs and faith. Nobody is free from beliefs. Even atheists have beliefs. Your belief is good for you.

I believe in almost 330 million Gods! But the problem arises when I say, my belief is right and yours is wrong.

Psychologically, there is no difference between a modern man worshiping an unknown creator and a tribal man in African Aboriginal tribes worshiping a used empty bottle (that fell from a helicopter) as God. You can't say one belief is superior to the other.

As human being evolve and be aware, those HADD conditioning will disappear. Such irrational stories about the creators cannot survive.

(Recently Pope had to admit that the entire Genesis in the Testament was false).

Whatever created will be destroyed. That's universal physical law.

Only scientific, rational, logical, inclusive and cosmic order will survive. And in Sanskrit language it is called Sanatan (eternal, never beginning nor ending). And the Sanskrit word for 'eternal order' is Sanatan Dharma!

Chapter - 8

We Hindus Have 330 Million+ Gods, Seriously!

"Do you really believe in 33 crore (330 million) Gods?"

"Yes, I do. I suspect there could be more," I said.

The question was from Abdul Saleem, a co-passenger in the Chennai-Ernakulam Express. He was discussing about the concepts for Gods with his friend Natesh Iyer. They were college mates. I was sharing the compartment with them.

"You are wrong Mr.Uday. You have mistaken the meaning of Sanskrit word 'Koti' as crore (=ten million). It's normal for a layman." Natesh said.

"Koti means crores, right?" I asked him.

"Hahaha," he laughed out aloud. "Koti has another meaning - 'type' and 'family'. Our Puranas say that there are only 33 devas (8 Vasu, 11 Rudra, 12 Aditya, 1 Prajapati and 1 Shatkaar). We only have 33 Gods in Hinduism that is mis-interpreted as 33 crores by ignorant people like you" Natesh said.

"Mr.Natesh, there are three issues here. One - In Sanskrit Koti (Kodi) means crore. There are many other meanings for that word, but, of course, not 'type' or 'category' or 'family' etc..." I told him.

I had the same doubt long ago so cross-checked with Sanskrit scholars.

"And the second issue?" he asked.

"The 33 Vedic devas concept is not in Puranas, but it is mentioned in Brihadaranyaka Upanishad. It says that there are 33 devas in the celestial world, in terms of performance of yagna (a ritual sacrifice). It doesn't mention the word "koti" there," I said.

"Ok"

"When some apologetic Hindus saw the number 33 there, they might have mixed it up with a different concept of 33 crore devas that mentioned in Puranas. But Vedas also lists many other Gods.

Rig-Veda itself mentions about 3,339 devas have worshipped Agni (fire God). It also describes Vishnu as younger brother to Indra. If there are only 33 devas, what about those inhabitants in Swargaloka?" I asked him.

I added: "There are 14 Indras. His army, his sons, members of his court - millions of devas are supposed to be there. Then there are many Gods in Kailasam (Shiva's abode), Vaikuntam (Vishnu's abode) etc. What about Vishnu's 24 avatars?"

"What's the third issue? "Abdul asked.

"Mr.Natesh should explain the Tamil phrase, 'Muppathu Mukkodi Devargal'? Does it mean 33 types of Gods? Most of the old texts and regional scriptures talk about 33 crore Gods..."

"But sir, seriously, do you really believe in such non-sense? There is only one God..."Abdul said.

"Yes, yes only one God in Hinduism too. Yes, there is only one God - Brahmam. We call it in many names, that's it..."Natesh said aloud.

"Brahmam is not God. It is the Ultimate Reality - it is all inclusive. There is nothing separate from Brahmam...The God in question is a totally different concept." I said,

God is not English translation for any of these words- Devta, Deva, Ishwar, Bhagwan, Daivam etc. They are not one and the same. The words 'Ishvara' and 'Devatha' are often translated as "God" leading to such common misunderstanding. Diety could be a better word for deva.

"Mr.Uday, there is only one God in this universe. He is infinite. He cannot be captured in images and idols. Only pagan idiots will worship as images..." Abdul said. I could see Natesh's face changing into red.

"I doubt whether God is he, she or it. If God is infinite, and cannot be captured in images or idols, tell me Abdul, how can he be captured in mere words? The vocabulary is used only to describe that is reachable.

An image is worth more than thousand words. Therefore, an image is far better than words. The definitions and description of God in all religious books are, in a way, an attempt to image God.

At least, Idol worshippers are sincere enough not to say that idols are what God looks like!" I said.

I saw Abdul's face becoming red.

He said: "God is one. The God Almighty - praise be upon him - has clearly declared: You will worship none but me that you will associate none with me, and that none of you shall set up mortals as deities besides me. If you commit the foulest sin by worshipping any other Gods (other than me) or associating partner with me, I shall throw you in hell fire as a punishment for this sin...He creates and controls everything."

"Is that statement from God? Fine. If there was only one God, how was it possible for man to find many other Gods to worship?

If the single God is so confident that there are no other Gods except him, why is he showing envy to another God that is obvious in his own words?

If he really knew that there is no other God, wouldn't he be confident that people will not find any another God to worship?

His own statement is contradictory - it clearly shows that he is always suspicious and insecure that there may be other Gods and people may worship those Gods instead of him. " (I remembered this as I had a similar experience earlier – see next chapter)

"Those are non-sense questions..."Abdul interrupted

"But Abdul, he is asking very pertinent questions..."Natesh said.

"I have more questions on your God's statement, Abdul. The word "One" itself is a selfish definition.

The word "One" exists here because there is a concept of 'Many'. The irony is obvious here. When you say that God is "One", you restrict him to be materialistically a standalone entity in the Universe with the almighty capability. And if God is not material, either no mathematical finite can be applied to him, or all sorts of counts apply."

"But our concept of single God is the best and most scientific till date..."Abdul repeated.

"When you say "my concept of God is correct" and "his concept is wrong", it immediately frames an arrogance, envy and ego that eventually results in hatred, anger, onslaughts and war.

Hindus don't have the right to say: "Krishna is the only God. All other beliefs are bullshit" Similarly, you can only say: "Allah is my God. I believe in him" But you shouldn't say "Allah is the only God, there are no other Gods".

"You are misguiding. Even, Vedas approve the concept of single God...Isn't it Natesh?" Abdul said.

This time Natesh didn't reply. He looked confused.

"If you need approval and acknowledgement for what is stated in your some 1500-year-old text from 7000 years old Vedas, then why don't you follow Vedas itself?" I asked him.

"I have been seeing Semitic faith followers' quote from Vedas and ancient Hindu texts to justify sentences in their religious texts. There is absolutely nothing common. All quotes they make are out-of-context," I added.

"But there is only One God - isn't it Natesh?" Abdul asked.

No reply from Natesh. He was just looking at me expecting reply.

"I am sorry guys, but the concept or notion of a personal whole sale God, hiding behind the clouds of secrecy, telling us irrational stories through few men whom he sends as messengers, demanding us to worship him or punish us, does not make any sense.

I don't think that God is as silly as an autocratic emperor who demands others to respect him or fear him." I told him, "I prefer to go with peaceful small time retail Gods than such monopoly fascist Gods."

"But I don't understand why would you endorse such superstitious beliefs of 33 crore Gods. Why can't you believe in real that there is only one God? "Abdul again asked.

"All beliefs are superstitious, as long as it is NOT proven in an empirical and scientific method. Single God and multiple Gods - both are beliefs only. You cannot say I have only 55 percent superstition and others have 95%, so I am better. You can't measure superstitions like that," I said.

"If there is one God, why can't there by many?" I asked him.

"But fanatic single God belief is unacceptable for a civilized and cultured society, as it always creates separation, splits, conflicts and violence in this world.

The fundamentalist one-God-domination concept has led to terrorism, fanaticism, insecurity, fear and killing whereas flexible multiple Gods create tolerance and co-operation. That's why our ancestors created so many Gods."

After a minute of thought Abdul said, "I understand - people can have many beliefs but tolerance to each other's belief is the key. I am very tolerant..." Then he asked me: "Seriously sir, is there any rationale behind the Hindu concept of 33 crore Gods?"

"Yes, there should be some science in it and you might know that too. Mr.Uday sir, I am sorry, I mistook you for an ignorant layman," Natesh enquired.

"I am an ignorant layman only. Little bit knowledge that I gained in my life doesn't elevate me to your standards. So, don't worry," I smiled.

I added: "Modern science cannot support any of our beliefs. But our ancestors have mastered the natural science. They have realized the divine presence everywhere. They have listed down 33 crore different forms of natural power or manifestations that is holding this Universe."

Incidentally, our ancestors have also listed around 8.4 million species, while science have just reached the figure of 1.75 and is predicting the figure to be between 8 to 10 million).

"Sir, what does your Puranas say about it?" Abdul asked.

"Puranas talk about various Gods or Devathas just to make a human being understand the vastness of the concept of God.

Otherwise it will be too abstract to understand for ordinary ignorant men like me. The stories in Puranas are metaphorical in nature. Natesh let me tell you - the Sanskrit phrase 'trayastrimsati koti' is also mentioned in Atharva Veda, Yajur Veda, and Satapatha-Brahmama.

And there also 'koti' doesn't mean type. It means 'supreme'. It lists supreme 33 devas for very specific purpose. But it acknowledges other Gods..."

"Sir, it appears like you really support the concept of 33 crore plus Gods. How could you convince yourself about it?" Natesh asked me.

"Our ancestors have simplified the process of selecting your 'own' God from the long list of 330 million. They have identified three principal deities. They are Kula or Gotra (clan) Devatha (Family Deity), Grama Devatha (Village Deity) and Ishta Devatha (Favourite Deity)...."

"Can you explain that sir?" both asked together.

"For instance, my family or Gotra Devatha is Mahalasa Narayani - that is Mohini Avatar of Vishnu (Not mentioned in your 33 types). I belong to Vishwamitra-Ahamarshana-Kamsi Gotra (clan) that supposed to be 1000s of years old. So, when I pray to my Kula Devatha - it is for the entire family, which would be spread to hundreds of thousands now.

They are all my family members, though I don't know most of them. Then comes Grama Devatha - mine is Narasimha.

The entire village is dedicated to Narasimha and the prayer is for the entire village and its inhabitants.

God's place is punyabhoomi. In today's world, the village concept is replaced with country. That's why for real Hindus their country - India - is 'Punyabhoomi' (sacred land) but for others it is just a real estate."

"And what is Ishta Devatha?"

"We can choose one from these 33 crores. So, for a Hindu, family, community and country were important than his personal likes and dislikes...

You will see this cultural aspect in everything related to Sanatan Dharma - there was no selfish importance for individuals, even in marriages." I said.

"Amazing sir —our thoughts have never ever gone this deep..."Natesh said.

"I believe in Allah, I am a Muslim. But now I know why should I also consider my country as a Punyabhoomi," Abdul said.

"You must...our ancestors believed that the world population is approximately 100 crores (and it was almost true then). 0.33 is the decimal representation of the ratio 1/3. They have classified human basically into three 'gunas' (qualities) namely deva (divine) guna, asura (demonic) guna and manushya (humane) guna. The ratio 1/3 refers to the deva guna in us. Thus, it comes to 33.33 crores of Gods! For a mathematical adjustment it is said 33"

"This is very convincing Sir. Salutes... Let there be billion Gods then..." Natesh said.

He added: "I suspect the 330 million numbers could actually be corresponded to the assumed population of the world at the time of composition of those scriptures. Going by what you said, our ancestors believed in divine existence in all human, it would mean that each individual has one God. In other words, the concept of God was being advocates as a personal experience."

"Could be," I said.

"Yes - Let all humans in this planet be Gods..." Abdul said.

I told them: "I don't have any problems in praying to Allah, Jehovah, Yahweh, Elohim, Abba or Krishna, Shiv, Vinayak, Vishnu, Durga - whoever....

Because, our ancestors taught us, 'Akashat patitam toyam, yada gachchati sagaram, Sarva devo namaskaraha, Keshavm pratigachchati...'(the entire water fell from the sky goes to the sea, similarly salutations to all the Gods reaches to Keshav).

Keshav is not a single Hindu God. The word represents cosmos. Let's all co-exist.

Let all Gods co-exist. Let's don't be fanatic to any single idea of God. Let there be billions of Godly humans. Let noble thoughts come to us from every side. Remember, our ancestors accepted even atheists as saints.

Our ancestors taught us to see God in every entity of the existence. That's the real oneness!

Chapter - 9

Is Single God Theory Ridiculous?

I recalled an old incident. My friend from Egypt told me that all religions say there is only one God. He ridiculed me for worshiping many Gods.

He quoted the religious texts that he believes to be God's own statements: "You will worship none but me that you will associate none with me, and that none of you shall set up mortals as deities besides me. If you commit the foulest sin by worshiping any other Gods (other than me) or associating partner with me, I shall throw you in hell fire as a punishment for this sin."

I beg to differ. I asked him following questions based on the above statement of the so-called God. He didn't have any answers. Nobody has ever answered me till now.

1. Had there been really only one God, it would not have been possible for man to find another God to worship, right?

2. Had the God been confident that there is no other God except him, he should not have been jealous of another God, right?

3. If the GOD knew that there is no other God, he would have been confident that people will not find any another God to worship, right?

4. The behavioural pattern of any single GOD in such concepts suggests that he is not confident that he is the only God.

He seems to always be suspicious that there may be other Gods and people may worship those Gods instead of him.

5. So the insecure GOD warns man not to worship another God.

Can't you clearly see the insecurity, whims and fancies of a narrow-minded human being behind this message?

6. Can any GOD always feel threatened that a member of his followers' gang may slip out of his grip and start to worship another God?

So he had to enforce strict law that if any one of his gang tries to desert Him, he should immediately be put to death for apostasy.

7. How can any GOD be so insecure? The single insecure God theory converts the basic instinct to insecurity right from childhood.

The followers' behavior may be fostered by GOD's violent teachings for establishing Himself as the sole proprietary God of the world.

8. And one more thing – you say, your singular God does everything. If there is only one powerful God who controls everything, doesn't that also mean he creates bad things and causes bad things to happen?

"I am sorry, but the concept or notion of a personal God, hiding behind the clouds of secrecy, telling us irrational stories through few men whom he sends as messengers, demanding us to worship him or punish us, does not make sense. I don't think that God is as silly as an autocratic emperor who demands others to respect him or fear him," I told him.

The single God theory can be one major reason to create terrorism, fundamentalism, fanaticism, insecurity, fear and violence, whereas multiple Gods create tolerance and co-operation.

"Uday, belief in multiple Gods is primitive," he uttered loudly.

Our ancestors taught us: "As all the water falling from the sky ultimately ends up in the ocean, the prayers/bows offered to all the Gods ultimately reach the Keshav (supreme cosmic power - the divine energy). That's a statement of confidence, unlike the insecure God.

If there is one God, going by the same logic, why can't there be many?

"When you believe in something, let me also believe in whatever I feel right. You have no right to say your belief is truth and mine is not...let me believe in multiple Gods, what's your problem?" I said.

Many research studies have shown that polytheism (the worship or belief in multiple deities) is more tolerant.

Nobody has the right to say: "Krishna is the only God. All other beliefs are bullshit."

Similarly, one can say: "Allah is my God. I believe in him." But he/she doesn't have the right to say "Allah is the only God, there are no other Gods."

Let us pray to all Gods. Let's not be fanatic to any single idea. Remember, our ancestors accepted even atheists as saints. All our 'Shad Darshanas' (shad means six, Darshana means views or insights.

It is about six Hindu philosophies), Bauddham and Charvakam are accommodating the no-God (Nastik) theory. Our ancestors were so broad-minded even to accept Nastiks.

Accepting any God is OK with me. We already have 330 million Gods! Adding one or two more doesn't make any big difference.

Let's accept all noble thoughts that come from anywhere. This is what our ancestors wanted us to follow. That's why our land - Bharat - was called Punya Bhumi (sacred land)!

"India has never invaded any country since last 10,000 years" - the statement which India often proudly speaks of about non-violence.

What would be the reason? The inherent tolerance derived from multi-faith system. So, why can't we co-exist peacefully accepting and respecting each other's beliefs?

India is the ONLY country in the world that gives special privileges (concessions, reservations and financial aids) to people who believe in Gods outside Hindu scriptures!

Let's follow the culture and civilization of our own broad-minded ancestors - why should we mimic different cultures that are not suitable for our DNA, environment, ambience and climate?

"But what's wrong in accepting and propagating a single God theory?"

"What's right in it? If you learn history, sociology and psychology you will understand dangers in that sort of propaganda"

Why Am I a Hindu?

The advantages of pantheistic or polytheistic religions are that they do not force their religion or God on others since they are bound to accept God in any form unlike monotheistic religions.

Single God concept has more chances to make its follower fanatic when one tries to prove the superiority of his/her God. Accepting God in many names and many forms on the other hand shows more liberty.

The single God theory not helped any countries so far. Europeans and Arabs have single God but Many countries.

The Arabian God, though hails 'universal brotherhood' could not unite Iran and Iraq or Paksitan and Afghanistan. They say 'peace', but cannot find peace in their own regions.

India had 330 million Gods but remains as one peaceful country, despite we have totally different languages and traditions.

Hindus have many Gods but one united country. That's unity in diversity.

"I understand Hindus have suffered plenty of brutal attack and inquisitions by religious fanatics. There are fanatics in every religion. But we teach love and peace only," he said.

"Though love and peace are preached in all religions, then why monotheistic (single God) religions resort to swords to spread their beliefs? So how does the single God and single moral code book justify all these deeds?

A single God is always insecure which makes the preaching of peace of the Single God go in vain, and finally resort to violence, and show intolerance and even deaths."

"Why is it that single God religions populated all around the world?," he asked.

"Isn't it mostly through different forms of violence like genocide, abduction of women and children, putting a forceful ban on indigenous faiths and their cultures, belittling the value of other cultures etc? However, I know there were many good missionaries and sober messengers too."

Chapter - 10

Do Hindu Gods eat food?

My friend, Mohamed Ashiq Naseeruddin from Birmingham, UK told me: "Your Gods might be getting indigestion! Millions of people offer them food every day...."

I initially thought it was a harmless joke.

Neither our Gods won't get angry or insecure on jokes on them, nor do real Hindus get hurt on innocent jokes. I laughed. "Yeah, especially with those loads of chemicals in the food now-a-days"

"Seriously Uday Sir, I see Hindus offer food to idols and believe that Gods can eat! I am not a religious hater. But isn't this foolish and nonsense?"

"Yes. Hindus do offer food to God. What we offer to God is Naivedyam. When it comes back to us, it becomes Prasadam. I also do that at home, during holy days or celebrations and in temples."

"See, even an educated journalist like you too... Don't you know God won't eat this food? Idol can't open its mouth. God won't eat or talk the way we human do. Offering food to God is very materialistic thinking. There is no spirituality in that. You people are so superstitious and Idiotic..."

"Hmm"

"In fact, God doesn't need anything from you. But you need everything from God. So, all we should do is, pray to God.

That's what 21st century's modern, cultured, educated people do...A sincere, dedicated prayer with utmost devotion is enough to please God."

"So, God will hear your prayer..." I asked him.

"Yes. He can hear the prayer. God doesn't want anything, let alone food. He is perfect and complete. Everything in this universe happens as per God's will and wish..." Ashiq said.

"Ashiq, you mean to say, God (or idols in question here) doesn't eat food, it doesn't even open its mouth. It won't talk, right?"

"Yes"

"You said God will hear your prayer. So, according to you, all we can do is to pray and worship him. Everything in this universe happens only by his wish and will. God doesn't need anything from us. He is perfect and complete. This is what you say as modern and scientific. Am I correct?"

"Exactly" he beamed. "Yes sir. I know you are very open and you can understand fast. This is crystal clear. So, you will stop your pre-historic Hindu tradition of offering food to God."

"No Ashiq."

"Why?" he was surprised.

"I am not convinced about what you said. You said, your God doesn't eat, he doesn't speak or behave as humans do, right?" I paused.

"Yes...yes..."

"Then how can he hear to what we humans say?

Why Am I a Hindu?

The very concept of delivering prayers through words (in any language) brings God to possess hearing capability as we humans...If God doesn't eat and talk, how can he hear?"

"That...but God can hear, right?"

"God can't talk or eat. But he can hear what kind of logic is that? Does it mean that God has only selective few sensory organs? Who told you that? Did God tell you that?"

"No, he talks through Prophets...All religions have prophets..."

"Is it so? Then, what prevents God from eating food through his people?"

"It's not right. Everything happens as per God's will and wish."

"Ashiq, will and wish are related of human thinking. You are saying that God also thinks as we humans do. And he has will and wish!

God's will or God understanding our wish is proof of material relation of God. Theoretically, how is it different from materialistic offering food to God?"

"It's not like that. We can just pray.... God will listen to us...all the Holy books say we have to pray for it..."

"But you just said he doesn't need anything from us. Then why did your God order in Holy books to worship him and pray to him?"

"Prayer is for us...God knows everything" Ashiq said."You are contradicting again. If your God is powerful enough to know about everything why should you tell anything to God?

God knows what is happening and what will happen. Then why ask for anything to God when God already knows what is going to happen to us?

Or is he so egoistic that he wants you to plead? Does he enjoy such ego? And if God is perfect and complete, then anything offered to him (including Prayers) which if accepted by him, would prove to fill up some void. It makes God incomplete. So as per your own arguments based on your Holy Scriptures, rendering of prayers itself binds God..."I said.

He didn't talk for a moment. We were talking over WhatsApp. I sent him a question mark. He replied: "I am thinking for answers..."

"You won't get. Ashiq, before ridiculing other's beliefs, we have to check if our path is right. When it comes to irrational beliefs, no religion is better..." I told him.

Then he asked: "Seriously, why are you people offering food to God? What's the rationale behind it?"

"Why do you offer flowers to your girlfriend? It is to express your love, right? Offering food is a symbolic gesture of love. It is a way of thanking God for the food provided. It's an act of gratitude.

We prepare Naivedyam with utmost devotion, dedication with purity of mind and body. Then offer the sacred food (Bhagwan Bhog) to God. We know God won't eat directly. It's just symbolic. After rituals, we distribute the Prasadam to everyone around us for blessings.

The idol won't eat. God eats through us. We are also the integral part of God." I added.

-When we offer food and flowers to God, we say 'Samarpayaamee' means it is yours and you have the first right on it. The words Prasad has many meanings too.

We seek God's blessings (Prasad), we believe God has blessed (Prasad) the food; we distribute the Prasad (blessings) of God with devotion.

And we accept and eat the Prasad (blessings) of God with utmost devotion. It also believed that offering 'Prasad' daily to Gods showers food and prosperity on the house.

-We offer food to God at prayer room in home and in the temple. We also celebrate festivals (like Pongal, Makarasankrathi, Diwali) when we make and share the food.

In every temple in India, it is customary to make a small offering of sweets or other food, as a mark of our devotion and gratefulness towards the God or Goddess.

"Is this mentioned in any of your scriptures?"

"All the scriptures talk about offerings to God. Bhagavad-Gita says, all that you do, all that you eat, all that you offer and give away, as well as all austerities that you may perform, should be done as an offering unto Me (Me=Brahmam or cosmos). So, offering food to God before eating is an integral part of our culture to make the food blessed..."

- Our ancestors found that food is the source of human body and mind.

It should be eaten for the survival and strength of the body, with a humble attitude, to practice austerities and gain awareness, and not just for pleasure.

All disease - related to body and mind - derives from food. They have scientifically developed a traditional medicinal system, Ayurveda that highlights the Viruddha Ahara (incompatible foods) and pathyam or parhes (dietary restrictions).

According to Ayurveda scriptures, if you follow this concept you can live up to 120 years without any major pain and miseries. So, food is considered as divine.

- Since their economic system was based on the temple, they have charted out the list of Naivedyas in temple for each month based on seasonal and environmental relevance and its impact on human body.

If a person follows the similar diet strictly, you won't have any physical problems... They wanted us eat Sattvik food with gratitude and devotion.

They wished that their descendant should follow this great system. So, they have mixed it up beliefs and temple, so that people would earnestly follow it.

I don't know if modern concrete business centres in the name of temples and those religious crooks that are behind this would follow this tradition. Modern priests won't even know about this divine food system.

"I am really sorry - I didn't know the significance of Prasadam and divinity of food..." he said.

"But Ashiq, it is a lost art in India. I wouldn't be surprised if modern temples offer you Pizzas, Chicken Biriyani and Mutton pulav as Prasadams, instead of pure Sattvik food.

Given the trend among fraud priests and the brain-washed zombie Hindu communities, instead of Milk Abhisheka (bathing a deity in milk), an alcohol Abhisheka can also be expected."

Before ridiculing others you should think - Why do Christians offer Mass (liturgy) and Candle to God? Why do Semitic religions offer fast? What is the reason to offer a Chadar (blanket) by Muslims at Dargah?

Does that mean God is feeling cold and needs a blanket? No - it's all a matter of faith. In fact, to construct a permanent structure over the grave is against the teaching of Islam, as it leads ignorant people to do Shirk (Belief on other than Allah). People follow many customs and rituals. Let's don't ridicule or mock it until and unless you have a foolproof system.

Chapter - 11
Stone is God, but God is Not Stone!

A reader has written to me: "Why do Hindus worship Idols? Why don't they understand it is just a stone? Why don't they try to learn from the modern religions like Islam and Christianity and stop this childish Idol Worship, Uday?"

I wrote back to him: "The only religion in the world that doesn't need to worship an idol is Hinduism. It is optional for Hindus to worship idols or not. But for all other religions, it is a MUST and mandatory."

Surprised? Many people have raised similar question on Hinduism.

The Webster's Dictionary says: "Idolatry is the worship of a physical object as a God of any object, person."

That means Idol is an image or representation of a God. One that is adored, often blindly or excessively can also be called Idol worship.

All religions have been engaging in idolatry without knowing it - it's always hard to see whether someone is really worshipping something, or just using it as a symbol of a totally different thing.

Are Christians idol worshippers?

Exodus 20:4, 5: "You must not make for yourself a carved image or a form like anything that is in the heavens above or that is on the earth underneath or that is in the waters under the earth.

You must not bow down to them nor be induced to serve them, because I Jehovah your God am a God exacting exclusive devotion."

The Christians worship the statue of Jesus or the Cross or Jesus in the cross in their Church. Catholics pray to Mary and have statues of her. Isn't that idolatry?

If you come to India, especially South India, you can see thousands of new Churches made as replica of Hindu temples, with Dwaja Sthamba (flag banner high column) among other things, creating more idols to worship.

I don't think anything other than the cemetery in the Churches that doesn't fit into external culture. Christianity is almost Indianised.

During first few centuries Jesus was pictured as Asiatic - bald, bearded and short - because of Asian origin. Later all images of Jesus became that of a European white man.

So, their idol clearly is Jesus Christ of European race. Can a Christian worship a black or Asian Jesus? Their main idols are Christ and Cross.

Islam doesn't have direct "idol worship" as Christians or Hindus do. The first condition to be a Muslim is: the act of worship should be devoted to Allah Alone.

Allah says (interpretation of the meaning): "And they were commanded not, but that they should worship Allah, and worship none but Him Alone (abstaining from ascribing partners to Him)." [Al-Bayyinah 98:5]

But you can see Idolatry in that religion too. Islam asks Muslims to pray towards Mecca. Direction or destination is focal point - an idol as per definition.

Something becomes sacred only when you worship it. Many Muslims worship the black Kaaba Stone in Mecca.

There are three explanations for the stone - (1) As per Islamic belief- it is sent by the Islamic God, Allah. (2) Some serious historians say it's a Shiv Linga (Abstract representation of the Hindu deity, Shiva.

Hindu beliefs were spread all over Asia then). (3) Some people claim it's a Meteorite. Whatever it is, Kaaba is an important icon that they worship. Zamzam water in Makkah is also sacred for them.

Let alone idols, Islam strictly prohibits worshipping any man-made objects. Millions of copies of Holy Quran are printed in many printing presses by men and made into book form by man.

Isn't it a man-made object? How can it be worshipped? If you say it is a representation of God's words, it is an idol by definition.

The printed quotes are photo-framed, kept in the wall and worshipped. It's also man-made. Alphabets used to describe God are also man-made images.

Most of the Mosques (place of worship) have photograph of Kaaba. Some are visiting Dargah (grave of a revered religious figure) to offer worship.

To my understanding, Muslims are forbidden to, and therefore do not, worship Prophet Mohammed. Muslims shouldn't even keep images of him.

But indirectly they do. Will they allow anybody to criticize him? If anybody talks one word against him, he/she will be cut into pieces. Isn't that fanatic worship?

Millions of Muslims worship holy hair of Prophet Mohammed and now building India's biggest mosque Sha're Mubarak Masjid (literally: Blessed Hair Grand Mosque) in Kerala, the southern state of India.

You can also find images of Muhammad's face in manuscript illustrations from hundreds of years ago, some of which are on display at the Metropolitan Museum of Art in New York.

Some of the earliest Islamic coins were minted with Muhammad's face on them! The celebration of Muhammad birthday is contradictory to Islamic law.

But India has official Holiday on Prophet's birthday like Christmas and Krishna Jayanti (Krishna's birth day). What is it other than iconic worship?

"All Muslims are not like that…"

"Similarly all Hindus are not idol worshippers. Only a section of Hindus do."

I agree many Muslims still worship only the formless God. But, they are still praying to a God which has all other attributes except that of "form".

Therefore, they only seem to be rejecting the attribute of "form", whereas they still seem to accept all other attributes in God (omnipotence, omnipresence etc.) which are also accepted by people from other religions who worship and pray to God using idols.

When you keep the photos or images of any holy places, ancestors and give due respect to those images, it is also like worshiping idols.

Even atheist philosophies like Marxism follow Idolatry. They have created Martyrs who they worship with garland and flowers. They call it "Rakthasakshi Mandapm" (Temple for martyrs).

The world capital of superstitious worship is communist China. Even African tribal are better than Chinese when it comes to superstitions and idol worships.

From a Western viewpoint, Hindus are still worst. They worship almost everything.

Apart from 33 crores (330 million) Gods and Goddesses, they worship rat, cow, stones, birds, sexual organs, mountain, weapons etc.

They have made idols or icons out of almost everything in this universe. But Hindus have the honesty and courage to admit that, "Yes we do have idol worship and that is important to our religion."

"Can you explain the rationale behind idol worship?" she askd.

As a matter of fact, Hindus don't worship idols; they worship the ideal behind the idol.

An Idol is an adjective of God.

Idol is NOT an equivalent word for Vigraha (body or form) and Bimba (image, picture or object) in Sanskrit.

The word 'idol' may be inadequate to mean 'Vigraha', except to indicate that the 'shilpa' or 'figure' indicates a kind of 'model' through which to visualize God.

In Sanskrit, "Viseshal Grahyathe ithi Vigraha" (The One which is acceptable or liked or holds passionately) is Vigraham.

In early stages of one's quest for divinity, a representative form becomes necessary. That's how the concept of Vigrahas (idols) came up in all religions. Vigraha (Vishesham Grihamiti = Special abode), Pratima (Mam prati = In front of me), Bimba or Moorti are synonyms of Vigraha.

The purpose of Vigraha is to help the seekers to focus on the concepts. So, the seekers are seeing the manifestation of a divine power in such idol.

They believe use of an idol or a physical symbol in worship and prayer is intended to enhance the focus on Brahmam (the universal or supreme God) with respect to a certain attribute (Saguna) of Brahmam.

Such Idol worship is called "Saguna Aradhana" (Worshipping forms and names) in India.

Contrary to popular misconceptions, idol is not the God for Hindus.

For the beginners, it is like this: Those who wish to offer worship to the Brahmam in whichever form he/she prefers, invite 'That' into the favourite 'Vigraha'.

Aavahayami (I invite), Sthapayami (I establish/seat), Poojayami (I worship). Then we offer water, flowers and leaves, fragrant substances, delicious food, music, dance etc. as part of worship to 'That'. Then we ask 'That' to grant our wishes and needs.

At the end of the day or period of worship, we offer the Pooja again and ask 'That' to leave the Vigraha. This process is called Visarjana (disperse). Then it becomes just an idol.

In short, if you carefully observe you can see all religions and ideologies have some form of idol worship - it may be a statue, book, person, symbol, icon or thing.

Everybody worships either images and/or political symbols. The only differences would be in the method or degree in worshipping.

It is thus quite apparent for the entire mankind - all religions - whether it is atheism, pluralism, animism, fanaticism, fundamentalism, gurudom, kingdom of priests and extreme materialism, the idol worship comes natural.

All idols and images were created by men only. They the followers get stuck there. They fight and kill for those idols. So, there is no point in anybody holding a "Holier than Thou" attitude.

Why can't a believer move beyond idols or images?

Because human mind needs some form of image or imagery for its very survival. This is the limitation of all religions.

So, our ancestors, the great sages, found that humans should move beyond beliefs if he/she wants to realize the truth. They should go beyond idolatry - it is Nirguna Aradhana.

The only religion that talks about truly formless and undefined God is Sanatan Dharma. It says the Brahmam - the divine power - is truly without a form, a gender or anything for that matter, while all other religions believe that God has a gender, a race and a language.

As Sankracharya says, "to describe Brahmam even the words recoil." Anybody trying to describe God through words or images (Idolatry) is like blinds describing elephant. You have to go beyond a name and a form (shape) to realise the Brahmam. (Lalitha Sahasranamam says 'Nama roopa vivarjitha')

Vedas say the Brahmam is formless, ineffable (nirguna) and Unmoved Mover. Upanishads describe Nirguna Brahmam- the ineffable God as, "Whole is that, whole too is this and from the whole, whole cometh and take whole, yet whole remains." This cannot be understood with using mind as the mind CANNOT go beyond images (idols) or beliefs.

That's the reason our ancestors said God is an experience to be experienced by the experiencer. It cannot be explained. It cannot be described.

In his final stages of quest, a Sanatan Dharma follower realizes and sees God's presence in everything in the universe (Isavasyam idam sarvam). That's why he prays "May all beings be happy" (Lokah Samastah Sukhino BHavantu).

That's how the universal compassion develops. That's how the inclusive philosophy of non-violence, equality and tolerance develops.

That's why ancient Indians could welcome and accept all religions, ideologies and philosophies including Atheism. No beliefs in the world can take a human being to such elevated higher dimension.

Put simply, a Hindu believes God exists in stones. But he understands that, it doesn't mean God is the stone.

Chapter - 12

Are Puranas Real?

"Why do you believe in Gods like Rama and Krishna? They are just mythological heroes or Puranic story characters and of course NOT real Gods..." a question from another ABCD (American-Born Confused Desi). (Desi=Indian) His name is Jayanth Mathews - born to Hindu mother and Christian father from Kerala.

Jayanth has some exposure to Indian and Christian literature. He is a kind of agnostic. He continued: "Uday uncle, I can accept that life of Jesus Christ as history. But Rama and Krishna are just myths..."

"It is, in fact, the other way around. Apart from Bible there is hardly any contemporary literature that even mentions about Jesus Christ. But there are more than 300 literatures, scriptures or versions of Ramayana from many countries around the world that talk about the biography of Rama. Krishna was also mentioned in hundreds of scriptures during his time. I am sure Jesus Christ as well as Rama and Krishna were historical characters.

There could be some exaggeration in their stories, like, even today, we accept a movie hero who bashes hundreds of villain with bare hands..."

"What about the Trimurti (Brahma, Vishnu and Shiv) - were they also historical characters?"

"There are God concepts in all culture and religions. In the Semitic culture God is Jehovah in Latin and Allah in Arabian culture.

Trimurtis are Indian ancestral concepts of Gods. It is both real and unreal or manifested and unmanifested depending upon the seeker or the worshipper." I said.

"But Semitic religions endorse the personal God concept, a male who creates man and judges him. Are Trimurtis like that?"

"No. The Trimurtis are different concepts altogether. They don't demand you to worship them. The sages, who developed Indian concept of God, didn't believe in a personal creator. The creator and created are the same and the cosmos survives in a cyclical process - even galaxies are born and die. The entire cosmos and the process altogether is called Brahmam..."

"But I asked about Trimurti, you are digressing from the topic, Uday uncle..." he said.

"No. To explain that you should know about Brahmam (Cosmic consciousness or the 'force' or universal energy, whatever - it means all inclusive).

There are billions of universes. Puranas talk about these things. Nothing ever happened from Brahmam, and nothing will happen from Brahmam. If anything/anybody originates from Brahmam, Brahmam cannot be called Brahmam."

"Ok..."
"We, human beings, experience time and space. I am not going into physics.

For laymen like us, sages have divided this Brahmam into three distinctive categories- the creative force (Brahma), maintainer or preserver (Vishnu) and transformer or destroyer (Shiv).

It is for us to understand as we experience all three realities (birth, life and death) in our life. Energy is transformed from one form to another. When it changes form, it looks like destruction and when it acquires new form it looks like newly created."

"Yes, I know, it is scientific. But how would Trimurti's roles be applicable here?"

"We consider Brahma as ancestor, not as creator. However, for the sake of explaining to your conditioned mind, let's consider Brahma as the creator for a moment. What do you need for any creation?"

"First and foremost, you need intelligence, education or talent for any creation." Jayanth said.

"Yes, so sages introduced a Goddess for it, sitting near Brahma -Saraswati..."

"Ah, Beautiful. So that was it...."

"One more thing - you need to look at the past, present and future when you create something, right?"

"I understood that - Brahma has three faces representing that. And fourth one is for unknown dimension. But what about Vishnu and Shiva..."

"What do you need to sustain or maintain anything?" I asked.

"Of course...dollars...I mean money, wealth..."

"Lakshmi is the Goddess of material wealth. She aids Vishnu to sustain this world. The Dharma sustains the universe. It is backed by the materials in that."

"Wow! What about Shiva then?"

"Shiva is the transformer, but it looks like destruction as we don't look at what's happening next. What do you need to destruct anything?" I asked.

"Power" he said.

"In Sanskrit it is called Shakti. Parvati is representative of Shakti. I have already discussed about Vishnu and Shiv after destruction, there should be a flawless creation. A great beginning should be without any obstacles. So Shiv and Parvati had a son Vinayak, who destroys 'Vighna' (obstacles). Hence he is known as Vighneswhara. (Lord of all obstacles).

The cyclical transformation yields to something new. Even destruction needs some intelligence that is represented by the second son, Shanmukha (Arumugan or Murugan) with six heads that symbolizes six Vedangas."

"It is very interesting and amusing Uday uncle. Can I get the books that explain these things?"

"Oh, these are all just thoughts. There are no specific books."

"I mean in books on Vedic and Puranic characters like Rama and Krishna?"

"You are really truly confused here. Rama and Krishna are not in Vedic period.

They are not mythological characters, but historical characters. Both of them lived in India.

They were strictly Dharmic that people elevated them to the level of Vishnu's avatar..." I explained to him:" First you need to understand the difference between Vedic literature, Puranic literature, Itihas and Sastras..."

"Can you please explain?"

"Vedic literature is founded by four Vedas Rig-Veda, Samaveda, Yajurveda and Atharvaveda. Then there are Samhitas, Embedded Vedic texts or Brahmamas, Aranyakas and Upanishads.

Then there are Vedangas (limbs of the Veda) - Phonetics (Śikṣā), Ritual (Kalpa), Grammar (Vyākaraṇa), Etymology (Nirukta), Meter (Chandas), Astronomy (Jyotiṣa)...There are hundreds of sub-texts, analysis, texts and scriptures related to this subject that are still available."

"Like?"

"Kalpa has Śrautasūtras and Smartasūtras. The latter is divided into two again - Gṛhyasutras and Dharmasutras. There are 29 Dharmasutras. It contains the manuals for individual, family, society, country explaining life styles, customs, social duties, banking, economics, documentation to the minutest details like the qualities of a witness in a legal case."

"Oh, those are Vedic literature?"

"Apart from that supplements or Pariśiṣṭa - Āśvalāyana Gṛhya, Gobhila Gṛhya, Kātiya, Āpastamba Hautra, Vārāha Śrauta Sūtra - there are hundreds of texts related to this."
"Great. Anything more?"
"Yes. Upaveda (applied knowledge) Archery (Dhanurveda), associated with the Rigveda Architecture (Sthapatyaveda), associated with the Yajurveda. Music and sacred dance (Gāndharvaveda), associated with the Samaveda Medicine (Āyurveda), associated with the Atharvaveda..."
"Oh...so much. All of them were in Sanskrit?"
"No. There was Vernacular Vedic literature known as Divya Prabandha. For e.g., Tiruvaymoli is a term used for canonical Tamil texts."

"So, Bhagavad Gita and all"
"Those texts came in a later stage. There are Gitas (nearly 39 Gitas) or the Vedanta Sutras. But strictly speaking, Bhagavad Gita is not Vedic literature. It comes in Itihas"
"What is Itihas?"
"History. Ramayana and Mahabharata are historical epics.
Then comes Puranas- a vast genre of encyclopedic Indian literature about a wide range of topics particularly myths, legends and other traditional lore...."
"So Puranas are stories."

"Yes, it is applied Vedic literature. The stories are not important. The messages the Purana give are what matter.

However, Puranas also have a great deal of science and innovations in it.

For instance, while world believed earth is flat and Sun revolved around the earth, Puranas, even in stories, reveal that earth is globe and is revolving around the sun. It has applied science and technology in it."

"How many Puranas are there...?"

"Several of these texts are named Vishnu, Shiva and Devi. There are 18 Maha Puranas (Great Puranas) and 18 Upa Puranas (Minor Puranas), with over 400,000 verses."

"Oh, it requires few hundred years to read and finish" Jayanth said.

Then there are thousands of other literatures - Sutras and Shastras texts - compilations of technical or specialized knowledge in a defined area.

The Dharma-shastras (law books), derivatives of the Dharma-sutras.

Other examples were bhautikashastra (physics), rasayanashastra (chemistry), jīvashastra (biology), vastushastra (architectural science), shilpashastra (science of sculpture), arthashastra (economics) and nītishastra (political science).

It also includes Tantra and Agama literature. Our ancestors touched everything in this universe. Even for sex we had 100s of manuals (Kama Shastras) and one among it is the most popular Kama Sutra written by Vatsyayana.

Books like Yoga Vashista and Abhinavagupta's Tantraloka are surgical tools to dissect untruth to find the Truth"

"Hmm...It's an ocean of knowledge. How many of it has you read?"

"Very few, mostly Puranas. I may have read it and stored in the consciousness many life times. I don't read anything now. Whatever I write is from downloaded from the memory – incidentally, in daily life, I have very poor memory too.

Somehow, when I write about our Dharma, thanks to my ancestral blessings, some information will be downloaded to my brain so that I can write." I smiled at him.

Chapter - 13
Anytime Hindu!

Is Sanatan Dharma relevant today? Can I Practice it in Other Countries? Can a Non-Hindu Practice it? Why is Hindu Dharma the Logical and Scientific Way of Life?

"I want my children to follow our Hindu culture. But they say it is not applicable to the modern world. How can I explain it to them?"

"Everything about our Hindu practices appears confusing, complicated and contradicting. It is so complex that it cannot be practiced in the modern context and in the developed world..."

"I want to bring my child up in the path of Sanatan Dharma. In our country, the systems and life style are totally different. So how can I bring up my children according to Hinduism?"

These are the gist of some letters, e-mails and messages that I get from many non-resident Indian (NRI) parents, especially those who are working in non-democratic countries.

The only requisite to follow Sanatan Dharma is logical reasoning and scientific temperament.

The very meaning of 'Sanatan' is eternal, natural and everlasting. 'Dharma' is law, duty and responsibility. There is no confusion or contradiction.

"The TRUE practice of our Dharma has nothing to do with time, age, place, space, culture, country and religion.

It has nothing to do with caste, creed, colour, boundaries or ideologies. It can be practiced everywhere and anywhere, anytime" I used to reply to all.

Avantika Subramanian from Riyad recently asked me if I can simplify it in layman's language.

"Every human being is a unique expression - just like the finger prints. No two persons are similar. Everybody is perfect with his/her imperfections. Therefore, we cannot compare two human beings. Isn't this the basic principle of life?" I asked.

"Yes Uday, I agree, it's scientific" she said: "I know comparison would mostly end up with dangerous emotions - jealousy, hatred, anger. Comparison will make life unhappy"

"So, our ancestors (some 7000 years ago) said it would be better letting people do things and live according to their taste, ability and skills. They said that the classification of society should be based on actions (karma) and nature of a person (guna).

When everyone is dedicated to his/her work (action) and doing it happily that will lead to the well-being of healthy society and harmony in the earth. So, the ancients developed a culture based upon a system of social division for individual's and social development."

"Yes, it is most essential for living..."

"The system of classification by profession and skills was named as "Varna" in Sanskrit.

We always need four powers for a harmonious society- intelligence, decision making, planning and execution.

They named these four powers as Brahmama, Kshatriya, Vaishya and Shudra. This is just a broad classification; there are hundreds of subdivisions for each one."

"Ok"

"Varna system is NOT vertical it is horizontal where everyone is equal. No work or job has been considered as lower or higher (Uttamam Cha Adhamam Cha Ethat Karma Na Vidyathe - says the scriptures) you have the freedom to choose the work as per your nature. It was totally transparent and democratic. Is there any problem in it? Is that not timely?" I asked.

"It can be practiced at any time Uday. Such system is applicable to anywhere in the world..."

"They have done research and study on genetics. They said it would be better (but not as a mandatory commandment) if you marry from the families that follow same Varna.

For instance, it would be better if a blacksmith's daughter marries to a blacksmith's son. Their children will most probably carry some genetically-ordained skills, ability and characteristics plus acquired extra innings of their parents.

And from childhood they get familiarized to the profession (karma) that their parents are doing. This is the best way of learning and progressing in life...Should this principle be limited to India?"

"No, it's a universal truth – son of a blacksmith couple can most probably turn out to be better blacksmith. It has psychological, sociological and genetic factors in it..." she agreed.

"For the betterment of families and society our ancestors have divided human life into four phases based on natural part of the human journey from cradle to grave. Phase 1- For education or acquiring skills.

Phase 2 - for married and householder phase. Phase 3 - For gradually retiring, it is the time for return to contemplation and for guiding society.

Finally, phase 4- Renunciation - you are ready for a happy death. Is it difficult to follow?"

"No Uday - everybody's life is like that only..."she said.

"Our ancients called the phase (stages of life) as 'Ashram' in Sanskrit language. The four ashrams are Brahmacharya (student), Grihastha (householder), Vanaprastha (retired) and Sannyasa (renunciation) respectively. Should it be confined to a geographical area or religion? "

"No. It can be applied anywhere in the world."

"The ancients meditated and researched about the aim or purpose of human life and ways to reach fulfill that purpose. They had developed a convenient, simple and flexible life-system to live happily and with contentment.

That too was in tune with the nature. They called this integrated living and development as Purushartha (Purusha = human being, Artha = meaning or purpose. Artha also means wealth)"

"Yes, I heard about it. But this part is confusing for me..."

"Purusharthas are four - Dharma (righteousness, moral values), Artha (prosperity, economic values), Kama (pleasure, desire, love, psychological values) and Moksha (awareness and readying for death). These aspects will take care of every aspect of life - physiological, physical, safety, social, esteem, Self-actualization..."

"How do we follow it, Uday?"

"An individual has certain duties, responsibilities and privileges. They called this righteous living as Dharma.

Take for instance, I have the Dharma of a father, husband, son, brother, lover, community member, journalist, wrier, citizen, teacher, student etc.

I have to take up the responsibility of all these duties and take care of those people in question; the earth and environment. A Dharmic person should live with freedom, responsibility and discipline."

"Till this day the word was confusing for me..." she said.

"The basis of all true pleasantness (sukha) is or righteous conduct (Dharma). (Hence it is said: Sukhasya Mulam Dharmah = means the basis of happiness is righteousness or ethics.)

A person must do his karma (work) with untiring sincerity and honestly to fulfill his various Dharma. Is it difficult to understand?"

"Not at all. A person should be dedicated to what he or she does. I understood."

"Now, if you follow the Brahmacharya Asharam, your Dharma is learning. To understand the value of learning the teachers (acharyas) should be paid by the student itself and not by the parents.

A student must work hard to pay his/her fees. One can even beg for his fee or work in the institution. This makes sure that the boy/girl learns humility and humanity and exposed to hardships and miseries of the life…."

"In fact, in the West students follow it better than in India," she said.

"So, you tell me if there is any other method existing in this world to make a boy/girl a perfect human being and good citizen?"

"You are right. Now-a-days we pamper our children and make them morons...

Now I understood about the first segment of Purushartha. What about the other three aspects - Artha, Kama and Moksha?"

"Artha = pursuit of wealth, guided by Dharma. Acquire as much money as you want, but in a Dharmic (ethical or righteous) way, without hurting or cheating any. Earn money only according to the rules and regulations of the country he/she lives in. That's all about Artha."

"Ok. Easy."

"That means, after the studentship, as you enter into the next phase (Grihastha Ashram), work (ethically) hard to create wealth to meet basic needs - food, money, clothing and shelter or to maintain a comfortable home, raise a family, fulfill a successful career and perform your duties. Is that clear?"

"Yes, very clear..."

"The ancients said: 'Dharmasya moolam Artha'. The prosperity (resources) is the root of righteousness."

"Right..."

"To make it simple for laymen and to explain to illiterate, they have created a concept of Vishnu (Hindu God representing Dharma) and Lakshmi (Hindu Goddess representing Wealth, Vishnu's wife).

Lakshmi is sitting near Vishnu's feet, and not near his head. It is to convey you that wealth will be with you, at your disposal, if you follow Dharma."

"Yes...hard work with ethics will bring you money and happiness, that's true even today..."

"Dharma and Artha are needed for mental happiness and physical pleasure. You can also use this wealth to certain extend to avoid physical pain and mental sorrow.

You can fulfill most of your desires or needs -like high position in power, wealth, property, name and fame - using the Artha.

These desires are called Kama. Kama (desire for pleasure or comforts) is an integral part of life. You cannot avoid or suppress it."

"Yes"

"The Artha and Kama include financial independence, freedom from debt, worthy children, good friends, leisure time, love, aesthetic and cultural fulfillment, pleasures of the world (including sexual), the joys of family, intellectual satisfaction.

You can do whatever you desire - enjoying every moment of it, but remember, you are accountable to your Dharma. So Artha and Kama fulfillment come with responsibility and self-discipline"

"And moksha?"

"If you follow the Varna-Ashrama Dharma, you will automatically become entitled to Moksha."

"Moksha is liberation, right? Moksha takes you to heaven..." she asked.

"I don't know about heaven - it is a religious superstitious belief. We are talking about scientific way of living. Moksha is all about developing awareness. You have fulfilled your desires.

Your duties and responsibilities are over and getting ready to die. You are at the phase of Sanyasa. That is all about 'art of dying'"

"Art of Dying, a good phrase!" she said.

"If you had done everything as per Varna-Asharama Dharma - that's with dedication, determination and devotion, you will naturally get Moksha.

That means you will be contended and happy to embrace your end...There wouldn't be any fear and sorrow."

"That's all..."

"Yes, that's all. Now tell me, which one of above is not timely or not fit into your country or today's life style?"

"Nothing. Everything is natural, humane and universally acceptable, Uday. Everything is rational, scientific and logical" she said.

"And that's the charm of Sanatan Dharma, the ever-lasting Hindu Dharma..."

The Dharma concept is developed based upon the principle of 'the world is one family' (Vasudhaiva Kutumbakam) that call for mutual love, respect and belongingness.

"What about the traditions, Poojas, rituals, beliefs and other things?"

"Fundamentally your life moves by your Karma. Those things are not mandatory. But it would be better for you if you follow scientific rituals earnestly for your betterment.

You always have choice and many options there. But I would insist you to follow those rituals; it is not for beliefs or Gods. It's for you, family and the society."

"Why do you insist?"

"All our rituals will have either or any or all these results: Psychological effect, physiological affect, physical benefits, spiritual family bondage, social bondage and national integration, environmental protection, sustainable healthy living. We will discuss about it later."

"Can we do it outside India or can non-Hindus do it?"

"Yes. We don't have any superstitious or illogical rituals.

    Our ancients worked out 16 rituals or sacraments during the lifetime of a person - that's called Shodasa (=16) Sanskar (=culture). There is nothing religious or exclusiveness in it.

   These 16 rituals have nothing to do with temples, Gods or beliefs. Anybody who wants betterment in life, family and society can do it. As I said, it's for psychological, physiological and social health that will bring happiness and contentment for entire world."

   "What about belief in God?"

   "That's also optional. If you have some beliefs, you may follow it in any country - but without hurting or implementing on others.

   If you follow superstitions, then you are not a follower of Sanatan Dharma. Nobody prevents you from following your beliefs inside your house, until and unless you take it to the streets. "

   Sanatan Dharma in a nut shell = Varna+Ashrama+Dharma and Purushartha plus Shodasha Sanskar. Our sages have written nearly 29 books on Dharma Sastra (the science of Dharma) for each and every role of human being. If you don't know about your Dharma you can refer to those books.

   For your mental, physical and social health, they have given us yoga, Ayurveda, pranayama etc. For Kama, they have provided authentic scriptures on arts, science, KamaSastra.

   Everything that's needed for the world is thus already provided with abundance. All we have to do is live happily so that the entire world would be happy.

We are never taught to hate someone because he follows a different path than us. This is the basic philosophy of our Dharma. Everybody should follow his own path. I hope the world will understand it sooner.

Hindu Dharma presents life as a present. It says you are here to experience, understand, act, make mistakes, learn from it and walk ahead, know yourself, know how you are related to everything around you.

Chapter - 14
Dharma, Religion and my Muslim Friend

Abdul Yusuf Ali, a reader asked me this question: "Udayji, Can you please explain Dharma in layman's language. What's the difference between Sanatan Dharma and Hinduism? I asked many Hindu friends who couldn't explain this properly, that's why I am writing to you..."

"Ali, it is simple. Dharma is the way to be followed by every individual as per their roles in life. Dharma is your duty, inherent nature, responsibility and privilege together. Dharma is a Sanskrit word and there is no equivalent single word in English"

"Who decides your Dharma? God?"

"God is a belief. We cannot explain anything based on beliefs. There are no beliefs, God and so-called spiritualism in the Dharma. It is evolved based upon logic and science. Dharma can be explained as the power that keeps the world in motion and keeps society ticking.

It keeps the trees blooming, the grass growing and the birds singing. It's the inherent nature of each and everything. It's the principle/law of nature which keeps the Universe in balance"

Dharma is responsibility of an individual and the community to lead life to ensure peaceful co-existence, principals of non-violence and in harmony with nature, respecting for all life on Earth.

"Can you be more specific, Udayji?" he asked.

"Hmmm. Simply put, the Dharma of sugar is to be sweet, the Dharma of salt is to be salty, and the Dharma of fire is to produce heat and light," I said: "In other words, Sun is to give light, cloud is to give rain, water to quench thirst...and so on..."

"But, my question is, what about human beings?"

"We, humans have intelligence and we can develop intuition too. So, we can perform our Dharma with awareness. It should be maintained through personal duty."

"I still don't understand Udayji...be more simple"

"Ali, it's our duty to keep the world operating smoothly. So, Dharma is both universal and circumstantial, or personal. It's our occupational or constitutional position or duty."

"Let me ask this way, what is my Dharma?"

"You are a father. So, you have father's (pitru) Dharma - your duties and responsibilities as a responsible father.

You are also a Son (putra) which means you have putra Dharma - your duty towards your parents. You also have husband (Bharta) Dharma, brother (Brata) Dharma, friend (Mitra) Dharma, Citizen (Paura) Dharma; country (Rashtra) Dharma...the list is endless.

Our ancestors clearly mastered the art and science of being human. To my understanding there are more than 50 Dharma Sastras.

It clearly explains the Dharma of a King to Dharma of an account clerk in the palace. Dharma of each and every person in tune with the nature and cosmos...Now, what's your profession?"

"I am a business man..."

"That means, you are a Vysia (Businessman/Trader). That's your Varna (Profession).

They have divided the society into four - Brahmin, Kshatriya, Vysya and Sudra, depending upon the job they do. It's not a vertical division, but a horizontal one. Each had his/her Dharma. As a Vysia, you have the Dharma of a businessman or trader. Now, what's your age?"

"I am 38, Udayji"

"That means you are a family man (Grihastha). What will happen if a 70-year-old man acts like a teen-age boy eve-teasing a girl? The society will bang him, right?

So, there should be an age-based Dharma for the well-being of the society and world. As said earlier, there are four age-based life stages (Asramas): Brahmacharya (student), Grihastha (householder), Vanaprastha (retired) and Sannyasa (renunciation)...."

"Okay, I understand logic and reasoning...But there should be somebody to control it, right? A God, spiritual head, King or Judge - whoever - to oversee everybody should follow his/her Dharma. And there should be a fear factor like if you don't follow these moral codes, you will be punished."

"In fact, in a Dharmic society, there is no scope for such control. Let me quote a verse from our scriptures:

"Na Rajyam Naiva Rajasit Na Dando na cha Dandikaha

Dharmenaiva Praja Sarvaha Rakshantisma Parasparam"

- There need not be a King or Kingdom. There is no boundary. Neither criminal nor any judge to give the penalty to the criminal.

All the people protect each other by the virtue of Dharma. Everybody acted according to Dharma. Everybody protected each other with a sense of Dharma. That is our notion of Dharma"

"That's a Utopian philosophy..."

"On the contrary, it was followed in India - that's why ancient kingdoms in our land like Kosala Kingdom was known as Dharma Rayam (Righteous Nation)."

"Hmmm...But you didn't tell about Santan Dharma"

"I did. All these Dharma together is known as Sanatan Dharma..."

"So, what's Hinduism? Isn't it a religion name for Dharma?"

"Hinduism is founded upon some of the ideals of Sanatan Dharma. That doesn't mean Hindus follow Sanatan Dharma. A Sanatan Dharmi need not be a Hindu. Sanatan Dharma is only about the reality of life as it is through the experiential knowledge."

"You mean to say Santan Dharma is NOT a religion?"

"No way. Santan Dharma is no way superstitious and superficial. Any religion is superstitious, superficial, and often hypocritical. Religion is focusing on devotion, beliefs, and non-critical thinking. A religion is anthropocentric while Dharma is universal."

"But religions are important to humans"

"No. A religion is about believing in a particular scripture that talks about a God who is external to creation.

Religion is often theory, dogma, concept, or intellectual and/or emotional following without any personal experience.

Sanatan Dharma is an eternal path to Truth for seekers. One has to seek the Truth. It has scriptures but the essential thing is not belief but seeking."

"But when people follow it, it becomes religion. In other words, Santan Dharma is a religion as it wants people to follow it?"

"No. Dharma doesn't ask you to follow it and divide humanity into believers and infidels as religions do. We also have amongst us those who are Nastikas (Athiests and non-believers).

Nastikas are those who don't accept the Vedas as a valid means of knowledge. Will any religion tolerate such things?

A religion is founded upon the opinion (viewpoint) and beliefs of a Messiah or Prophet or Godman or Avatar or Saints.

But Dharma is not founded by anybody - it is not an opinion. It is the ONLY known scientific way of life."

"You are wrong. Your Dharma also has founders and Gods. Who are Rama and Krishna then?"

"Dharma was not founded by any individuals as in Monotheistic religions. Krishna or Rama did not start our Dharma. They were born into our Dharma. They were born as Vaidikas. Since they followed Dharma to its perfection, we called them God. Dharma has nothing to do with religion or beliefs..."

"But there should be somebody - a prophet, avatar or messiah who founded this Dharma..." Ali said.

"It is just evolved and perfected by trial and error method. If I ask you when did Physics start? What would be your answer? Did the laws of Physics start on a particular day?

Isn't it that the laws of Physics have always been there as long as this cosmos sprung into being? Dharma is art and science of cosmic order. No. It's not religion and there is no founder."

"So, we can follow any religion and still follow Dharma, that's what you mean?"

"Yes, of course. You can be a believer or non-believe. Dharma is not Hindu or Christian or Islam or Buddhist. All we need to be Dharmic in our life."

-Dharma just tells you how can you make this world a better place, that there is a part of the divine lying within you, that you can raise yourself and let that part take on yourself and that part can become you. It's such a magnificent concept.

"It's not right, Udayji. Non-believers are outcasted in your Dharma too. Otherwise why do you people believe in a God that protects Dharma? They say your supreme God Vishnu takes avatar to protect Dharma"

"There is confusion here. If you perform your Dharma with the awareness that 'I am part of the cosmic and it's my duty and responsibility to maintain cosmic order', you are called enlightened or avatar.

Hence it is said: dharayati -iti-Dharmah: that which protects is Dharma. Dharma will motivate you, inspire you, will instruct what to do, guide you, appreciate you and bless you."

"If there is no protector, then what's the meaning of this Sanskrit verse: 'Dharma Eva hate hanta, Dharma rakshati rakshitah' (One who destroys Dharma is destroyed by Dharma/ One who protects Dharma is protected by Dharma). To punish Adhramic there is a God, the creator, right?" he asked.

"It doesn't mean that an outside Avatar will appear to protect Dharma.

It means: Dharma does not destroy, nor Dharma can be destroyed. For instance, the Dharma of the earth is its gravitational force. If it is destroyed, everything on earth will fall apart.

We know the gravitational force keeps everything protected on earth. Neither Gravitational Force can be destroyed, nor does gravitational force destroy. It's just the statement of fact. There is no belief or spirituality in it."

"Hmm. Then why did Krishna warned that if you don't follow your Karma properly, you will be punished by God? He cautioned about result of the wrong Karma"

"Krishna didn't say that anywhere. Dharma is the way. Karma is the action. Karma, the action, should be based on Dharma, the Way.

Dharma is one's duty and responsibility, karma is the actions performed to complete the duty.

Karma has ONE meaning that is Action or Deed. Krishna said, you have right (Adhikara) to do your Karma and NO right over its results.

The results of your action can be good or bad depending upon the action. Sowing Neem seeds expecting Mango fruits is unnatural! That's all he said. What's spiritual or non-scientific in it?" I asked.

For every action, there is an equal reaction. As we sow so we reap. This is the law of nature, that's all Gita says.

It is just logical and scientific. In human beings, the intellect is the one which is used to understand what Dharma is in a certain context, and the Karma to undertake, to uphold this Dharma.Sanatan Dharma is surviving for the past 7000 years. Because it is not associated with any language, sect or religion factors of world.

Chapter - 15
Why Should You Question Hindu Rituals?

Many readers used to send me letters with plenty queries related to Hindu rituals.

Yesterday, I received a call from Anantha Krishnan: "Udayji, I am a regular reader of your website. A famous astrologer advised me to conduct a "Maha Mrityunjaya Homamm" (Its a ritual for healing - to survive and rejuvenates a man or woman who is under a life threat and fighting against death.

It is is dedicated to Shiva or Mahamrityunjaya, the conqueror of death) to protect my father from the unfortunate event of death."

He continued: "I am in USA now. The priest, who recommended by the astrologer, said that he can do it in his house and send Prasadam (religious offering) to my father. He said the total cost would be around $1500 (above one lakh).

This has to be done with immediate effect or my father will die. Is this right? What's your advice? I appreciate your rational perspective and logical explanation. I don't have anybody else to consult. Please advice."

"Anantha, I am not an expert in Achars (rituals and customs). All I can do is sharing my limited understanding of Achars in Hinduism," I said.

"Yes, that's what I need. I wanted an unbiased opinion," he said.

Broadly, we have three types of rituals and traditions.

First one is Vaidikam - Vaidik karma (Vedic customs and traditions) is purely based on Vedas and hence do not change. All rituals (Homamm, Havanam, yagam, jagna, Yajnaetc) through the medium of fire (Agni) is Vaidikam.

We offer 'Homam Dravyas' or Havan Samagri (materials for sacred offering) to fire. Here, we use Veda mantras (sacred hymns) and the swaram (note in the octave) of hymns is most important here. There is no idol worship in Vaidika karma, and hence, rituals are not related to temples.

Second one is Pauranikam - it is based on Puranas. All rituals using the medium as an Idol or a Lamp can be termed as Pauranikam. Here we use keerthanam (singing the glories) of the favourite Gods and also some Veda mantras.

However, instead of Swaram, the thrust is given to raaga (melodic modes used in Indian classical music).

"Shodasa Upachara Pooja" (complete process of performing the rituals of Pooja, the worship) - which constitute of Dhyanam (prayer), Avahana invocation, Aaasana (offering seating), Paadya (washing of feet), Arghya (washing of hands), Aachamana (Offering water to drink) etc - is the integral part of this... Most of such rituals are done at temples or Pooja (family prayer) rooms.

The third one is Loukikam - It is part of any functions. It has local flavour.

Most celebrations that happen at homes or halls fall under this category.

This changes as per the status of the person conducting the function and his/her locality. Sometimes few rituals from Vaidikam and Pauranikam are seen mixed here.

The mantras from Veda, Itihasa (epic) and Puranas may be used in Loukikam. Sometimes poem in local languages are also used. The housewarming, Shashti Poorthi (60th birthday), Birthday celebrations, Namakarana (Naming the child) etc come under this. The rituals can be elongated or shortened.

"However, there exist numerous local Gods around the country who are neither Vedic nor Puranic. Naturally there are rituals that do not fall in any of these categories. A traditional Hindu marriage is a mix of all three.

There are also umpteen rituals in the marriage, which has nothing to do with Veda or Puranas or even the religion. For instance, there was no practice of exchanging rings during marriages in Hindu ritual. This practice was not a wedding or betrothal rituals but considered as a wedding gift only," I said.

Now, about the practical side of all these rituals and customs...

"All our rituals in Sanatan Dharma MUST HAVE either or any or all these results: Psychological effect, physiological affect, physical benefits, family bondage, social bondage and national integration, environmental protection and sustainable healthy living!"

Dharma Sastra tells that Achars are for a long happy and healthy life and for sustainable and permanent positive results.

By practicing those rituals, you become happy, prosperous and wealthy (not necessarily in tangible forms). Rituals are followed for strong family and social bondage. Those Achars will take you from darkness to light. It develops a Sattvik character in you.

"So, we have to follow all rituals as is..." Anantha asked.

"No. We have to be careful about Anachars and Durachars ."

- The rituals not relevant for 21st century are known as Anachar (malpractices). When you discriminate people based on caste, creed and sex or follow superstitions, it is called Anachar.

-The rituals which produce negative results are Durachars (vice offends, evil practices) - animal sacrifice, offering liquor as a part of religious rituals, etc

- The rituals which produce good results or effects are Sadhachars - that is what we have to follow. Dharma Sastras say that one should eradicate Anachars and Durachars based on our wisdom, time, location and science.

Most of the Hindu rituals have founded upon strong scientific rationale.

Take for instance, 'Ganapathi Homamm' in which we burn coconuts.

The fibrous part of the husk (coir) produces moderate sulfur oxides (Sulfur dioxide (SO_2) and sulfur trioxide (SO_3), the coconut Shell, when burned produce phenol and when you burn coconut with ghee, it produces pyrazine (a heterocyclic aromatic organic compound).

Please ask any school students, they will teach you how these can prevent virus, bacteria and germs that create cholera, typhoid, tetanus, pneumonia, chicken pox etc. It is Antimicrobial. The ritual of burning medicinal plants is to produce 'purifying' smoke.

Please check yourself about how the burning wood and odoriferous and medicinal herbs during the Vedic rituals can effectively reduce pathogens in the air. Each item of the ritual material is significant.

These materials are offered in the fire after completion of every mantra chant. It is supposedly the sacred food for the deities. But we know deities won't eat it. Hence, it has an effect only on us and our surroundings.

Evaluate materials used for each 'Havan' and analyse the chemical reactions when each material is burned in combination of others.

Combustion of fatty substances, photochemical process, purification of environment, removal of bacteria, the antiseptic and antibiotic effects, removal of insects, effects on plants and vegetation, role of CO_2 generated in Yagna (is not free CO_2.

It is mixed with the vapors of other aromatic oils and antiseptic products) – you will say "wow".

The mixture of various dried herbal, roots and leaves is offered in the ablaze fire disseminates in micro form, in the air, to purify the environment besides activating the air as disinfectant germicidal agent. It is anti-bacterial.

Another example is house-warming Homam (when you start living in a new house) that has an effect of modulated fire test. The wood burned emits white smoke and you will know if your place is properly ventilated to allow smoke to go away.

But in present environment of sprinklers fire extinguishers, air conditioners, fans, exhausts, the science behind house warming Homam is going to see a limiting effect.

As described in Rig-Veda's, saints used to perform Agnihotra-Yagnas (Agnihotra is a process that uses healing fire to purify the surroundings mostly done by Nambudiri Brahmins of Kerala) to purify the environment by sublimating the ritual materials in fire.

There are psychological and physical benefits too, depending upon the Homam.

However, Agni rituals have declined in the last 40 years. Life has changed. Today most of the priests do not know about these rituals.

Hence, if you are a truth seeker or Hindu, you should question each and every ritual. There is NO scope for blind beliefs or fanaticism in our Dharma. Everything needs logical explanation.

For, you must develop a healthy dis-respect to these rituals. Use your rational brain. Everything in Sanatan Dharma needs rationale and reasoning.

Our rituals, as noted above, are not belief-based non-sense. It has multiple meaning.

So, ask your priest all about the rituals. Why should you do it? Ask him to explain the process and Upakarma in scientific terms. If he cannot, well, he is just like a parrot repeating words he learnt.

He is doing it just for livelihood and not thoroughly studied. If priests cannot explain the basis of what he does, what's the point in performing such rituals?

Unfortunately, mostly what go around now are pure business- oriented rituals. Jyothishi (astrologer) - priest combine utilizes the mental weakness of people just as the doctor- test lab combine rob people with medical/ physical ailments. In both cases, basic awareness is the remedy.

Another issue is the genuineness of materials. Most of the Havan Samagris (materials) are Chinese. Even the camphor that you are using is NOT natural, it is artificial. You should make sure if materials used are original or duplicate.

"So, if you want to perform a ritual, first you have to learn about it. Just because a fake-astrologer-fraud-priest-mafia provided you bid or quotation for their revenue, you don't have to do a Homam." I told Anantha Krishnan.

"So, there is no point in performing this ritual?"

"Please perform the ritual with the help of a genuine priest at your home in presence of all family members. The genuine priest will explain whatever he does. He shouldn't demand money from you.

Instead, you should give him a reasonable Dakshina (a financial remuneration or honorarium to the priests in exchange for their services) according to your wish."

"Okay, so I will try to find a genuine learnt person in our area. But what about time frame? He said soon..."

"God knows everything. If you are delayed by few months, no God will charge additional interest, tax or put fine on you. The moment your mind think about performing a ritual, God knows it, so don't worry," I told him: "Get your father's health checked properly immediately in a good hospital and make sure that he doesn't have any medical problem. And pray for ayur (longevity), arogya (health), aishwarya (wealth) of all of you."

"What should I say, if that priest calls again?"

"Tell him you will pay $1500. But you need a receipt clearly mentioning the warranty period of 'his' Mruthunjaya Homam.

If something happens to your father within that warranty period, go to consumer court and file a case for few million dollars' compensation from the priest and astrologer."

I would like to answer two more frequently asked questions here:

Is it true that only Brahmin can perform Homamm?

No. It is the other way around. Those who learnt Vedas and performing these rituals are Brahmins.

Just because you born in today's Brahmin caste, you are not a real Brahmin as per Sanatan Dharma. It is a position, a position earned, not gained by birth. Of course, a person born in Brahmin caste has some advantages over others - easy access to all those things coupled with traditional knowledge and DNA advantage.

It is just like a doctor's children have more information on that profession than others. But anybody can learn and perform rituals - Maharshi Viswamitra, who taught the Gayatri mantra, was not Brahmin. Maharshi Valmiki, who taught Brahma Jnana to Maharshi Bharadwaja, was a tribal by birth.

Are these Achars written by Brahmins?

These Achars were written by Rishis (Saints) from all Varnas and from different parts of India. They are also written in different languages.

During the period when Achars were written, none of the Rishis was known in their caste name. The present type of caste system did NOT exist during that period.

Can women perform Homamm?

At the level of subtle body there is no difference based on gender.

All spiritual practices operate mainly at the subtle level. So, it makes no sense to have a total ban on women performing rituals.

In fact, NO major ritual in Sanatan Dharma is possible without your wife sitting beside you.

Unmarried priests are not allowed to do Pooja in temples. As I have discussed in many articles, discrimination based on caste and sex introduced to India by foreigners.

The taboo for women is product of male chauvinistic beliefs that thrust upon our country and that is NOT part of Hinduism. If any woman is interested, she should be encouraged to perform ritual.

Chapter - 16
Are You Superstitious?

My friend in who had migrated to Canada long back recently saw a photograph related to my daughter's engagement ceremony and told me: "It is very funny to see a person like you perform ancient tribal rituals. Your religion is plagued by enormous superstitions, wrong customs, bad and ugly rituals, ceremonial impurity and immoral traditions. It is high time that your religion is modernized and moves according to the times like the Semitic religions in the West..."

"I have two questions. (1) Can you show me a single superstition in the original Sanatan Dharma scriptures? (2) Can you show me a single scientific truth in any of your religions?" I asked.

He sent me a "LOL" smiley and laughs!

"Seriously," I said, "I want to learn...as far as I know there is not even one single superstition in any of our scriptures like the Vedas, Upanishads, Dharma Sastra, Shrauta Sutra, Brahma Sutra, 40 Gitas (including Bhagavad Gita), Yoga Vasistha etc..."

Ridiculing me he said, "Oh, come on, everybody knows India is a land of superstitions and foolish beliefs...and how will people know about your scriptures? Non-Brahmins were not even allowed to learn Vedas, right?"

I said, "You are a non-Hindu, but you can learn the Vedas. The Vedas are freely available for download on the internet.

The scriptures said, "Brahmajnanana Eva Brahmama" means only if you learn the Vedas you will become a Brahmin.

It has been misinterpreted as "'Only Brahmins should learn the Vedas'. Please don't go by mis-quoted postings on the Internet or talks by people who intentionally denygrate Sanatan Dharma for vested interest. Seek the truth and read it for yourself..."

"Really? You mean to say that all your customs, rituals and beliefs represent truth?" He asked mockingly.

I replied, "I didn't say that. There are Anachars (irreverent, obsolete, outdated rituals, not useful in this century, but it might have been useful in the olden times) and Durachars (negative rituals like black magic, killing animals etc.) that crept into Sanatan Dharma at a later stage. A person with common sense can remove those rituals and focus only on Sadhachars..."

"What do you mean by Sadhachars...?" He asked.

I answered, "Sanatan Dharma advocates rituals, customs, traditions and beliefs that have any of or all of eight benefits..."

"8 benefits?" He asked with raised eyebrows.

"Yes, all our rituals have either one or any or all of these results: Psychological effects, physiological effects, physical benefits, spiritual family bondage, social bondage, national integration, environmental protection and sustainable healthy living.

But, all rituals that you people follow are ONLY to get linked with God or to reserve a seat in heaven nearer to God," I said.

"Let's not compare," he got angry, and then he said, "I am curious to know, your Achars are not to link up with God or heaven?"

Giving an account of Achars, I said, "Nowhere it is said that you will reach God if you follow Achars. Dharma Sastra says that Achars are for a long, happy and healthy life and for sustainable and permanent positive results.

By practicing those rituals, you become happy, prosperous and wealthy (not in material terms). Those Achars will take you from darkness to light. It develops a Sattvik character in you. It also says that you should eradicate Anachars and Durachars by logical, scientific and rational analysis..."

"And, what are those good Achars?" He questioned.

I asked, "Have you heard about Pranayama (breathing exercise), Yogasana (or Yoga), Surya Namaskar (Salutation to sun) etc..."

"I know...all have excellent proven benefits...I asked my children to follow those," He remarked.

"But you just said we follow superstitions and thousands of years of tribal rituals," I said with a laugh.

"There could be other bad rituals," he stated.

I enumerated, "Yes, we have lighting lamps, chanting mantras, singing Bhajans (devotional songs), reading the Gita, Satsang (spiritual discourse or sacred gathering), seeking blessings from elders by touching their feet, offering sweets to everybody after offering it to the deity. you think these are superstitious bad things? You please try to attend a function to learn any of those benefits..."

"Interesting...what are other Achars?" he quizzed me back.

I continued, "Going for pilgrimage all over India - the followers of Sanatan Dharma consider the land of "Bharat" as their mother.

They were patriots (in non-violent terms), hence national integration was their major agenda. The invaders considered India as just a piece of commercial real estate. Our ancestors believed that rivers like the Ganges are Gods. Now environmental protection groups can explain better to you the logic behind my ancestors worshipping rivers, mountains and trees..."

He said, "I know all those things...the people elsewhere think that these resources are meant for exploitation. I agree with you."

I further added,"Then we have festivals to concrete the social bondages - like Diwali, Vinayak Chathurthi, Holi, Onam, Dussera, Durgashtami, Navaratri etc..."

"But, what about those people doing Poojas and Homams?" He wanted to know.

I elucidated, "Hmmm...even those Homams and rituals have strong foundations" (Already explained)

"But your people propagate superstitions like astrology and horoscope matching," he complained.

I clarified, "Our teacher, Swami Vivekananda said: 'Anything of western origin- verify it and then accept it. Anything of Indian origin- accept it and verify it if necessary.' The signs of the Zodiac are of Babylonian origin. Astrology originated in Egypt. Hora means hour and Horoscope examining time/hour or fate. Indian Astrology is a modification of Egyptian system. Astrology doesn't have Indian origin. We had Vedic knowledge of Astronomy (Jyothisha). Idiots interpreted it as Astrology to make money. The cosmological science Astronomy has its origin in India."

Vivekananda also said: Astrology and all these mystical things are generally signs of a weak mind; therefore, as soon as they are becoming prominent in our minds, we should see a physician, take good food, and rest.

"Hmm. So all scriptures in Sanatan Dharma teach you to imbibe an inclusive, sustainable and eco-friendly way of living," he remarked.

I said, "I can't say "all" scriptures...Most of the Vedic literature, yes. But some Puranas are not. Take for instance, Bhavishya Purana, which has been manipulated by Vamana Shastri who was actually the brother in law of Akbar, the Mughal King.

Sometimes names are misleading about their true religion. So, there could be false elements that got added into some scriptures by die-hard fans of invaders, Chinese and Russian communists, and the European evangelists..."

He paused for a while and told, "Hmmm....you made your points. The Semitic ideas are not scientific. And the basic principles of Sanatan Dharma are truly scientific and far advanced...But what about the ground reality? The man on the street is just superstitious and idiotic..."

I smiled and said, "You have the answer in that question. He/she who follows superstitious rituals is an idiot. Nobody can correct idiots. We can tell people to follow only Sadhachars. If they don't listen to the truth, what can we do? Can it be blamed on our Dharma or Shastra? We cannot kill or die for religion. Ours is an inclusive Dharma."

There are reverse Achars too.

For example, usually when a dead body is taken out from a house, it is customary that the house is then cleaned and people in the house take the bath immediately to get purified (from the impurifications caused due to the bacteria or germs which decompose the dead body).

However, some people have reversed this practice and say that after someone goes out from house, then the persons staying in the house should not bath immediately as it will cause inauspiciousness to the person who left the house.

India is probably plagued with more superstitions than any other countries. All our Shad Darshanas (six views), Upanishads and Buddha's Darshanas never support any superstitions. But human mind is more comfortable with superstitions rather than bitter truth.

Dharma is not superstitious, but today's Hindu way of life, may be. Culture and religion are so entangled in many places that it is difficult to know where one begins and the other ends.

The Vedic Dharma has established a way of living irrespective of caste and creed that is 100 % eco-friendly. There was nothing in this life style as unprogressive.

Superstitions are not part of Vedic custom. It has been created by people who don't want to be logical about what to take and what to leave and not wanting to use their common sense.

Chapter - 17
Snake Worship and Idiotic Superstitions

Few months ago, my friend's son, a teen ABCD (=American Born Confused Desi), came to visit me. He said: "Uncle, my grandparents are superstitious and pushy. My dada told me to listen to them. But they are talking utter non-sense and ridiculous things..."

"What's it all about Arun?" I asked him.

"They want me to participate in Naga Pooja (Snake worship) at the Sarpa Kavu (also known as nagabana, nagavana, nagamoola Sthana, Sarpa puja sthana - it's a small abode or shrine dedicated to the serpent (snake) God). They believe in all those absurd things like - snakes drink milk, snakes will listen and sway according to the tune of the pulluvan paattu (naavur paattu = traditional song to worship snake Gods), a snake will take revenge if you kill its spouse and worst part of it is the story of Nagamanikyam (a myth that certain cobras produce magical snake-pearls)...."

I couldn't help laughing at the way he presented and explained this through his American slang.

"Aren't those idiotic beliefs?"

"Yes. Snakes are cold blooded and carnivorous animals, whereas milk is often consumed by the mammals, normally a snake wouldn't drink milk

Snakes do not have ears and are deaf. When the charmer plays his Been or Pungi (wind instrument played by snake charmers) he is giving a particular motion- so the snake may sway according to the movement or tapping on the ground. The stories of Nagamanikyam and snake revenge are just childish fallacies or folklore - there is no element of truth in it," I said.

"Yeah, that is what I told them," Arun said, "Why do these oldies worship snake? Isn't it stupidity?"

"Did you see the new movies in Avengers and Spiderman series?"

"Yes, of course - what's that to do with snake worship, those are just movies..."

"The movie makes you believe things and you really enjoy and believe it during that point of time. I have seen a South Indian movie in which the sixty years old weak hero with heavy make-up/alterations hits at 100s of strong villains single-handedly - but you will still believe it and enjoy it."

"But, that's a movie, Uncle."

"True. In movie, the content is fiction, non-sense or ridiculous. But the technology, the science and ambiance behind the movie is truth, right?"

"Yes"

"Similarly, there could be something behind all those snake fictions.... Have you ever visited a Sarpakavu?"

"Yeah...It's there inside the compound in which my ancestral home stood. It's in is a corner and dark. It looks scary in the night.

It is rather a miniature forest - a cluster of trees, old, crowded, hissing and rustling. There is a pond and a rock stage where stone carved snake shapes are kept. My old family members put turmeric powder, kumkumam, milk, salt etc there..."

"There may be or may not be snakes in such groves. But instilling fear was the means adopted by our ancestors to evoke in the community the need to respect every species and to respect boundaries."

The belief of (or real) venomous snakes kept the greedy man away and did NOT allow him to rape that virgin grove of eco-system. To make the fear more solid and to prevent public from axing the forests, our ancestors may have added spicy stories or even worshiped such places. The snake abode is a micro-forest where you can see a great green spot that should open up the mysteries of the nature for a true observer.

Every grove is a perfect blend of fauna and flora that represents the ancient Indian way of conservation of bio-diversity.

It had preserved many rare and endemic wild plant species, various endangered reptiles, animals, birds and numerous herbs having significance in the world of medicine and agriculture.

The ponds and streams adjoining the groves are perennial water sources too.

These condensed forest or natural green spots preserved abundant exotic and rare species of plants like naalppamaram (group of four medicinal plants Ficus carica, Ficus infectoria, Ficus religiosa and Ficus bengalensis), dashapushpam (ten sacred flowers) and many more.

It's a place where land, religion, myth culture and civilization harmoniously blend together with greenery.

It is essential for a peaceful environment. It's a beautiful concept for preserving bio, socio-cultural diversity.

You know about symbiosis- interaction between two different organisms living in close physical association, right? All trees are grown together in a grove in co-operation. They communicate. Sometimes, when the bigger tree pollinates, the small trees below it too will do it..."

"Oh, I didn't know that"

"Yes Arun. I have observed this in a grove. During summer time, the grass in the grove may dry up. The big trees then would absorb water from the pond and let its green leaves (NOT dry leaves) fall. The grass would thus get water content. I have seen such a co-operation in groves. They live like a family. They ARE a family. It's a micro forest. If something lacks in one tree other trees will come for help.....It is unbelievable, but true."

In the groves, they have a free and fearless life, without any threats from hunters or other interference by man.

The trees and the vegetation tiers in the serpent grove help produce life sustaining oxygen and prevent soil erosion, conserve water and purify air.

"Uday uncle, my grandma used to say, "Kavu theendiyal, kulam vattum" (Destruction of this greenery will lead to drought)"

Our ancestors said- all are connected. Our ancestors didn't know the modern scientific words like eco-system, ecological balance, environmental protection, humidity control and food-chain.

But they have seen the unseen bondage between each and everything. You know, in a food-chain, if one creature is extinct, that will affect all creatures - it will lead to mass destruction of human life...

Hence these micro forests are very essential for a peaceful environment. In a dire situation of drought or famine, this micro forest can be developed in to a macro one...It would develop itself into a power house of nature...It was a backup storage plan kept intact by our ancestors for future generations to come. They cared for us."

"Uncle, I believe you..."

"Have you noticed the molehills inside those sacred snake groves...? Our ancestors would prevent us from touching or destroying it. I don't know the science behind it, but ask a biology or genetics scientist who know about mutation, species (animal and plant) and new species that are produced in molehills during thunder, lightning and rain..."

"Oh! Awesome....But why do you worship such grove? Can't you reveal those truths as matter of fact?"

"Whatever I told you about snake worship, is based on today's scientific knowledge. If tomorrow science finds something else about snakes? Worshiping nature and various living beings have been practiced in India, from time immemorial.

During later age, people didn't know the Sastra (wisdom) behind it, they just followed it... The common man of this land who believed in the existence of divine presence in all the animate and inanimate things around him worshiped all the elements and phenomenon of nature. And that's the ONLY perfect way of living in the universe."

These forests are priceless treasures of great ecological, biological, cultural and historical value; and these forests are never axed. Strict religious and cultural taboos observed by believers had curbed the removal of even dead twigs in many such groves.

"But do you believe in Sarpadosha (snake sin) related to infertility?"

"I don't think so. But killing any creature is unacceptable. There is a pain and violence in killing. The nature has memory and can record any sounds. Scientific studies say that sound energy of ancient time can be extracted from the atmosphere and replicated. Snake is an important creature in the food-chain. We can't rule out energy level communications between the memories of the cells.

So it can definitely effect on human too. When you destroy a sacred grove, it affects rain and ecological balance. It affects farming and the nutrients around. Nutrients are important to produce enough sperm..."

This nature spot plays an important role in stabilizing the ecosystem of the land by conserving soil and water of a region. The small ponds and streams adjoining the grove are perennial sources of water. The rich debris composition enriches the soil and the nutrients thus generated find their way into the nearby agri-system.

The land, religion, myth, culture and civilization harmoniously blend together in a small space replete with greenery. It is a unique and ancient ecological heaven.

"Our grandparents were in green party!" exclaimed Arun.

"Thousands of these sacred serpent groves have been destroyed and the land used for building houses. Usually this land was sold to non-Hindus as Hindus were scared to destroy the grove. There were hundreds of thousands of groves - now only few thousands are remaining.

Hundreds of thousands of people destroyed the groves and built huge mansions and commercial buildings. Nothing happened to them. No snake came for revenge. But they would not understand the damage they have done to the cosmic system. Probably they never will."

"Why did they sell it? It was very bad..."

"The atheists, communists, socialists and social reformers of yesterdays didn't have the facility in their brain to think beyond superficial manifestos and ideologies. They were in power and pooh-poohed such groves as superstitions. And some blind religious followers, who believed that everything in the universe is made for man to enjoy, destroyed these groves.

Even today, the remaining few thousands snake temples owned by families through generations are facing a threat to their existence due to collapse of the joint family system and the changing socio-economic scenario and neo-liberalization."

"OMG"

"Fortunately, some of the environmentalists and eco-lovers realized the truth about such groves and prompted the state government to step in to conserve them. Will the short-term thinkers in the government run by greedy and petty-minded politicians protect such groves?"

"Somebody should save it..."

"Why should wait for somebody? You can do whatever you can - by sharing this information and creating awareness among individuals

So, before branding something as superstition, try to find the facts behind it. Let me tell you, the urban market-media superstitions make our ancestral superstitions look so pun," I said.

Snake is one of the most dreaded creations of nature. Instead of instilling fear in us, our ancestors taught us to respect everything. Why?

Our ancestors lived in a much more natural way and they were bold and daring.

They could pardon someone or something only out of respect or sympathy. Instead of being ruthless and arrogant, they taught us to live in peace. The simple philosophy of life is to love each other; respect each other. This shows their generosity and principled living.

When someone understands that the earth is not for humans alone, they will appreciate and respect the ecosystem and live and let live, not only humans, but other living things.

Practitioners of Modern medicine use a straight staff around which two serpents are coiled. Medicinally the two serpents represent poison and its antidote, or venom and serum. This imagery comprises the caduceus, an attribute of Hermes, messenger of the Greek Gods. We don't have a problem in accepting that.

Practitioners of ancient Yoga say that the force (they call it Kundalini) is depicted as a serpent, reposing in a coiled base around the spine.

When activated, this force travels through three channels (nadis) - the sushumna, the ida, and the pingala. The sushumna, like the staff, is vertical and straight, traveling in parallel motion with the spine. The ida and pingala channels twist together like that of the two snakes, intersecting at a handful of point (chakra centers) - Just a coincidence?

Chapter - 18
The Clear and Present Danger for Hinduism!

I get countless messages and letters..."Islam and Christianity are threats to Hinduism", "All leaders appease Minorities", "Foreign Media attacks only Hindus", "International conspiracy to destroy Hindus in India" "Save Hinduism", "Save Hindus" - I wonder how much insecure Hindus feel in India.

"Nothing, no ideology, no philosophy, no religion have inherent strength or depth to even come near Sanatan Dharma even in the wildest dreams! So, the real threat for Sanatan Dharma is not from outside but from inside the religion..."

"What's that?"

"Unfortunately, today's Hinduism designed and advocated based on Semitic thoughts. Nobody understands the difference between Dharma and religion. This is going to be very dangerous..."

For, Hinduism as you see today is the distorted version of Sanatan Dharma.

"What's the difference between Sanatan Dharma and Hinduism?"

It is very simple. Today's Hinduism is a process of semiticalization the great Sanatan Dharma tradition into a trivial narrow-minded religion. Our so-called Hindu intellectuals are blindly imitating Semitic ideas. Today, Hindus are moving away from Sanatan Dharma and tend to follow Semitic religious concepts.

HERE IS A FACT CHECKER TO FIND HOW MUCH YOU KNOW ABOUT YOUR DHARMA

1. Many Hindus say: "I believe in creator". No problem in believing whatever you want. But our ancestors had pooh-poohed the irrational belief in the creator God as a childish idea 7000 years ago. Please do not compare the Semitic belief of a creator God with Brahma. Brahma is not creator; he is the "ancestor".

2. Hindus apologetically say that "there is only single God, we call it in many names and worship in many forms". "We have only one God, Brahmam - all Gods are many forms of it," even learned pundits would tell you the same. Brahmam is NOT God, though Gods are also the manifestation of Brahmam like everything else. World needs multiple Gods to accommodate all. It should contain atheists too. Single God theory has given rise to fanaticism and terrorism.

3. The RIP culture. In many Facebook posts, I have seen Hindus write "May his/her soul Rest in Peace" Soul is a funny irrational and illogical concept. We have JeevAtma but it is something else. It doesn't rest and wait in peace - it recycles till it attains moksha. "What should we say instead of RIP?"

"That depends. If you believe Vishnu as Parabrahmam, you can say, "May the departed jeevAtma be one with the lotus feet of Mahavishnu"

4. Another major disastrous trend is, converting our Devalaya (God's abode - temples) into "Aradhanalaya" (prayer halls) like Churches and Mosques. Today most of the Hindu temples are anti-Sanatan Dharmic. A Hindu will not even go to temple for at least 7 days if a birth or death happens at home.

But for Semitic organized religions, birth and death are related only to their prayer places. Hindus were not conducting marriages in temples (except in some rare cases) - marriage has nothing to do with temple. But today, most of the temples have marriage halls and make it a huge business like Churches. All basic rituals in Sanatan Dharma (Shodasha Samskara) have absolutely NOTHING to do with GOD.

5. I hear Hindus saying "I am spiritual", "She is very spiritual" or "My spiritual partner" - I really don't understand the difference between "spiritual" and "material". Our ancestors taught us everything is divine. Then how come the "spiritual" concept came into being?

The difference in spirituality and materialism had come from 19th century evangelists, Europeans and the British. They had a concept of Church vs State. Or Science vs Religion. On the contrary, in India, Sages were scientists ranging from astronomy to Ayurveda. Science was the foundation stones of Sanatan Dharma.

Why Am I a Hindu?

6. Priesthood and superstitions. Sanatan Dharma doesn't support any superstitions - When it comes to marriage, Sanatan Dharmi didn't believe in superstitions like horoscope matching. They checked for Gotra and parambara only for scientific reasons.

Today a large chunk of Hindus follow Vasthu too. Earlier, the priests (mostly Brahmins) were starving as Hindus didn't depend upon them. Today (most of the) Hindu priests are no different from (most of the) Semitic priests - exploitative and greedy.

7. Inviting death on Birthdays: Ask your parents - how did we celebrate our birth days? By lighting lamps and praying to the light energy (Agni Deva)"Thamasoma Jyothir Gamaya".

Today, how do the modern Semitic Hindus celebrate birthday? They blow off the lamps. Throwing spit on the god of light!

8. Gita is NOT a Holy-book like Bible or Quran: I have seen people propagate Bhagawad Gita as Holy book. Why? They want to imitate a standardization developed by other religions (Because, Semitic followers believe in one God, one book and one prophet theory). It is also shameful on Hindus.

There are 39 Gitas. We have thousands of sacred texts. The one book concept is for LKG kids. You are not following a single book when you reach at post-graduate level. You must refer to a huge collection of books.

9. God fearing - Hindus never ever fear God. For us, God is everywhere and we are also integral part of God. God is not a separate entity to fear.

10. Falling prey to organized structure: Many Babas, Mathas, Gurus (self-styled God men and God women) forms cult and spread their own version of Hinduism for making money. Anything organized will be commercialized, corrupt and perished.

There are many other things too - Sanatan Dharma doesn't believe in Caste system. But Hindus follow it. The evils like Sati and Child marriage came in our culture through the influence of brutal invaders.

A Hindu is not a sinner. We only have Dharma and Adharma. I hear many people talk about sin. Paapa is not sin, it is Adharma.

Please don't fall into traps of setting ridiculous fanatics' concepts as the 'benchmark' and ignoring our ancestors' ideals.

Read history - the religions do not bring peace; it always makes you piece-piece or piece meat. Our ancestors had a broader universal view. Let's follow that.

There are no superstitions in Dharma - but just look around you. Hindus indulge in all sorts of superstitions. A true Hindu MUST be a rational and logical thinker who believes that he/she is divine. The most obvious misconception about Hinduism is that we tend to see it as a religious faith.

Why Am I a Hindu?

To be precise, Hinduism is a way of life, a Dharma. Dharma does not mean religion. It is the law that governs all action. Thus, contrary to popular perception, Hinduism is not a religion. Out of this misinterpretation, have come most of the misconceptions about Hinduism.

To obtain a true understanding of sacred writings, such as the Upanishads or the Bhagavad Gita, one must read them on their own terms and not from the perspective of another religious tradition.

Because the Hinduism now developing in the West is being reflected through the lens of Christianity, Judaism and Islam, the theological uniqueness of Hinduism is being compromised or completely lost.

Karl Marx said: "Religion is the opium of the people". It's true - he was talking about Semitic religions. He was not aware of a Dharma where even atheists are considered as Sages and there was no discrimination based on caste, creed, race and colour.

Hinduism doesn't have missionaries, crusades and process of conversion - still millions of educated people want to be a Hindu - why?

There is no official authority controlling Hindus.

There is no Pope/Caliph/ any living prophets/intermediaries. Priests are not given targets and incentives to "Spread the Word".

Despite attack from everywhere, Hinduism survived. How?

Look at the history - whichever country Islamic invaders entered - Indonesia, Iran, Afganistan, African countries - a total annihilation of indigenous culture happened and the country became 100% Islam. Despite ruling India for 800 years killing millions of Indians, burning libraries and demolishing lakhs of temple, why couldn't they convert all Hindus?

Because Indians believed Dharmo rakshati rakshitaha (Dharma protects those who protect it) - the power of Dharma was divine than blind faiths. But it is naive to think that Dharma can never be in danger. When a huge number of people in a society violate Dharma, then the society is in danger resulting in major upheaval.

An avatar may appear to protect Dharma - but it may take few more centuries. Till then, we must do our little bit by creating awareness about our Dharma and Universality - not with violence like organized religions do, but with non-violence.

So, ask yourself - do you want to follow Sanatan Dharma or compete with those religions?

Chapter - 19

Hindu Economics

Ten years ago, I was travelling from Mumbai to Frankfurt by Lufthansa. My fellow passenger, a young Briton - Rohan Stanley - talked to me.

Rohan Stanley's ancestors were South Indians who settled in UK long ago. He is doing honors in fine arts.

I said I am a finance journalist and working for a US-based newswire. Our talk touched economics when he said: "India has never focused on economics from the time immemorial...Hence it remains as poor, underdeveloped and intolerant country...Even great economic theories like communism and socialism failed in India."

"I know my country has many shortcomings. I also don't see any great progress in the next couple of decades. But don't say India never knew anything about economy...As a matter of fact, the only humane and sustainable economic theory - the best ever in the world - was developed and practiced by our ancestors."

"Mr. Uday, over-patriotism is a sickness! What economic theory India has apart from some non-practical spiritual idiotism? Your theories never address poor working class and downtrodden. Your ancestors were big zero in finance. They didn't even have a currency or coin. Even dessert dwelling Middle East Arabs had Dinar as currency..."

"You are wrong here. Early punched coins were minted and used for many centuries in India. These coins were made of gold, silver, or copper.

12 Dhanakas = 1 SuVarna, 3 SuVarnas=1 Dinara. An equivalent of Indian Dinara was Greek coin denarius. So, even the word dinar comes from India. Modem currency codes Dinar, Rupee, Rupiah, Taka etc. all have equivalent terms in Sanskrit (Dinara, Rupyaka, Tankaka etc).

Incidentally, the 'Dinar' was introduced in Kuwait in 1960 as a replacement for the Rupee!" I told him: "Our ancestors had an economic theory that was the best in the word... And India was never a spiritual country - it's a misconception."

"That's amusing, can you please explain?" Rohan asked. Then he suddenly laughed. "Sorry, Mr. Uday, don't think I am rude but I can't help laughing. India's ancient economic theory is non-existing...Since my forefather's hail from India, I also have done a good deal of research..."

"If you are an independent thinker and learnt well about the history, tell me if your Platos and Pythagorases had not traveled to Hindu civilization what would they have known of philosophy, science and mathematics?"

"I agree that pretty much whole known world was under Vedic wisdom till the advent of aggressive cults in the names of Semitic religions attacked and destroyed your country. I also know Pythagoras studied in India and he was a vegetarian blah blah blah

Why Am I a Hindu?

.The world owes lot of things to ancient Indians...But we are talking about economics, sir...Your ancestor's contribution is zero!"

"Did you know that India or then Hindu civilization was the largest economy and richest civilization in the world till AD 500, when barbarians and religious fanatics from Middle East looted trillions of dollars' worth of gold from Hindu temples?"

"Yes, but how is that connected to economic theory? Don't beat around the bush. Come to the point..."

"The economic principle introduced to the world by our ancestors is known as 'Madhukara Vritti'. ...No other system - Capitalism, Communism, Socialism, Fascism, Marxism or Mixed Economy- can't even be comparable to this practical, sustainable and scientific economic theory..." I said.

"That's a sweeping statement. Tell me specifically about this madhu…madkar..-whatever," he said.

"'Madhukara Vritti. The basis of economics was introduced in earth by great sages in Vedas some 7K years ago. RigVeda says: 'Earth bestows riches and various wealth and treasure…prosperity on all, sustainers of the region.

Let a man (or woman) ponder well on wealth, earn it by the path of ethics and with humility consulting own conscience, and heartily gain upright prosperity.'

You will agree to me that any philosophy without considering nature and its sustainability is not worth considering for human beings"

"I agree to that..."he nodded.

"Sanatan Dharma is not life-negating, otherworldly or pessimistic in its philosophy when it comes to finance. The four legitimate wants allowed include: Artha (material prosperity), Kama (pleasure or desire), Dharma (righteous conduct) and Moksha (liberation)"

"Can you explain in a way a 'human' can understand?" he asked.

"Wealth won't come without effort. Our Sastras say that wealth has to be earned by Dharmic and truthful means, and not by dishonest means.

It has to be earned with humility and not arrogance, because one owes it to the society of which one is a member for making it possible.

Consulting one's own conscience also is important in deciding the ways in which wealth is earned. To make it simple for the layman, our ancestors have picturized the concept as Vishnu and Lakshmi."

"You mean Vishnu?"

"Yes, Vishnu is Dharma and Lakshmi is wealth. The wealth should be at the feet of Dharma, not on the head. The heart of Hindu economics philosophy is not profit, employment or growth, but how it strengthens family and community, individual character and sensitivity. It is very practical because it touches all aspects of a human life and nature."

"Okay, but you didn't come to the basic principle of economics that is formulated by your ancestors."

"Yes, ancestors explained about three types of vrittis (mode of living) - Angahara Vritti (you burn the forest to get some coal or firewood), Malaka Vritti (you take the flowers from the forest, but leaving the trees or plants) and Madhukara Vritti (you are like a bee, which takes only honey from the flowers). Madhukara Vritti is the basis of Hindu economic theory."

"How does a Honeybee becomes principle of economics?"

"The honeybee doesn't exploit the flower. It helps flowers to bloom and populate. It takes nectar to its hive and converts into honey.

It saves honey for future and for future generations. It's a selfless activity considering ecology, environment and future generation. It is helpful to the entire world, not just few."

"Oh, that's a beauty! A clean green thing"

"The developed, rich countries based on all other economic principles destroyed the entire resources (that the earth stored for its living beings for millions of years), just for the sake of a couple of generations. Any resource in the earth belongs to all its population and all its creatures.

But the rich nations were considering that they are the owners of these resources.

The Semitic thoughts and religions spread the concept that the earth is made by God only for humans (believers) so that you can exploit and kill everything (including human) who do not believe in their concepts. But our country focused on culture, family bonding, judicious spending, and savings habits"

"Hmmm"

"Hindu economics did take a serious note of economy as a field of legitimate human activity as well as of political economy or economics as a field of thought and teaching. But for you people consider such concepts as pre-historic..."

"I don't think so. But you have a point here. But communism is still better..."

"7000 years ago, before communism, our ancestors said: "Let the rich satisfy the poor implorer, and bend his eye upon a longer pathway. Riches come now to one, now to another, and like the wheels of cars are ever rolling." (Rigveda). It also says God is with the labourers. The Veda says that "Not without toil are Gods inclined to friendship." (RigVeda).

"Gods befriend none but him who has toiled". Can your communism go to that extend to glorify labour? We had a clear distinction of labour which was horizontally divided into four and known as Varnas.

They have explained even food habits of each Varna for physical and mental health - that was also very scientific.

The entire system was green and sustainable - they consider everything in the nature is divine (even trees and rivers were Gods for them) hence we shouldn't exploit it. And their prayer was 'let the entire world be happy'

"Hmm. Yes, such principles are better than communist principles. But India had tyrannical kings..."

"On the contrary, barring few exceptions most of or kings were Dharmic. The economic center was temple in each village and not Kings. King was just a caretaker of the deity in the temple. Indian Kingdoms progressed based on this Hindu (human) economic principle.

Hence, unlike their counterparts elsewhere our Kings had always been democratic. The entire population was divided themselves on the basis of work they do. The division was based exclusively on profession (Varna). And all of them worked earnestly for the society in the name of the deity.

They promoted tolerance, equality, accept all religions and freedom, that's why our advanced ancient civilization could provide incredible contributions to the world of science and art"

"Why did it fail then?"

"The wealth of the village was concentrated in the temple. Just like honey hive, the hard-earned wealth was kept in the temple for the future generations.

It was an easy target. Barbaric invasive forces and non-righteous Kings up to the Mughal dynasty and the colonialists (British Imperialism) attacked out ancestors for this wealth.

For instance, when the Barbarian invader Mohammad Gajnavi took away nearly 10 tonnes of gold jewels and golden idols of God and Goddesses in Somnath temple (Gujarat) in 1025 AD, which was life savings of hardworking peaceful human beings (nearly 80,000) for their future generations.

When you ridicule our ancestors, you fail to see 1000s of such temple ransacked and Iconoclastic and Hindu Holocaustic Genocidal invasions"

"For us, Indian history starts with Mughals only. How come the world missed such great teachings?"

"India do not teach the real Indian history. For instance, India had the richest Kingdom in the world - an economic role model for the entire world - the great Vijayanagara Empire. It is a successful model of Hindu economics. Merchants sold precious gems in bucketsful in the streets of the markets. Its architecture was grand and its love of art breathtaking."

"Wow! This should be taught in the London School of Economics. Why don't they teach about such Kingdoms in India?"

"If you teach, then you will have to explain what happened to that Kingdom. They would then need to teach about barbaric invaders and holocaust of millions of Hindus. That would have political implications. Nobody would take up such risk."

"It's really amazing. I need to read and learn more about this. Are there books on Hindu economic theory?" he asked.

"Thousands of scriptures are still available. There are economic texts like ArthaSastra and many financial and economic analyses in Manu Dharma Shastra, Aapstamba Dharma Sutraas, Gautama smruti etc.

Texts like Yaajnavalkya Smrutee (in the chapter Runaadaana prakaranam) deals with loans and the rates of interest to follow according to the risks involved, and who would clear off the debt in case the borrower expires etc, that is far better than today's credit rating systems."

"I have never heard about it," Rohan said, "I am sorry, but really I didn't know India had advanced economic theory and Kingdom that flourished with practical implementation of Hindu economics."

"Rohan, you are being used to an economic system in which human beings are mostly regarded as essentially economic beings, carrying out economic activities, producing goods and, in turn, consuming goods to complete the economic cycle.

Indian ancestors held that human beings are not just physical entities to be kept happy by producing and consuming.

Rather, humans comprise physical, mental and conscious aspects, and for the happiness of an individual all three should be taken into consideration.

For all economic activities, Dharma (righteousness) must be the guiding force and svAdharma (to find and follow the path of one's own being) should play a fundamental role in choosing your economic livelihood."

Chapter - 20

Do You Believe In Caste?

A friend who lives in Germany, Heidi Ryan, asked me: "India still has the evil caste system. Do you believe in caste, Uday?"

"Yes, Indian caste system is definitely evil in the current form," I agreed with her.

"But I saw a few pictures of you performing some funny rituals. Why do educated people like you follow the ancient ridiculous evil caste system? Do you still practice the inhuman untouchability too?" She asked mockingly.

I smiled and said, "I practice some rituals related to my culture and tradition, during special occasions such as a family function. But these rituals are not ridiculous. We do not practice untouchability. And I am not aware of any caste system that was prevailing in ancient India..."

"You mean to say there was no caste system in ancient India?" she laughed! "I know Indian history too. I have learned about Hinduism too."

In return, I said, "The Indian history books, curriculum and research papers were prepared by die-hard fans of invaders, missionaries and communists. Similar to what today's market-media does, they have successfully planted a false theory that caste system was prevailing in ancient India. They have publicized it as s traditional way of Hinduism. But, our social system was not like that of your western way of dividing society."

"How can you compare your barbaric system with the modern scientific western classification system?" she became angry.

I calmly said, "You divided the society based on race and hate...Indian caste system, even in the present rude form, pales when compared to South African apartheid and the feudal system that was in force in Europe. We never had a slavery system based on class or caste as you still can see in the Middle East."

"But you also had caste system based on Aryan and Dravidian races," she persisted in her argument.

I patiently explained, "You got it all wrong... For example, my community (I don't call it a caste) is Gawd Saraswat Brahmins (GSB) - There are black, white and brown colored people in our community - from all races. There is Uttar Chitpavana ethnic groups (Mongolic), Ratnagiri ethnic group (Indo-European race) or Aryan and Dravidian races. You can even find people with looks resembling Chinese facial features in our community. That shows Indian community (caste) system has nothing to do with race, colour or creed..."

"Hmmm...So I was misinformed..." she appeared confused and asked, "But what about caste based violence in India?"

I replied, "There was not even a single violence related to caste or community in India till the Mughal and British rule. In recent times, we have witnessed such unfortunate incidents.

But if you investigate, you would find that the real issue was not caste - there are many politics and personal vendetta involved in it. It's not like the Nazi holocaust of 10 million people and the immolation of innocent females in the name of race."

"But there were wars between religions in India," she said.

I explained, "It was not war. It was a one-sided attack and persecution by religions of non-Indian origin. According to an estimate, more than 100 million Hindus were persecuted by invaders starting from Mahmud Ghazni.

It was not war - it was a holocaust of the Hindus. Hindus never killed or fought for faith or religion. India has never had a religious war like the one where 50 million Africans were killed in slave boats during 200+ years of slavery with the Church justification of Africans having no soul.

Also, there are other examples such as decimation of Native Americans, Europe and Middle East raging a Holy Cross War, or Jihad violence against infidels...but India has never had such wars."

After listening to me she said, "I understand that Hindu philosophy always stood for peace and universal love beyond religions. But, still, all your scriptures have promoted the caste system."

Patiently putting forward my points I said, "Please show me any Vedic scripture that promotes or even mentions about caste.

There was NO caste system in India.

We had a "Varna vyavastha" based on the karma (job or profession) people do.

Caste is not intrinsic to Hinduism. Jaati, Kula and Varna are cornerstones of the society that followed Sanatan Dharma (Hindus).

When the Portuguese colonized parts of India, they mistakenly translated "Varna vyavasthaa" as "caste system" and the mistake has stayed since then.

So "Caste" is not an Indian term to describe the complex mix of factors that made up a part of the ancient social system in India. It is an inaccurate Portuguese term grouping and mixing the separate ideas of jati and Varna, and the equally separate issue of ethnicity all into one."

"Everybody knows India had a caste system. You are in denial mode, Uday," she said slightly feeling annoyed.

I smilingly continued to explain, "Till about 400-600 A.D, Guna (character) and Karma defined the Varna system in India. But, after the invasions by foreigners everything had changed.

Europeans and Arabians came to India as invaders, conquerors, missionaries and evangelists for inquisition. They created the untouchable lower class in the Hindu society too and distorted the Varna-system and used it politically for their selfish purposes.

For, in the West and Middle East, you had a slavery system and treated the so-called "lower class" people like animals."

"Hmmm...But I follow Christianity which doesn't believe in any caste system," she declared confidently.

Suppressing my laugh I said, "There are approximately 41,000 denominations in Christianity. This also can be called caste, if Varna = caste. And most of these denominations fight against each other for increasing market share, converting each other. Such inter-caste conversion or fight for market share never ever happens among Hindu castes."

Confused she asked, "Hmmm...So, Islam is the only religion that doesn't differentiate people based on caste?"

Before she could carry that train of thought, I interrupted saying, "No single day passes without report of violence between Shia and Sunni castes in Islam.

There are many sects in Islam - Ahmadiyya, Shia, Sufism and Sunni. There is religious orientation within the sect (Isnashari, Ismaili, Ahmedi, etc.) and ethnic affiliation (e.g. Sindhi, Baloch, Punjabi, etc.). They don't even marry each other."

"So, all people in the earth follow caste system," she conceded as if appearing to agree with me.

There are always four classes of people brahmin (scholar), kshatriya(administrator), vaishya (bussinessman) and shudra (those other than the three) based on their own virtues.

Whether you like it or not - you will definitely find these 4 divisions of classes everywhere in the world in all the times. Our ancestors studied its scientific background of social divisions and developed it as a great "Varna system".

It was based on virtue (not on birth), but there are better chances for a child to learn skills of his family. Hence, it descended as birth system and later it was taken as granted and thus further deterioration took place.

I said, "Mahatma Gandhi announced that Varna (caste system) is 'inherent in human nature, and Hinduism has simply made a science of it. Thus, unlike racism and culturalism elsewhere, India has only ethnicism. Swami Vivekananda says 'Caste is the plan we want to follow. What caste really is, not one in a million understands'."

"So you support caste system!" She stated with confusion.

Clarifying I said, "I believe in Varna system, but not the caste system in the current form. Varna divisions are horizontal, not vertical.

There was no discrimination. A caste system dominated by superstitions, wrong rituals and discrimination is not acceptable to me. Today, the entire society is manipulated by greed and corruption. Hindu "Varna" system was one of the greatest social institutions.

I can perform one duty in social life, and you another; you can govern a country, and I can stitch a dress, but that is no reason why you are greater than I, for can you stitch my dress? Can I govern the country?

The seers of the early Vedic period knew nothing of caste. The four-fold Varna (mistaken as caste) is merely a theoretical division of society to which tribes, clans and family groups are affiliated. It is a sociological fiction. The earliest available literature gives instances of Brahmins carrying on the professions of medicine, arms and administration."

"But karma based caste system has later turned into birth right...," she nodded and said finally understanding my point of view.

I further explained, "Yes - even in democracy, you can see birth-based leaders.

You can see people who came into film field as actors, just because they are sons/daughters of actors. The social deterioration is not confined to caste. It exists in every sphere of life, especially more in political ideologies than in castes. Can you find any single leader in Communist Marxist Party who does daily physical labour, though its ideology was based on upliftment of working class and labourers?

Corruption and manipulation has crept in everywhere. So, why blame only the manipulated caste system? Blame it on manipulation and corruption in society."

"So, birth-based caste system is totally wrong?" She asked as if wanting a black and white conclusion.

I replied, "Again, I have a different view here. There are good and bad points in birth based privilege system too. A carpenter's son starts the profession from childhood.

There is a great quantity common sense, special skills and wisdom that has developed from the rich experience of generations. It may be imbibed or inherited in his genes. So, a carpenter's son can do better carpentry work than you or me. However, there can be exceptions to this"

"Why do you follow Brahminism, is it because you were born to Brahmin parents or going by karma?" She curiously asked.

I said, "Brahmamism is an invitation to live a virtuous, humble and noble life in accordance with nature. It is not a caste. A Brahmin follows the path of non-violence, vegetarianism and prays for the happiness of the entire universe (not just for believers or any caste).

For, a Brahmin sees the divine presence in everything - that's the gist of Brahmajnan. Every human being in this world should thrive to be a Brahmin. A person born to Brahmin parents has more access to these concepts, sacred scriptures and Sanskrit, than those born in other castes.But, whether they follow such noble traditions or not is a different question."

Is there any society where there are no divisions based on the work people do? Every society has such divisions.

The unfortunate thing that happened in India, was that along the way, Indians fossilized the caste system into permanent castes. India is doing it now in politics, business, movies etc.

"So, we in the West have a many misconceptions about the Hindu caste system," she admitted.

"Hinduism believes in "Vasudhaiva Kutumbakam" (the world is one family). So how can we follow a rigid caste system? The caste system was never a tenet of the Sanatan Dharma faith." I told her ending the conversation, "So, yes. I think this "caste" word should not be given so much importance. Unfortunately, India is ruled by evil caste system because all political parties support that system."

Now the present system is mostly corrupted, very few are trying to maintain those standards.

Chapter - 21
Hindus Don't Respect Women!

My college mate Zackaria Johne is an atheist. Few years ago, we had an opportunity to meet when he told me, "All religions are anti-women. All religious scriptures do picturise women in a very derogatory manner. Still, the womenfolk earnestly follow those religions...."

"If such disrespectful attitude existing in any religions, it's completely unacceptable for me as I believe in gender equality..."

"Ha-ha... And you are a practicing Hindu. 'Women don't deserve freedom' says your sacred texts of Hinduism...."

"But, Zack, I do not know anything of the sort mentioned in our Vedic texts..."

"You are turning blind eyes to your scriptures. The ancient Hindu law-giver Manu clearly says, 'Pitha rakshathi kaumare, Bharta rakhshathi yauvane, Puthro rakshathi vaardhakye, Na, sthree swathanthryam arhati'. Manu Smriti, Chapter 9 Verse 3. This means, a woman is protected by her father in childhood, by husband in her youth, and by son in her old age, and hence she doesn't deserve freedom...."

"If that's the meaning of the verse, it is shameful for Sanatan Dharma and highly deplorable." I said. "But, I have a question - being an atheist why did you write an article "I believe in God"?"

"What? I have never written such rubbish thing. I am a confirmed atheist. Didn't we fight in many debates in the college arts-club? I have never written such an article..." he raised his voice and his face became red hot.

"No Zack, you have written. I remember reading your article - 'I believe in God' - in our college magazine." I argued.

"Uday, don't make a fool out of yourself. You know very well that I had written an article in English - which was my first article in English - 'Why don't I believe in God'. It appeared in the very next page of your state award winning short story in Malayalam..."

"Zack, if you are being selective in quotes, I can also do the same. I have selected few words from the headline 'Why don't I believe in God'. I have just deleted first two words, but you are neglecting a whole book just for a verse." I smiled at him.

"What do you mean?" he raised his eye brows.

"You have taken a stanza from Manusmriti out of context and quoting it. So, I can also do like that, right? Why are you getting angry about it?"

"Sorry...But do you mean to say that quote was not fully represented?"

"Not only that, you have given a wrong meaning and incorrect interpretation too...This verse is most mis-quoted and intentionally mis-interpreted to project Manu as 'anti-woman'"

"How come?"

"Zack, before interpreting this verse, we have to go through the other verses before and after that one, and then you will see that Manu holds women in high esteem.

Wherever (family / household) women are worshiped or held in high esteem, the Gods and Deities reside there happily. Where they are not honored, no sacred rite yields rewards." (Manu Smriti 3.56).

He clearly says all actions remain un-fruitful, if women are not worshipped. "Those women who can protect themselves (are the only ones) who are actually secure." (9.12) "Nobody can protect women by force." (9.10)...."

"I didn't know that..."

"Before jumping into something based on the anti-Indian-brain-washing teachings created by evangelists, secular morons and ignorant communists, you should have, at least, tried to read it..." I told him. "Zack what would you do if a molester catch hold of your daughter, sister, wife or mother?"

"I will fight and try to protect them with my life..." he said.

"So, how can it be wrong if Manu says the same thing? He is giving men a huge moral RESPONSIBILITY...All he said was to respect and take care of your women. It was something written more than 5000 years ago, a time when even the King's wife was snatched by Asuras (Barbarians). How can it be wrong?"

"But...but... that's...."

Why Am I a Hindu?

"Now let's interpret the (in) famous verse of Manu. In Manu's perception, a woman is, by her very nature, so divine and unique that she should never be left to fend for herself. It is the duty of society to protect and take good care of her — by her father during childhood, husband in her youth, and son in her old age. That is what the 9.3 sloka (verse) says.

It is wrongly translated as a woman does not deserve independence. The word 'swathanthryam' here does not mean "independence," but refers to the state or condition of "depending on one's own self for sustenance."

"Uday, you are mis-guiding me.... The person who accused Manu as anti-women is a Sanskrit scholar...You are not..."

"I am not an expert in Sanskrit. But the interpretations that you had learned are NOT stemming from inadequate or improper understanding of the original Sanskrit text, but intentional distortions made by the die-hard fans of Arabian invaders, British, missionaries, evangelists, communist and so-called socialists-secularists. Since I am not a brain-washed zombie like you, I am not buying such arguments that say Manu was anti-women...."

"You mean to say Manu was supporting women liberation..."

"This one line, 'Na sthree swathanthryam arhati', which means that a woman is not fit for independence because somebody has to take care of her, is not right.

I don't agree with that. Maybe, at that point of time, such advice was needed in the society."

"But women were not free in India at any point of time. They were treated as slaves..." Zack said.

"I agree with you that the status of women has deteriorated in India after brutal barbaric forces attacked our country and violently converted peaceful Indians to non-civilized blind cults. India was the only country in the world where slavery never existed.

Vedic Women in India enjoyed high status in society - in education and other rights and facilities. Along with invasion, child marriage, widow burning, the purdah and polygamy worsened the women's position."

- There were two types of scholarly women in ancient India — the Brahmavadinis (the women who never married and cultured the Vedas throughout their lives) and the Sadyodvahas (who studied the Vedas till they are married).

- It is amazing to know that there were HARDLY any illiterate women in India 5000 years ago! Among the proponents of Vedas - the foundation of Sanatan Dharma - were women sages like Ghosha, Lopamudra, Sulabha Maitreyi, and Gargi. Yami Vaivasvathi, Sraddha , Vasukra pathni , Ghosha , Soorya , Indrani , Urvasi , Sarama , Joohu , Vagambhruni and Poulomi Sachi were revered and associated with individual Rig Veda Manthras.

- Women were encouraged to undergo Upanayana rite of passage in ancient India, either before they started Vedic studies or before their wedding. All women were wearing the "Sacred Thread" (Yajnyopavitdharan "Juneev" or "Punool")

- Man was (even today) not allowed to perform any religious rites without his wife sitting near to him. Gobhila Gruhya Sutras state that the wife should be educated to be able to take part in Yagam or Yajna (a Hindu ritual of sacrifice) and Havan.

- No man is complete without woman - try to understand the Ardhanareeswara (half man and half woman) concept. The supreme Hindu God is neither "She" nor "He". Even our country -India - itself is regarded as "female" (Bharat Mata = mother India).

- The status of woman comes first than anything, anybody in India."Matha Pitha Guru Deivam" is a very popular adage or phrase in Sanskrit. First comes the mother (Matha or Mata). Next comes the father (Pitha or Pita), third is the teacher (Guru) and God (Deivam or Devam) comes last.

- Woman is considered as a "Lakshmi" (Goddess of Prosperity) of a Hindu home. She is the one who creates bond amongst all family members, thus keep entire family united and together. We see her in different roles such as daughter, wife, sister or mother. She is the one who gives good "samskar" based on traditions to the children, thus decides the fate of next generation.

"So, Zack, you have to tell me one single quote or sloka that is derogatory for women in our ancient Sanskrit sacred scriptures.... Just an out-of-context quote won't do. You have to explain the situation that leads to the verse." I said: "I totally agree with you that the situation in India has deteriorated and women are being harassed and insulted by male chauvinistic pigs. It starts from home when a mother gives more importance to her son than her daughter. It started with the decline of Varnashrama Dharma..."

"Is it?"

"Do you know, it's been clearly said in all Vedas and Suktas that the Jati (not to be mixed up with today's caste) of a child is that of mother's and not father's. What more proof you want?"

"Okay, let's forget the past. This disrespectful attitude towards women in our country should disappear...Religion is a major culprit today."

"I agree with that. People follow superstitions and wrong practices. They don't learn the teaching of our ancestors. However, there is only one way out..."

"What's it?"

"Follow the teaching of Manu Smriti earnestly. Which is = Women must be honored and adorned by their fathers, brothers, husbands and brothers-in-law, who desire their own welfare. Where women are honored, the Gods are pleased, but where they are not honored, no sacred rite yields rewards.

When women are cared for, they can perform well their roles of creators, nourishers, educators of children and inspirers. So the entire society becomes happy." I told him.

Chapter - 22
Misquoting all Scriptures

Few readers quoted Tulasidas who said in Ramcharit Manas "Dhol gawar sudra pashu nari sakal tadan ke adhikari" = animals, illiterates, lower castes and women should be subjected to beating. This is a typical example of misquoting and out-of-context quoting happen in India.

Our great "think tank" says that this explains about untouchability (on caste basis) and state of women in ancient India. These issues have deep Vedic roots in past. This means Women and Shudras=Animals!! How degrading is that?

My first thought was that, Goswami Tulsidas might have written correctly. As I said in two articles, caste system and discrimination based on sex arrived in India from 1400-1500AD by invaders. Tulasidas life period was during that time. In all probabilities, he might have influenced by social changes. Therefore, it should be correct.

I am not good in Hindi. I asked the meaning of that sentence to my father who was a Hindi teacher and Hindi pundit.

"Tulasidas was a great saint and bhakt of Rama - how could he discriminate human on basis of caste or sex?" he asked me. I felt ashamed about doubting the great saint for a moment.

He further explained the real meaning. The context was when Samudra (Sea) seeking forgiveness to Rama.

Dhol = drum, Gawanr = Ignorant and illiterate. Samudra says "I am like Dhol Ganvar" an idiotic person who keeps beating his own drum without listening to others. Shudra = Worker (wrongly translated as lower caste), Pashu = animal and Nari = woman.

But, here it is written "Shudra Pashu Naari" which means women who behaves like a working animal and thus breaks the social order. (During those times, Chastity was considered as a great virtue. A woman goes to many men was guided or punished by authorities during those time).

Samudra says that I acted like such a woman so forgive me and please guide/punish me. And for the sake of argument you can say the real meaning is "drum, idiot, worker, animal and woman should be punished." But there is an issue with this. The word "tadan" has a different meaning.

A friend of mine quoted his mother who belongs to Awadh region of U.P (Awdhi is the language - Dialect - in which Tulsi Ramayan is written here).

According to him the word TADANA means to be taken care of or to be looked after with care (Tadna means looking) but self-styled "scholars" confused it with PRATADANA (meaning beating someone)!

If you learn history of English language you will know how the word "mistress" is used in various places during different time - its meaning ranges from "rich lady" to "extramarital girlfriend"!

Not only Indian historians, but "scholars and thinkers" under payroll of evangelists-invaders combination with their greed can say anything to taint the scriptures and our great ancestors. It is a pity that many of us believe these totally baseless and misguided statements without researching and thinking for themselves.

Chapter - 23

The Truth about Sati Practice

I met Shahnawaz Hussain during a trip to Mumbai. He was my fellow traveller from London to Mumbai. He is an Indian desi in the UK with a very modern outlook. He expressed his views regarding the superstitions and wrong traditions plaguing India. I agreed with most of his observations.

"Hinduism is a curse for its women - evil people were practicing SATI everywhere in India until the British rule," he said.('Sati' was the name of the custom, in which the widow was placed on the pyre of her deceased husband and burnt alive - it was a barbaric and inhumane act).

"I agree with you regarding SATI. It is highly deplorable. But how come you blame Hinduism for that?" I asked.

"Hindu scriptures glorify Sati system, he confidently declared.

Countering this I said, "So far there is no word in Hindu scripture for "Bride burning". Sati is the feminine of 'sat', which means "true".

"But Hindus were practicing it and encouraging it, resulting in genocide," he argued.

"Hmm," I understood that he is yet another misled educated person and said, "Shahnawaz, Can I ask you a question?"

"Yes, please," he was all ears.

Putting forward my question I said, "Even in modern America, female genital mutilation (FGM) - also known as female genital cutting and female circumcision is being practiced among some Muslims. They believe that females have no right to enjoy sexual pleasure. Isn't that, right? "

"That's not true," he raised his voice. His face turned red.

I calmly said, "You please get your facts checked. FGM is done in the name of preservation of virginity and reduction of female desire, and further to enhance male pleasure. The practice is prevalent in some of the Muslim - majority countries. Many girls bleed to death or die of infections, even today because of this practice."

Not liking what I said, he argued, "That's highly deplorable. We, the educated Muslims, seriously condemn such acts."

"But Islamic scholars have two opinions about this - some say no obligatory rules exist while others refer to the mention of female circumcision in the Hadith. I do not know, you tell me," I invited him to clarify.

He became defensive, "Sir, All Muslims are not practicing it. Don't blame Muslims or Islam for some people doing wrong things..."

In a mellowed tone, I told, "I totally agree with you. As in any religion, wrong customs are practiced by the ignorant followers. I also agree that just a minority among Islam uphold terrorism, but unfortunately the blame falls on the entire religion."

"I got your point, Uday. You mean to say that just because a few people among billions of Hindus practice it, doesn't mean that Hinduism supports Sati," he admitted.

Further explaining I said, "Not only that - Sanatan Dharma or the eternal philosophy of life established in India is the only tradition in the world that gives equal importance to all without any gender, colour and racial discrimination. So how is it possible to force something like Sati on females?"

"Uday, a scholar told me about the mention of a widow's burning in the Rig-Veda," he stated.

In an attempt to clarify things to him, I said, "Yes, I have also read about it. Rig Veda, Mandala 10, Chapter 18 mentions about widowed dames.

The hymn calls for a widow to rise from the pier of her dead husband and now move on to take the hand of her new husband. As in all cases, Hindu-bashers have misinterpreted it into a terrible falsification signifying the burning of widows to demean Hinduism."

He said, "Mahabharata, the Hindu epic, mentions that Madri was burned with her husband Pandu. I explained, Pandu had another wife - Kunti - why didn't she die? There are hundreds of characters in the Mahabharata. Madri's case was exceptional.

The epic is broader in universality. -It showcases all evil and good things that had been prevailing in the society during that time.

How can you generalize things by a singled-out example? In the Ramayana, when Dasaratha died, none of his three wives jumped into the pyre.

There is not even a single case of forceful widow burning in any of our scriptures. The story of Sati and Shiv has nothing to do with Sati system. Sati didn't die in her Husband's funeral pyre."

If Sati was a Hindu system, then it should have been everywhere. I have never heard of any Sati incident anywhere in South India.

"Then what, really, is Sati?" He exclaimed.

Narrating the concept, I said, "Sati is an ancient Sanskrit word, meaning a chaste woman who thinks of no other man than her own husband. The famous examples are Sati Anusuya, Seelavati, Savitri, Ahilya etc. None of them committed suicide, let alone being forcibly burned. So how is it that they are called Sati?"

"But there is proof that Sati was practiced in India," he insisted.

Nodding I said, "Yes, it began with invaders bearing Muslim names. Please note I am not calling them 'Muslim invaders' (as popularly known) as I know that there are good people in all religions. Rape, genocide and gross human rights violations against innocent Hindus induced the victims to adopt defensive mechanisms. Hindu women in India adopted the Sati traditions to protect themselves from invaders, who perpetrated the largest holocaust in history against Hindus."

The barbaric and inhuman invaders did record with glee their genocide of Hindus, because they felt all along that they were doing their duty; that killing, plundering and enslaving Hindus, and ransacking Indian temples was their duty.

It was standard practice for cruel warlords like Ghori and Ghazni to unleash the mass rape and enslavement of hundreds of thousands of women after the slaughter of all peace-loving innocent Hindu males.

The tradition of sati, where Hindu women voluntarily cast themselves onto burning cremation grounds after their husbands' death, gained widespread acceptance during the invasions.

Apart from looting and conversion, there was another reason for the fanatic religious invaders to attack foreign lands - the shortage of women in their land, since a male could marry many woman, many males had to remain unmarried.

So, invaders have been capturing any females - from child to grown-up. Many women had to commit suicide to protect their dignity. Widows had no other option left, but to die with their husbands.

The most famous instance took place when invaders overran Chittorgarh (Chittor) in 1568: rather than submit to the rape and slavery that would follow, eight thousand heroic Hindu women committed sati en masse.

The word "Sati-Pratha" (forcible widow burning) was coined by British and foreign Missionaries in India to de-mean Hindus.

Hindus were victims of the crime. This is a typical case where the perpetrators of crime are glorified and the victims are penalized. Just like any other durachara (wrong practices such as black magic, astrology, mantravada etc) Sati might have been in practice among some ignorant Hindus".

"Sorry, I didn't know about these facts. I thought that Sati was part of your Sanatan Dharma," he admitted apologetically.

"It is NOT. Shahnawaz, let us absorb good things in all traditions. Things that are not relevant today are anachara and superstitions. We can't use violence or force to change this.

Our Dharma is to learn the truth and teach the truth. When people become aware, they will naturally stop such practices. The historians (unforgivable criminals) in India have done gross injustice to our culture for fistfuls of money," I told him.

Prior to the arrival of invaders, Sati was only a mythical term to describe Shiva's wife (named Sati) burning herself. Sati is not a practice.

It was a mechanism adopted by women of defeated kings to escape slavery in the hands of moguls. However, this Sati distortion created by British had given the Evangelists and Islamists gleeful reason to degrade Hinduism as a whole for centuries.

Chapter - 24

Is Wearing a Bindhi Relevant Today?

I have been to Hong Kong few years back. I had a press conference there. I took my family along with me. One day evening, I found the group of journalists from Mainland China taking photographs of my children. I asked them why.

A lady who can speak English (I remember her English first name only - its Vicky) said: "The red dot tattoo above their noses is beautiful..."

I said: "Oh Vicky, it is not tattoo, it's known as Bindhi."

"Why do they wear it?" she asked.

"It's part of our tradition, our culture," I said.

"Then, why are you not wearing it Uday?" her friend asked. Very logical question!

My wife laughed and said: "Men do not wear bindhis. It's only for females."

"Vicky - it is like this. Females wear kumkum (vermilion), a mixture of turmeric and lime, between their eyebrows. It is known as Bindhi. Males also wear, but mostly sandalwood (Chandan), a bigger mark. It is called tilak..." I explained.

"Uday, your wife has put that powdered red material in her forehead, that's not seen in your daughters' head!" her next question.

"Vicky, married Indian woman apply vermilion in the parting of their hair every day. It is called Sindoor"

"Is it to ward off evil spirits?" asked her companion.

"No - we do not believe in evil spirits and there is no superstition attached to it. It's purely a traditional and cultural." I told her. My wife gave Bindhi to all females in the group and one should see their excitement in wearing it.

Making a mark on the forehead is a very old tradition among Indian men and women. Bindhi is derived from the Sanskrit word bindhu meaning dot or drop. There are many terms for it in various Indian languages: Kunkuma, Pottu, Bottu, Phot, Tip, Chukka, Kunkoo,

Tilakam, Tilaka etc. In my mother tongue, Konkani, it is called Tilo. The men's Tilaka is made with coloured earth, ashes of Yajna (the fire offering), sandalwood paste or unguent. The term tika or tikka is a distorted form of the term tilaka. It's also known as 'Pattai' or 'Naamam' in south India.

The colour of tilak was depended upon the Varna (profession). The priests or academicians (Brahmins) wore a tilak of white sandal wood signifying purity. Kings, Warriors and Administrators (Khatriyas) wore red tilak to signify valor.

Business men and traders (Vaishyas) wore a yellow tilak signifying prosperity. The service class, workers and laborers (Shudra) wore black tilak to signify service.

Shaivites typically use ashes (called Vibhuti) and draw their tilaks as three horizontal lines (tripundra).

Vaishnavites apply clay (preferably from holy rivers) or sandalwood paste. They apply the material in two vertical lines, which may be connected at the bottom, forming either a simple U shape.

Once I heard a television swami saying: " Wearing Bindhi is the most scientific and advanced technology.

Bindhi is worn on forehead where there is Ajna chakra or Brahma sthana. This is 6th chakra (of seven) meaning "command" which aids concentration.

The central point on the forehead is an outlet of potent energy. Thus, it is believed that the red kumkum retains our inner energy. It's also a cosmic window to receive and give power and energy"

He went on saying: "Today's science found that pituitary gland is attached to Ajna Chakra...Negative energy in the form of negative thoughts and black magic enters the body through this chakra. When you place a Bindhi, you block the negative energy from entering the body"

There's absolutely no proof regarding any of these claims being made by those television gurus or propagators of pseudo-scientific concepts.

I don't know about such negative energy. The pituitary gland lies under your brain and is somewhere behind your nose.

The hypothesis that it cools the pituitary or activates it doesn't have a base.

I don't know why we need a scientific validation for each and everything that we follow. This in turn propagates pseudo-science, which is very harmful. It makes us a laughing stock in front of a modern scientific society.

We have much stronger traditional and cultural significance. No one knows exactly when the tradition of putting a Bindhi started. Some say, it started with the concept of Shiv and Parvati.

It is believed that Parvati protects all those men whose wives apply vermilion to their parting of hair.

For Vaishnavites, it is one of the 5 places Mother Lakshmi (Goddess of Wealth and prosperity) resides on Earth.

So, wearing Kumkum shows your respect for Mother and gives prosperity to your family.

The book 'Shishtasamacharat' written by Bhabadeb Bhatt and Pashupati talked about this Vedic practice, which gives instructions to wear vermilion.

Adi Shankaracharya writes in Soundarya Lahari: "Oh mother, let the line parting thine hairs, which looks like a canal, through which the rushing waves of your beauty ebbs, and which on both sides imprisons, your Vermillion, which is like a rising sun, by using your hair which is dark like the platoon of soldiers of the enemy, protect us and give us peace."

Radha the consort of Krishna turned the kumkum into a flame-like design on her forehead. Mahabharata says, Draupadi (wife of the Pandavas) wipes off her sindoor in disgust and despair at the happenings in Hastinapur.

Usage of Bindhi and Sindhoor is also found in Sanskrit books of Kalidasa, Panchatantra and Kathasarita Sagara. Tulsidas mentions it in his Ram Charit Manas at the time of the marriage between Ram and Sita.

The original Kumkum has some medicinal properties. Turmeric's anti-bacterial properties and sandalwood's 'cooling' properties are well known.

Today's Sindoor is red or orange-red colored cosmetic chemical powder - an artificial powder. Bindhis are not traditionally prepared one anymore, it is just those stickers.

I don't know how those things are supposed to keep the place cool and thus healthy? Kumkum is known to contain high levels of lead and can cause health problems. However, it has some practical uses - sindhoor is the cultural equivalent of the West's wedding ring.

No doubt, it also is a message to potential suitors that 'the games over.' It has just become a traditional show off, more than anything.

Now, coming back to personal experience, I asked my wife: "Why are you wearing Sindhoor?"

"I just love it. In fact, the first reason for me to get married was to wear it..."

But I think it has much more into it. It is symbolic expression of love. At the time of the wedding the groom applies red vermillion to the parting of the bride's hair - the love begins...

In the West, the newly marrieds say 'I love you' umpteen times every day. They wanted to be assured of the love every now and then - so they say "I love you" whenever they talk. Or they express their love through kisses, even publicly.

Indian society was and is not very vocal. Symbols are used to convey many sentiments. India followed a joint family system - so expression of love was not possible in the public. So, symbols were used to express.

There are historical reasons too. When barbaric invaders indulged in plunder, rape and abduction of young girls, no women's honor was safe. Later the locals discovered Islam forbids touching of another man's wife and most of religious fanatic soldiers abided by the tenets of their religion.

Thus, Indian women displayed vermillion prominently to announce their married status. Sindoor became the women's savior. The practice continued when the British arrived.

According to tradition, if the husband dies, the widow won't wear Sindoor.

"Do you wear tilak?" many people asked me. "Yes, I do." The Tilak invokes a psychological feeling of sanctity in the wearer and others.

The tilak is traditionally applied with the prayer, "May I remember the Brahmam! May this pious feeling pervade all my activities. May I be righteous in my deeds."

The tilak is thus a blessing of the Lord and a protection against wrong tendencies and forces. The scriptures say that a Hindu without tilak is worthy of condemnation and is compared to intellect without clarity.

I remember in my childhood, our community (GSB or Amchigelle) there were various such observance that is a part of our culture spanning many centuries.

Clean courtyard with flowering shrubs, a pampered tulsi, bilva, kamkasturi, watered daily and kumkum applied and arathi performed gives an auspicious identity to the home of community members. It's a great tradition.

However, wearing a bindhi is a lot less common with younger urban women. Today's young generation don't wear Bindhi or tilak, especially in the offices and education institutions. Most of them only wear them on special occasions with traditional attire.

My daughters used to wear every day. I can't say they are very excited about it! They know that their mother would get angry if they don't, hence no questions asked. My daughter says she is the only person to wear Bindhi in her college class.

My cousin's daughter once asked me: "Uncle, bindhi is old-gen stuff. Why should a modern girl wear it?"

"There is nothing mandatory in our culture. It's up to you. I like my daughters wear Bindhi because their grand-parents were doing it.

My mother loved to see them wearing it. When they inherit the health and mind from their grandparents, why can't they follow their likes and dislikes, especially if it does not create any hazards in your or others life?" That was my indirect answer to my kids too, if at all they had the same question in mind and didn't ask.

"Why should I please them, Uncle?" she asked.

"In your case, especially, it is a MUST. Your parents and yours source of living is the wealth created by your grandparents. You people are totally dependent on them - so you have to please them. When you are on your own, you can take whatever decision that you want."

Chapter - 25

Hindu Hypocrisy over Sex and Chastity

"On the one hand, there is the cult of the Kama Sutra and erotic temple carvings and on the other prudery, hypocrisy and lip service to the ideal of chastity..."said my friend's son Adi.

"Very true...Indians have a notoriously ambivalent attitude towards sex..." Adi's friend said.

"Yes, the Hindu Mahasabha burnt effigies symbolizing the western culture celebrating Valentine's Day. That too in a country which has a temple in Khajuraho filled with couples in explicit sexual positions..." an elderly person said. Then he turned to me: "What's your take in it, Uday?"

The venue was a marriage hall for evening get-together connected with relative's wedding. The subject of discussion was Indian's hypocrisy over sex.

"I have a couple doubts- if you can answer it, I can join your talk..." I told them. They agreed.

"Adi, what is the best comment that boys make at girls in the college?" I asked.

"'You are sexy"

"Till few years ago, calling a girl 'sexy' was considered as insulting...Now, it is a common usage. Do today's women enjoy that comment?" (Citation needed from female folk). During my teens, the boys would say: "You look beautiful".

Recently, I have witnessed this incident in an apparel store: A 12-year girl came out of trial room with new dress and asked her mother, "Mom, do I look sexy in this dress?" And you should see the proud mom's beaming face!

"Now I have two questions to you uncles..."I looked at the elders. "One. Do you remember your grandma, uncle? How was she looked like?"

"Yeah, she was 80 when I was born. She was looking graceful. We still have her photo in the wall. She appears so serene and divine in the pic..." he said.

"Right. Yesterday's females never went to beauty parlour - make up set was unheard then. Except the turmeric and sandal, they didn't use anything in their face. Even at 70s they looked beautiful and serene...They used to decorate themselves was fresh flowers in the hair - they have never used any perfumes or deodorants. But there was no foul smell when they come near you. Today, instead of serene beauties, Indian society wants seductive beauties...Same goes for males too...The concepts of looks and appearance have changed..." I said.

"Yes, I agree with you"

"Now my second question, uncle. In your childhood, what was the usual dress of womenfolk?"

"Most of them wore just a blouse and a half dhoti."

"This means they were 75% naked. Still nobody looked at them with burning desire. And remember, there were no secure doors in 90% of the houses. The toilets and closets were at least 100 meters away from the house (not attached to house, mostly they do it in open).

So, in night time, they have to go bit away alone. They took bath in public ponds and rivers. But have you ever heard of any rape happening then?"

"That's true...Even if cameras existed then, nobody would have fixed cameras in anybody's bathrooms," he added as half-joke.

"Why?" I asked. "Why?" they also asked.

"Simple. In those days, we had followed a comprehensive life style based on "Sringara" - today it is replaced with "Kama" or extreme desire"

"I didn't get you. It's something new...Can you explain that?" he said. Adi and other two also were keen.

"Sringara (Srungara = love, beauty and grace) Rasa (=expression, no exact word in English) is considered as the top one in nine rasas. Sringara is aesthetic. It's the most intimate secret of lovers - it was depicted in the classical Indian dance, all art forms (writing, sculpture) and life..."

The idea of Shiva and Sakthi or Prakruti (nature -female) and Purusha (Male) could have been developed from the concept of Sringara.

Maha Vishnu's Mohini avatar in Indian mythology is based altogether on a feminine mood of Sringara. (Moham= charming enchantment exercised by a one on the opposite sex. Mohini = the creator of Moham).

Sringara was considered as the noble and divine feminine qualities. Natya Shastra says that Vishnu is the presiding deity of the Sringara rasa.

Krishna is regarded as the complete incarnation of Vishnu - do you know why? Because he incorporates within himself all attributes of human refinement, on top of it is the Sringara Rasa! Krishna has three meanings. "Krishyathi iti Krishnah" (The one who cultivates is Krishna), "Karshathi iti Krishnah." (The one who attracts is Krishna) and "Kushyathi iti Krishnah" (one who is always blissful).

Sringara should comprise of all these state to reach bliss.

"But what about Kama?"

"Kamadev is the God of love. The word Kama should not be erroneously interpreted as merely an erotic urge. It does not represent sensual pleasure.

But in today's context the word Kama is used for extreme desire, sexual desire etc." (I am also using the word Kama in today's concept to explain things).

There is huge difference between Sringara and Kama, though the Western concept says both are same. Hence they erroneously use the word "love making" for physical relation.

, some sages say Sringara is part of Kama. Kama has two perspectives - Kama-Bhaavana and Kama-vaasana. The former propagates shringara while the later one promotes the lust.

Our ancestors conveyed much deeper sense by this term. As said, Sringara means "Love" and often also "beauty".

Narrowly speaking, Sringara means to enjoy the company of the opposite sex, in a very lovely and romantic manner. This ensures a long, happy and healthy life (ayurarogya soukhyam).

Soundarya = beauty. That is why Sringara Lahari is also known as soundarya Lahari. Love is not just Rati (Kama) the amorous attitude.

Sringara is truth and naturally it is considered to be the king of the Rasas.

In modern world, it is mistaken for seductive, passionate or amorous love. Our ancestors believed that the life will always be beautiful, if you have the Sringara Rasa - unfortunately today we don't even know about it.

"Can you explain bit more, Uncle," Adi said.

"Sringara is not sex or romance - it is romantic love! (Check your dictionary if you don't know difference between romance and romantic).

It is clearly explained in classical Sanskrit Sringara literature, where Sringara is bordered by ethics and aesthetic love.

It has two bases namely Sambhoga (Love in Union) and Vipralambha (Love in Separation)."

The romantic imagery of the first romantic poets in the earth Kalidasa, Amaru and Bhartrhari, followed a certain structure of restraint and dignity based on 'Dharma'.

Kalidas's "Kumarasambhavam" is as elegant as it was Sringara, as romantic as it was sublime. Two other important works of Kalidasa are 'Ritusamharam' and 'Meghadutam', where the lovers enjoy Sringara yet sublime love with an unspoken understanding between one another.

Bhartrhari's 'Shatakatrayi' comprises the 'Shringarashataka' – 100 romantic verses, in which he combines thoughts of renunciation (vairagya). It was considered as the hallmark of 'Sringara Rasa Kavya'.

The 'Gita Govind', the highly impacting romantic songs by Jayadeva of the 12th century stands as absolute epitome of both 'Sringara rasa' and 'bhakti Sringara rasa.'

Anandavardhana had very rightly proclaimed that among all the 'rasas' Sringara is a very delectable and a great 'rasa' in giving extreme happiness and joy ("Sringara eva madhuraha, para prahlaadano rasaha.")

15th-century Tallapaka Annamacharya's songs are classified into the AdhyaAtma (spiritual) and Sringaara (romantic) sankeertanas genres.

His songs in the "Sringaara" genre worship Venkateswara by describing the romantic adventures of Venkateshwara and his consort Alamelu.

"Adi, have you ever gone through those great works? Reading those literatures won't make you feel horny; instead you will be elevated to a world of pure love with happy hormones and joyous mood which will create a fruitful progeny."

"Ohk, that's right. I never thought in this direction..." the elder uncle said.

"Please don't equate Western porno literature with Kama Sutra. The Kama sutra is not really a sex manual at all but rather is about 'the art of living'."

Similarly, looking at Khajuraho Group of Monuments (Madhya Pradesh, India), do you feel horny? Not at all. Instead you will develop a Sringara rasa.

What is decoded as the sexual depiction actually symbolizes nature worship of yesterdays.

There is a description of an unforgettable moment in Ramayana, in which Rama decorates Sita Devi's head with fresh beautiful flowers- it depicts the divine Sringara Rasa. If you read it, you won't feel Kama, but you will feel devotion.

Unfortunately, in the contemporary world, Sringara is replaced by Kama (=extreme sexual desire) and perversions - that creates violence, frustration and explosion.

The love as per your understanding derived from Romeo Juliet or Titanic or Valentine Day celebrations can be best termed as a superficial temporary emotion.

"Okay, now I understand your point. How did Sringara disappear from India?" Adi asked.

To please the 'educated' materialistic Indian elite and the 'civilized' British colonialists, this divine layer of Sringara was discarded almost totally.

The new notion of "secular" (SICK-ULAR) classical dances and arts started to be marketed for those who had no understanding of sacred life style based on Sringara. Even in singing 'his master's voice' became prominent.

The alien faiths, culture and superficial morality brought in by invaders and evangelists destroyed Sringara's purity.

This would've resulted in the mutations in religious and moral perceptions. The result - all art forms are mis-interpreted and transformed to please a West-looking elite class.

Sringara was not to the liking of Wesern culture where women are never to be pampered but only to be enjoyed, so when we imitated the West, we began indulging in bhoga rather than sringara and thus slowly we came to look women as something to be enjoyed and not share the love, and it became physical only.

Now we are living in an age of 'instant gratification'... instant food, instant money, instant relationships etc etc. As a result the word 'Beautiful' is replaced by 'Sexy and Hot'.

Then how will the new generation know about Sringara?

How will they know the romantic beauty of life is based on love and bliss and not on comforts and pleasures?

We have travelled a long away from a beautiful natural divine love in to an artificial chemical plastic chocolate world, in which people cannot even understand what real love (Sringara) is!

"And we make sweeping statements about hypocrisy of older generations and insult our own forefathers to please the ignoramus!" I said.

A note about Khajuraho temples were built between 950 and 1050 by the Chandela dynasty. There were 85 temples by 12th century, spread over 20 square kilometers.

Of these, only about 20 temples have survived; spread over 6 square kilometers after invaders attack. The Khajuraho temples feature a variety of art work, of which only 10% is sexual or erotic art.

In fact, the life style and dress code of only a certain class of women in that period, viz. the Courtesans, whose profession it was to entertain men.

However, in the same period, women of the common or noble class were very much subject to the restrictive code of conduct. All scriptures mentions that the women of India though enjoyed more freedom in till foreign invasion period were highly self-disciplined.

Chapter - 26

Souls, Soulmates and Other Funny Things

Few months ago, I met Sunil, my college mate now an NRI, who offered me to have tea with him. While we were having tea, the rain started. So, we had to spend some time together talking various things. In between he asked me: "How's your soulmate?"

"Soul mate?"

"Wife..."

"Ah, she is doing good..."

"You didn't understand the meaning of soulmate?"

"I understood. But why did you use heavy word like soulmate instead of simple word wife?"

"Don't you know, the soulmate is destined by God...Perfect marriages are made in Heaven as God decided who to marry whom...The men and women each have half of the same soul (like a unique matched pair of shoes)."

"The world population exceeded 7 billion as on March 12, 2012, which means anybody among them should be soulmate to anybody...If there is only one perfect mate for each of us, the odds of finding them are astronomical. So, the entire concept is silly"

"But, that's what all religions say..."

"In that case, I would say, God is a racist. God promotes religion, race, regionalism, and caste..."

"How can you say that?"

"You had married to a 'soulmate' who belongs to your own community, that too from Kerala.

We know all over India mostly religion/caste-based arranged marriages happen. All over the world it is almost same instead of caste many other things - nationality, race, colour of the skin etc. Only less than 3 percent marry out of caste, religion, race, country etc..."

"Yes"

"That's what I wonder. Going by your belief, the God makes sure that your soulmate is from your same caste, religion and race? Isn't that breaking every concept of God so far? How can a God be such a narrow-minded person?"

He didn't have answer. I asked him: "When one soulmate dies, many people marry again. Does that mean the heaven's customer service department has buffer stock for replacements? The entire concept of perfect soulmate is a katta comedy. Lifemate could have been a better word."

"Uday, don't you believe in soul?"

"What's it according to you?" I asked.

"You have a soul given by God. Every individual has unique 'soul' is conferred on each person at the time of conception. It's an entity separate from the body yet somehow located within it. If you do any sin, your soul will go to hell after your death. If you follow God's commandments the soul will go to heaven..."

"Sunil, that doesn't even qualify to be a bedtime story" I said.

"It's a scientific truth that whenever a spermatozoon penetrates the ovum a soul slips in also. Otherwise how can a life start?"

"You mean to say, God goes in for mass production of souls and allocate the appropriate amount to each fertilized ovum?

Almost two thirds of all fertilized ova may not develop to full term. So, what happens to all the 'souls' of the aborted ova and fetuses both naturally occurring and induced?"

"Only blessed fertilized egg has been given a living individual 'soul' by God" he said.

"Sometimes, blessed fertilized ova divide into twins, triplets and even up to sextets. So what happens about the 'soul'? Does it also subdivide to meet the changed circumstances or are new 'souls' provided at each division? Is the 'soul' of an aborted fertilized egg the same as that of the person who dies after reaching old age? "

"It goes to heaven to live with God..."

"Amusing. Where exactly is the blessed abode of 'souls' – the mansion where they live for happily ever after? Is it up there in the stratosphere, on in this earth, or in the infinite expanse of space at near absolute zero temperature? Are souls kept there in refrigeration?"

"Why do billions of people believe in soul then?" he asked a counter question.

"I guess, soul created by religions to keep their followers happy that they will have a better life after death and don't mind the hardships here in the earth.

It is also to scare those non-believers and non-followers saying after death you will rot, roasted, will be punished, etc.

We persist in believing in 'souls' is because we don't want to die. If death means the destruction of the body, then the only way we could possibly get some solace is to believe that we have a soul...."

"See Uday, don't be hypocrite for the sake of arguments. You also believe in those things. I know you just wanted to kill time till rain is over, that's why you are ridiculing this idea..."

"I don't have a problem to believe in anything. I believe in many things that modern people ridicule as superstitions. But there should be a clear idea behind it. I need to have clarity in thoughts and deeds."

"What's your take on soul, jeevAtma or prana whatever?"

"I don't think the concept of soul as you have explained can be compared to jeeva, prana and Atma...These words are used interchangeably in many places in many scriptures.

Our ancestors never separate anything from the divine. So, we don't have to even think the idea of soul coming from God and going back to God. Even if soul exists, it never was and will never be a separate entity in the spectrum of life..."

"That's a vague answer...Please tell, you should know about it..."

"I don't know much about it, Sunil - but I am meditating to find it. I think 'prana' is breath. I have read that there are five types of pranas (Panchaprana). Prana in Sanskrit means ' that by which one lives'. 'Pra' = the first and 'na' = flow. It should be oxygen."

"Oh, so what's jeeva?"

"There is no clear definition of jeeva or life in the medical science. In ancient texts, Jeeva = 'alive'. That which is born is Jeeva (Jaayate iti Jeeva). Life starts - when father's seed enters mother's egg. Where was it before - we don't know, so to be on the safer side people say jeeva is a God sent thing?"

"Atman?"

"It should be something more at micro-level. The Atman was there in the sperm. Atman was there in the ovum too.

Rigveda says Atman is 'ajobhaga' means the unborn part of human. This is different from and not to be confused with body and mind.

Atman is the real self. It derived from the Sanskrit root word "an" which means to breathe. Incidentally Atman is root for Old High German 'atum' (breath) and Dutch 'ademen' (to breathe).

When the Atman manifests as the body (+mind) - it will have both Jeeva+Atma= JeevAtma"

"That's very clear now. Even I was confused. But where does JeevAtma goes after death and how is it coming back to womb?"

About birth: According to our learnt ancestors, the main purpose of marriage is to have worthy children.

The ritual Garbhadana (that act by which the Jeeva embryo is well borne) is called by Sankhayana Grihya Sutra as Chaturtikarma.

Upanishads, Sastras, other Scriptures and the Ayurveda manuals talk a lot about the birth of worthy child. They call the son as AAtmaj and daughter as AaAtmaja, meaning the self or their own image.

While in all other parts of the world sex and reproduction was considered as mysterious and unknown thing, you know, our ancestors clearly said that it is a unification of father's 'beeja' and mother's 'andas'. (In Sanskrit words beeja = seed = sperm and anda = egg = ovam)

"Wow! Really?"

"There is an Upanishad called "Garbha Upanishad" (Anybody can search and find it). It talks about the uniting of the male and female reproductive fluids and how the embryo is in a mixed (semi-fluid) state.

It discusses about various states - like in two months, the head takes form. At the end of three months, the legs and foot are formed.

And by the fourth month, the wrist, stomach and the hip, waist etc. are formed - these things were written as if somebody seen every stage of pregnancy using most modern scanning technology!!! Thousands of years ago!

And it is most accurate...You should be proud to born as descendant of a scientifically advanced society."

"But what does it talk about soul or jeeva or whatever?"

"The Atma and jeeva has memories. Even every atom in your breathe has memories. The DNA research has proven about the genetic codes and memories.

The jeeva identifies through the brain, desires with the mind and speaks with the language. Scriptures say that previous birth memories and all the history will be cleansed the very moment he/she first inhales the air after coming to the earth.

These scriptures talk about genetics, DNA and how life is coming into being. It talks about secrets of getting good children too. The modern-day science is advancing towards it.

There are scriptures about Gynecology advances techniques of test tube embryo fertilization and also with transferring and implanting embryos to suitable situations - the applications are mentioned as stories in many places in Puranas. Even to imagine such things during that time...."

"You mean to say they were more advanced than us?" he interrupted.

"Probably yes. Thousands of years ago, they used the word 'Nara' for human being. And name given for monkeys was "Vanara". Va=alternate or like. Nar=Human.

Why Am I a Hindu?

How did they know that Old World monkeys have the same Rh factors of human group? How did they know that human is evolved from those monkeys?"

There has been not much research to understand if Atman is divinity or a bio-electric trigger, one or many, eternal or ad hoc and substantial or ethereal. We do not know how it changes bodies or how it becomes a courier of vasanas.

However, human mind (read ego) refuses to accept that the life has an end and conceptualises a continuation for itself in most esoteric terms that is how rubbish thoughts of soul pops up. No one who has died has and come back and reported that soul exists.

This is something to be pondered in further depths.

The rain stopped. We parted.

Chapter - 27
Are you a Sinner?

David Adefuye, an African-American, my fellow journalist, told me that we are all sinners.

"I don't think I am a sinner..." I said.

"Are you saying you are perfect?" he raised his eye brows.

"Yes, of course, I am perfect with all my imperfections..."

"That's ridiculous. Nobody is perfect... To not be a sinner means you've never broken any Law of God?"

"Law of God? What's that? Is God a law maker?"

"The One and Only God's book says so"

I knew what he is coming to. But I wanted to make it very light. So I said: "Oh, I didn't know God runs a printing press. Did he close it after publishing ONE single book? And what book is that? What does it say?"

"As a sinner, you are separated from God. But the God loves you enough to want you to be with him. Hence, the only way to have your sins forgiven is to put your trust in God and follow what God said... Otherwise, you will have to face him on your own on the Day of Judgment - that is what God says in his Holy Book Bible. God declares we all are sinners."

"David, many books may say many things.

There are lots of books that influenced people: Das Capital, The Communist Manifesto, Mein Kampf, Quran, Bible, The Republic etc.

Followers of each book believe that whatever said inside is truth. The followers consider it as a great book. Fair enough.

But for other people, those are just like any other books. Just because somebody in a book said some opinions that you believe to be true doesn't make it universal truth. You should respect others freedom not to believe in it. So as much you believe that you are a sinner as per your Holy book, I can believe that I am not."

"Are you criticizing our trust in God as just a set of beliefs or opinions?"

"Did I? Who I am to do that? I am just expressing my viewpoints which are different from yours. You can claim to be a born sinner. And be proud of that. But you don't have the right to say all others are sinners."

"So your religion doesn't say you are a sinner?" he asked.

"Sanatan Dharma or Hinduism is not a prescriptive religion. It doesn't give you a list of Do's and Don'ts. It gives a much freedom of thought so much so that a person who said there is no God is also referred to as Saint."

"That's bull *@#&"

"That's your intolerant reaction. I expected that. Because, I understand that you are conditioned by your blind beliefs. I don't have to believe in beliefs.

With conditioned-mind like that of yours, one can't understand truth. You can't even be a truth seeker as the absolute truth according to you is already given in your Holy book - all you have to do is follow it without questioning. You be happy with your beliefs. But please don't call others sinner."

His face turned red. He got really very angry. This is very strange.

Some belief-systems that have the world's largest numbers of followers are more insecure and feel hurt faster. I asked him: "Why do you people feel insecure and angry or get hurt when somebody says against your faith? Please give freedom to others to express their views..."

"I disagree with you. You are wrong, totally wrong" he angrily said.

"The concept of seeing things as good and bad or right and wrong is totally overly simplistic view of the world. All the goods and bads are relative and subjective."

"Uday, you don't even understand the meaning of the word Sin. Sin is an offence against God.

According to our theology, a mortal sin (a bad act committed with full knowledge and significant reflection) breaks a person's relationship with God and if he/she dies unrepentant in a state of mortal sin, he/she will go to hell...Man has inherited "original sin" from Adam.

Mankind then is inherently evil and is in need of forgiveness of sin.

By knowing right and wrong Christians choose their actions. Humans are a fallen, broken race in need of salvation and repair by God. Romans 3:23 says that 'all have sinned'."

"All those sayings are applicable ONLY for those who follow Bible. I neither believe your creation story nor the Adam story. You said every human is assumed to be a sinner right from birth, and therefore, must fear the God. Not just any God, but the exclusive Christian concept of God.

In other words, if you accept and convert to Christian, you will go to Heaven and your all sins are purified. This is just your belief. You are free to follow that. But why should you force it up on others?

Semitics believes that only when you go against the moral laws mentioned in those books considered as sin. Those books are written specifically for the human population (mostly consists of shepherds and desert dwellers) that lived in a particular geographical area at a point of time (irrelevant now). For you, killing an innocent non-believer is NOT a sin. "

"That's not correct. We deplore any sort of violence..."

"That's a lie. In fact, you venerate it. Otherwise, how can Francis Xavier, a barbarian who killed thousands of innocent Goans, canonized as the Saint? What's more, when you say everybody born is a sinner, your Pope, Bishops are also sinners. So how can a sinner canonize a dead man as saint?"

"There may be some mismatches in old texts; we can't blindly follow a religion. We have to move according to times. We cannot generalize" he said.

I just smiled. "Then how can you generalize all humans are sinners! The objective of the inventors of sin was to codify conduct in a simple childlike book of rules. They classified actions into transgressions and non-transgressions. This is a morally toxic idea.

An oversimplification causes profound harm. It leads good people to doing bad things because they are not pre-labeled as transgressions. It leads to the good people avoiding doing the right thing, because the rule book labeled them as transgressions."

"Uday, believe me, if you follow Jesus Christ you will be free from the burden of sin"

"I respect it as your belief. There is a difference between being "free from the burden of sin," and being "free from sin. However, Christians "feel free" because they believe Jesus died for their sins, right?

I contend that the "feeling" that Christians get is no different than the "feeling" that ISIS gets when killed innocent people."

"But Jesus died in the cross for all our sins. "

"Again, you can't say "our" sin as we are not sinners. You may claim that he died for the Christian's sin as part of your belief. For, the history is full of atrocities happened in the name of inquisitions your people committed.

Whatever, there is no logic in saying that a person died some 2000 years ago, for a sin that's being committed by people of 21st century. It's like saying I shouldn't be hungry today, as I have had a lunch 30 years ago!"

"So, for you, there is no sin at all?"

"David, we have a simple definition. There is a subhashita (eloquent saying) in Sanskrit: 'Slokaardhena Pravakshyaami yaduktham grantakotishu: Paropakaara:Punyaaya Paapaaya Parapeetanam' = What has been told in millions of scriptures, I shall tell in just half a sloka- actions that fetch good to others is Punya (pious deed) and actions that fetch difficulty to others is Paapa (sin). That's what we follow in life."

"Seriously, don't you have God's law of evil and sin?"

"We understand that everything is part of divine cosmic and God - for us the divine presence is there everywhere (Ishaavaasyam idam sarvam). I am part of God; I can never really be alienated from God by sin."

"How do you define 'your version' of sin then?" he asked teasingly.

"We use the term sin (paapa in Sanskrit) for Adharma (non-righteousness) to describe actions that is done against one's Dharma or against humanity and the nature. But it depends upon Varna-Ashrama Dharma - for each people Sin is different.

For instance an army man kills his enemy is not considered as a Sin.

The Mahabharata, Santi Parva, Section XV: "There is no act that is wholly meritorious, nor any that is wholly wicked. Right or wrong, in all acts, something of both is seen…" That's the broad-minded universal law we have"

"Will you not get punished for this Adharma? Won't your God send you to hell after death?"

"For us, even Gods are subjected to the law of karma. We don't have irrational beliefs like heaven and hell.

We believe that by doing good karma, we can create heaven in the earth itself. Hence, we consider our land as 'Punya Bhoomi' or pious land. For us, the ultimate liberation happens when one transcend punya and papa."

"So, you are not answerable to God. No wonder you people don't fear God…"

"We love God - God is not an intolerant tyrannical demon to be afraid of. We consider both good and bad deeds as a laggard in attaining the ultimate aim of eternal happiness and peace. Vedic scriptures say Punya or Papa are products of mind and does not hold any substance."

"You can't repent of sin?"

"No. And there is no forgiveness. There's no formal atonement for sin anywhere in Hindu scriptures.

He is responsible for his actions because of an inexorable law of Karma in the universe. Karma – it is just karma, good or bad depends upon situation, people and time.

The results depend upon action and reaction of the person, situations, space and time.... here again; we cannot describe it in simple black and white or in 'yes or no' platform..."

"But if I want to repent my sin, I mean - to reduce the backlash of the Adharma that I had done - what should I do?"

"You can do a fair amount of good karma - when you do manav seva (service to humanity) the existence will also support you. Our scriptures do not say if you pay money to Church/Temple, you will be saved from bad karma. You won't.

Here, you will be creating more Adharma by paying money to spiritual traders and greedy priests. One has to do individual seva to cover up his/her Adharma."

"So how can you achieve salvation?"

"As said, for us, there is no sin. Hence, no salvation is needed, only enlightenment. We must merely wake up to our innate divinity. If I am part of God, I can never really be alienated from God by sin. I just can't do anything against the cosmic will as I am aware that I am a part of everything.

So, I pray 'Om lokah samastha sukhino bhavanthu' meaning, let everybody live peacefully and happily. We can't pray 'only Hindus should live happily and let all infidels or non-believers die. Humanity should come first for a real Sanatan Dharmi, not religion."

- A real follower of Sanatan Dharma will not involve in sin (Papa) or Adharmic Karma. Why?

It is not because of fear of GOD as a Hindu never is taught to fear God. It is not because of an entry ban in the heaven, but out of his love to Brahmam or cosmic. A Hindu is answerable to himself, for, he knows he is part and parcel of the cosmic nature...that's called awareness...

According to the basic principles of Hinduism, the greatest sin is to call a person a sinner.

We believe the divine force in all living and non-living things...so, to call a person a sinner is to deny their divinity.

A Sanatan Dharmi taught to think this way: "I'm allowed to make my share of mistakes. Still the God loves me. Though I make mistakes he stands with me.

He will give me strength if I'm ready to stand. Is this not enough to make oneself a strong person?"

Will this not help to develop a better society?

To call a person a sinner is to deny his/her divinity.

Chapter - 28

Ridiculous Spirituality, Useless Knowledge

My friend Muthuswamy told me: "I have read almost all religious and spiritual scriptures. I have also visited most of the famous temples in India. I have done most of the rituals, Homams (Homamm or Havan) and Poojas (prayer ritual).

I do yoga regularly. Still I am not becoming Sthitaprajna (emotionally stable, tranquility, desireless, Satisfied etc) and get fully enlightened"

"Hmm"

"You are a spiritual person...Please help me in this regard..." he said.

"Muthu, if you slap in my face or call me names, I would have forgiven you. But calling me "spiritual" is very much insulting. That word is a cliché. The very word makes me feel nauseous.... It is okay if you call me selfish or materialistic. I do not see any separation between anything spiritual and material. I see the divine presence in everything..."

"But how can you be happy being materialistic? How can you be free or liberate yourself in this attached life?"

"Muthu, you are conditioned with a fair amount of concepts on spirituality and its marketing strategies. I am not.

If you think your freedom or happiness derives only from detachment, then your idea of these things is limited to detachment. I am free and happy in detachment as well as in attachment too...You are conditioned with many concepts, hence not feeling happy..."

"But our scriptures say..."
"I do not know if you have read original scriptures in its original form. What you must have read is interpretation or commentaries on scriptures...And you trust whatever that is printed or in Wikipedia or on the Net. I don't.

Our original scriptures never differentiate between spiritual and material. It is inclusive of everything. Nothing is excluded. Our scriptures vary from meditation to sex or from breathing technique to life medicines....

Our ancestors included everything and saw the presence of divinity in everything. You are confused because you are influenced by well-marketed Semitic concepts that exclude, compartmentalize and divide humanity..."

"May be.... I am a master in philosophy. I have knowledge in all religions...Both Western and eastern wisdom doesn't help me to cross over and become fully spiritual" he repeated his complaint again.

"Muthu, the knowledge will remain as information and it won't transform you. That is why Shiv Purana says "Jnanam Bandhanam".

Knowledge won't liberate you. Ramakrishna Paramahamsa and Ramana Maharshi were not PhDs..."

"Yes, but what about the spirituality then? ..."

"What's spirituality to an ordinary man? You call people who are following superstitions, anAchars, durAchars, wearing religious uniforms or marks, following blind faith etc as spiritual! An average man like me cannot understand the heavy definition that you attribute to spirituality"

"I agree...People who visit temples regularly, doing their rituals and Godly karmas are termed as spiritual..."

"In that case, Ravana was the most spiritual person; he was the greatest devotee of Shiva. He was master in 64 arts. He was a highly learned and knowledgeable man.

All religious terrorists are spiritual - and they kill or die for their concept of God. St Francis Xavier who killed millions of people during Goa inquisition is considered as a very spiritual man and saint by Christians.

Please scrap such wrong concepts - it is very naive to think that those who follow religion are good guys. It is very stupid to think like that knowledge and spirituality will help you overcoming your stress and tension."

"You made it appear so simple, I never thought in that line Uday..."

"Knowledge will not help you liberate or cross-over. For instance, we know everyone experiences death.

But when somebody near to you dies, you will be stricken with grief. Why don't the knowledge that 'death is the only truth', helps you here? Why don't you be calm, cool, happy and relaxed when somebody dies?"

"Because, we don't have emotional insight..."

"Yes..."

"So, you mean to say emotional insight is important than knowledge?"

"Is it relevant here if I answer yes or no? Why do you need everything in black and white? Because your mind wants an answer just to satisfy ego.... Otherwise the answer is not going to help you anyways."

"Hmmm"

"Muttu - Long ago, I had read about a conversation that took place between Krishna (good guy) and Duryodhana (bad guy). Krishna asked Duryodhana: "Why are you doing all these bad karmas? Don't you know this is really wrong?"

To which Duryodhana said: "Krishna, I know this is bad. But when it comes to a situation, I can't help doing such sins. Something inside me prompts me to do those bad karmas and I derive pleasure from that..."

The gist of the story is that the bad guy Duryodhana knows that he is doing bad things and he will eventually be punished. But that knowledge doesn't help him..."

"Yes - I also felt like that, but never thought in this line..."

"All diabetics' patients know that eating sugar is dangerous - still they get temptation to eat - sometimes they steal sweet from own home and eat, why?

You may ask any alcoholic, he will tell you the hazards of drinking alcohol better than any doctor. So, knowledge is stored as just information and it doesn't transform you."

"So, what's the way out Uday?"

"It is very simple. Be aware about this. Being materialistic or spiritual is not important in life, being aware is. Just be aware that there is a real me, and the manifested me."

(I have explained this in many of my articles, hence not repeating)

"But we mistake the manifested me as the real me. We cannot cross-over the conditioning of mind. We live in full control of conditioned mind and live a life run with auto-pilot..."

"That's why I am telling you to live a life with awareness..."

"What's the real awareness then?"

"My understanding about awareness is that - we are inclusive of the divine power. We are not separate from anything. WE ARE THE COSMOS.

And if God exists, it/he/she is not separate from us - the divine presence is same inside as well as outside. Hence we are all connected..."

"Is it not just a belief? You have always been ridiculing beliefs..." he teased me.

"No - it is a truth. We are all connected to each other, biologically. We are all connected to the earth, chemically.

We are all connected to the rest of the universe atomically. If you don't have this awareness, any knowledge won't help you. And if you are not aware, does it matter whether you are spiritual or materialistic...?" I asked him.

Chapter - 29

Why Am I NOT Spiritual?

Two years ago, Prajesh, one of my readers, came to meet me in my hotel in Mumbai with his father. He introduced me to his father: "Dad, Mr.Udaylal Pai is highly spiritual person"

I didn't say anything. I bowed and greeted him. But he continued using the word "spiritual" whenever he referred to me. And then his father said: "I had the opportunity to read few of your articles - I was amazed. It is very rare to see people at your age with so much spiritual knowledge and spiritual experience. You didn't chase materialistic gains. Your face also says you are very spiritual..."

"Sir, you are making a baseless accusation about me I am neither spiritual nor materialistic. I am just an ordinary human being doing my karma. I have absolutely nothing to do with spirituality..."

"It's surprising. You write about spirituality and its science. I know a couple of my friends who have turned into spirituality reading your articles."Prajesh said.

"I have never written about spirituality and never promoted it" I said.

"Confused, I don't understand. You are a staunch follower of Sanatan Dharma. You are devotee of all Hindu Gods. You go to temple.

You write about Dharma, mind, Atma etc. Still you say that you don't believe in spirituality. We are really confused" his father said.

"Sir, I am not responsible for your assumptions about me. But I am not spiritual. Seriously, can you explain what do you mean by spirituality?" I asked.

"Spirituality means "Chaitanyam" (consciousness).... Something that doesn't have this chaitanyam is material"

"Hmmm. My understanding is that there were no such boundaries in our culture.

Atharva Veda classifies everything into two (especially in life sciences and Ayurveda) - (1) Antar-chetana (internal consciousness) and (2) Bahih-chetana (external consciousness). They didn't even use the word Achetana (non-cosncious things) at all...."

"So according to them there was NO non-spiritual existence..."

"Yes, they said, the living things (biotic, animate) have both Antar and Bahih Chetana. The materials that you see as non-living things (inanimate, abiotic, life less, inorganic etc) has only Antar-chetana. It is said to be in a state of 'Jadatva' (senselessness, inert or stiffness), that's all. That's why we don't see the Chetana in them."

"Is it?"

"Yes, our ancient sages like Susrutha, Vagbhata and Charaka said that the Antar-chetana of the ('non-living') materials can be activated with suitable combination.

Why Am I a Hindu?

For instance, gold, which if consumed can damage internal organs, is used in some Ayurveda preparations by invoking its Bahih-chetana.

Now, the quantum physics also teaches us that matter (atoms/subatomic particles) does not exist at a single point of space/time until observed..."

"Yes, I have also learned it. Quantum physics says that as you go deeper and deeper into the workings of the atom, you see that there is nothing there – just energy waves. It says an atom is actually an invisible force field, a kind of miniature tornado, which emits waves of electrical energy. Oh, God, that's what they said thousands of years ago!"

"If you know that how can you classify things into spiritual and materials? Especially when, both Vedic Sastra and modern science do not approve it!"

"Okay, What I meant by spiritual was worshipping God or propitiation of the deities..."

"Sir, I have a problem in accepting that concept too.

According to Hindu Dharma, there are only two traditions for propitiation of Gods (Aradhana Smabradaya) - Vaidiki and Paurana. In both systems, we offer material objects (dravya) to God...."

"How come?"

"In Vaidiki Aradhana you offer 'Homam (Havan) dravyam' into a consecrated fire (Agni) saying: 'Agnaye swaáhá, Agnaye idam na mama' (=unto the fire I am offering all.

This offering is not mine, it is Thine). In Pauranic Aradhana we offer 'Pooja dravya' to the Gods (in the Puranas) in the temple. And look at those Gods - all are cladded with gold jewelries and precious gems...

All Hindu Gods are depicted as wearing expensive flashy ornaments and have all material characteristics. They have material weapons in their hand. Everything is about materialism only. We have two Gods - Lakshmi and Kubera - exclusively for material wealth."

"I mean, spirituality - it is above religious practice, it is about divinity..." his father said.

"Sir, still it is incorrect. Vedic Dharma says 'Isavasyam Idam Sarvam'. There is nothing else other than God. So how can you differentiate between spiritual and material? It is all inclusive..."

"But, then how come everybody talks about spirituality when relates to God?" Prajesh asked.

"Sanatan Dharma never had any traditions that cannot be explained based on logical, rational and scientific thinking. The idea of spirituality came to India from the West."

"Nonsense," his father's face changed into red, "It is idiotic to say that the West brought the idea of spirituality in India. How ridiculous"

I smiled at him and said: "Sir, the West had a concept of Church Vs. State. Or Science Vs. Religion.

Why Am I a Hindu?

They considered Physical science as the number one enemy of the Religion and punished scientists (like Galileo). Hence they believed that spirituality belongs to Church and Science belonged to material state."

"Oh...yeah, I had forgotten it," his face suddenly changed. "I am sorry Uday, yes - you are right. I know. I have learned European history...In fact, I was in the UK for some time" his father said.

"Their philosophy was: Give up science for religion or give up religion for science. That's how this separatism came in. That's how they classified spiritual (religion) and material (Science) into two."

- On the contrary, in India, all Sages were scientists and discussed about subjects ranging from astronomy to Ayurveda.

From metallurgy to navigation and from mathematics to quantum physics.... Even those atheists and Nastiks were considered as Sages. Charvaka, Lokayata and Brhaspatya who founded the Nastik (anti-spiritual in modern sense) schools of thoughts were also venerated as a great Sage.

Ramayana says that it was Charvaka who advised Rama to go back and rule Ayodhya after the War.

"Oh - we had never thought in that line. You look at things in totally different perspective, Uday Sir. I thought anything related to God is spiritual and all other things are materialistic..."Prajesh said.

"You are right Uday, the British and evangelists were successful in planting this idea among Indians to ruin our culture.

And they have been successful in that. Today, for a common man in Hinduism, spirituality means things related to greedy priests, fraud astrologers, new-built up commercial temples, con people in disguise of God-man or God-woman, going to religious institutions etc. I understand my mistake now" his father said.

"Yes - the practical meaning of spirituality today is greedy Hindu priests, cut-throat missionaries of trade, terrorists, religious industry etc, though they claim otherwise like politicians..."Prajesh added.

"And you wanted to put me in that segment?" I laughed.

"No Uday...you are doing yeoman service for our Dharma, apologies..."his father said."You said, our ancestors didn't classify into spirituality and materialism. Do we have any proof?"

"To make it very clear that there is no division between spirituality and materialism, they have created Upavedas for the four Vedas. For instance, Rig-Veda has a subsidiary ArthaSastram, the science of economics. Yajurvedam has dhanurvedam science of archery.

Samaveda has Gandharva vedam, the science of arts and music as upavedam. And Atharvevedam has science of health and food, called Ayurveda.

Yoga Sastra is the biggest proof about the unification of body, mind and consciousness.... For bodily pleasure we even have many scriptures on Kama Sastra"

"Okay, they didn't want to see things separately. How will you define divinity then?"

"I have already told you that. God is everywhere; God exists in every particle..." I said.

"He is right, there is a Malayalam song: 'mannilum vinnilum thoonilum thurumbilum daivamirikkunnu' meaning, divinity exists in soil, sky, pillar and rust," his father added.

"Yes, it is only to reveal this truth that the supreme God emerged out of a pillar as Narasimha," I said: "Our Sastra are based on this truth only.

While the entire world was groped in darkness about the universe and floating funny stories of creation and creator, our ancestors made it clear (7000 years) that the entire universe is the manifestation of the Brahmam and made up of Brahmam.

Nyaya-Vaiseshika Sutra said - the entire universe is composed of the panchabhuthas (5 elements) and the four non-physicals. It includes fluid, atomic elements, fields/force, energy, ether and space, time, mind and JeevAtma.

Each and everything has divine presence in it. And modern physics is also nearing to this concept…"

"Uday, you make things ridiculously simple. Let me ask you a personal question. Do you really believe that God exists everywhere?" Prajesh's father asked.

"The root of belief is "lief", meaning "wish". So, when somebody says, "I believe in God", the meaning is "I wish God were there". I don't have to believe, I can experience."

"Okay. I understood, so let me rephrase the question: Have you ever experienced the existence of God?"

"Yes, I do, every moment. With every breath I can experience it. Just look outside through that window. Can't you see the leaves of the tree swaying in the breeze happily, silently announcing their existence? Look at each and everything around you, you will know that everything - animate and inanimate things - is happy, lively and silently saying "yes, we exist here" What more you want?" I asked.

I use the word spiritual for the purpose of communicating an idea that is for something other than seemingly physical existence. That doesn't mean I am spiritual.

Chapter - 30

When Human Becomes Powerful than God

Do you know which the second longest text in Sanskrit is after the Mahabharata? No, it is not the epic poem Valmiki Ramayana - it contains only 24,000 verses.

It is 'Yoga Vasistha' (Jnana Vasistha) that contains about 32,000 verses. Its abridged version is known as the Laghu (Little) Yogavasistha contains 6,000 verses.

The content is a discourse of Sage Vasistha to Rama, the powerful Hindu God. It teachings are associated with Advaita Vedanta and Yoga, and explain the illusory nature of the manifest world and the principle of non-duality.

Have you noticed something special here?

A human being is advising the God - the avatar of the Supreme God, Maha Vishnu! Can you show anywhere - in any religion or any Holy books, where a human advising God and God considering him as a teacher?

Who had written Mahabharata, the largest ever text in the world with 107,281- verses? Sage Veda Vyasa.

Who was his stenographer?

Ganesha, the great God - the remover of obstacles! He is also known as Vinayak, Vighneshwer and Ganapathi.

No Hindu rituals start without praising Ganesha! Such a powerful God.

Ganesha is the first stenographer that the world ever had, and he had taken down the largest ever book composed in the world, viz. The Mahabharata dictated by a human being, Vyasa!

Veda Vyas, the celebrated compiler of the Vedas, is son of a fisher-woman - an ordinary human being born to sage Parasara.

According to Sanatan Dharma, the supreme reality is Brahmam (Ultimate Reality or the Absolute). It's also known as ParamAtma (Universal Self). Brahmam is NOT "God". The ancients said that "Everything is Brahmam" (Sarvam Khalvidam Brahma)

For starters, the learnt sages divided the Brahmam as three - Brahma (Ancestor or the creator and not to be confused with Brahmam), Vishnu (Dharma in charge of sustenance of the universe) and Shiva (represents contraction and expansion of universe). They are known as 'Trimurti', meaning "three forms".

There was an ordinary man who by deep penance became a great sage - Brigu.

He went to Brahmalok (residence of Brahma) and cursed him (the creator):"Brahma, you are not worth of being 'Supreme'. Let no one worship you."

Then Bhrigu visited Shiva at Kailash. Shiva and his wife Parvati were sporting fun. Bhrigu cursed him: "Shiva, you will only be worshipped in Linga (phallus) form."

With accumulated anger, he went to Vaikuntha, the abode of Vishnu, without Vishnu's permission and saw that he was in sleep.

Brigu couldn't wake him up. So he hit Vishnu on his chest (that strike by Bhrigu left a foot print on his chest and that foot print is known as "Shri Vatsa").

Vishnu got up and asked him, "Maharishi, are you hurt in your foot?"

Seeing the decorum and humbleness of Vishnu, Bhrigu was pleased and declared him superior amongst the Tridev. "Vishnu, let people worship you in many forms, many avatars!"

The point I want to make from this story is that, a human being Brigu was powerful enough to curse and bless the tri-murtis of Hinduism! So, where does man stand?

According to a story from Bhagavata Purana the 'famous Four Kumaras', Sanaka, Sanandana, Sanatan, and Sanatkumara appear to be mere children, though they are of great wisdom and strong with penance.

Once they visited Vaikuntha to see Vishnu. The two gate keepers of the Vaikuntha, Jaya and Vijaya, interrupt the Kumaras at the gate, considering them as silly children.

"Vishnu is resting and you cannot see him now," they said and tried to stop and ridicule them.

"You are lying. Vishnu is available for his devotees any time,"

Kumaras said and cursed them. "Both of you would have to give up your divinity, be born as mortals on Earth (bhuloka, or physical plane), and live like normal human beings"

Vishnu appeared before them and sought for pardon.

As a result, Jaya Vijaya be born three times on Earth even though it would have to be as enemies of Vishnu.

In the first life they were born as Hiranyakashipu and Hiranyaksha who were killed by Vishnu taking the form of Varaha, a boar and Narasimha, a man-lion.

In their second life, they were born as Ravana and Kumbhakarna and were killed by Vishnu who descended as Rama.

And in their third life as Shishupala and Dantavakra (in some places Dantavakra is replaced by Kamsa) who were killed Krishna (Vishnu's avatar).

In short, all major Avatars of Vishnu happened because of just four human beings who were powerful enough to control the cosmos.

What's the moral of all those stories? Is it that a human being can be elevated to the level of God or more than that?

It is said in Upanishads that "Brahmam is knowledge" (Prajnanam brahma) and "Brahmam is of the nature of truth, knowledge and infinity" (satyam jnanam anantam Brahmam).

Through awareness the human being can experience that Brahmam is existence, consciousness, and happiness. (Sachchidananda brahma).

He will realize that "Everything is Brahmam" Sarvam Khalvidam Brahma. Then he becomes Brahmam = "I am Brahmam" (aham brahmasmi).

Everything in this cosmos, including Gods, is the manifestation of Brahmam. A human being by deep awareness/penance (meditation) can realize it. 'I am Brahmam' means you are grown to the level of realizing it and becoming one with it.

For, the word Brahmam comes from the Sanskrit verb root brh, meaning "to grow". Brahmam means "that which grows" (brhati) and "which causes to grow" (brhmayati). A man can grow up to the cosmos.

Those Puranic stories are excellent examples of this cosmic revelation. Our ancient scientists never pictured God as not a separate entity that we ask and beg and he delivers.

Instead they have shown paths of Duality (Dwaitham) and relate ourselves with VishitAdvaitham (non-dual & non-brahmam) and Non Duality (Advaitham). It's an interesting energy of back and forth depending on our maturity.

The distressed seek God (aartha), the desirous seek God (artharthi), the curios seek God (the jijnasu) and the enlightened dwells in God (the jnani).

Chapter - 31
Why Am I NOT afraid of GOD?

Few years ago, my friend Rajsekhar introduced me to his family: "This is Mr.Uday Pai, my good friend and very God fearing person..."

Later, I asked him: "Raj, who told you I am afraid of God?"

"Everyone is God fearing. If we do not fear of God, how can we live in this world?"

"Human beings fear some living things which can cause us harm -Snakes, Rabies Dog, Tigers, Terrorists, Thieves, Dacoits, etc. Man, is also afraid of Thunder, Storm, Tsunami etc. But how can one be afraid of God? Is God a Person who causes considerable damages to you?"

"He is powerful, omnipotent, all-pervading...."

"Hmm...Okay. Forget the God for time being. Whom you are afraid of as of now?"

"I am afraid of a terrorist..."

"Have you ever felt respect, love or worship towards a terrorist?"

"No... I hate them."

"Are you a fan of any sportsman or film star?"

"I am a hardcore fan of Sachin Tendulkar"

"What do you want to do with Sachin?"

"I wish I could take a photograph along with him, get him signed in an autograph..."

"That means, you want to be near him"

"Yes, I wish I could touch him and handshake with him"

"Which movie you wanted to see the most in your life? I mean, which movie you eagerly waited to see?"

"E.T. the Extra-Terrestrial"

"Why?"

"I heard lot about it. I have been seen few clippings and photograph - that was amazing..."

"So, you felt curiosity. Jijnasa. You had the desire to know or see that movie. So, you went to see it..."

"Yes. I liked it very much...Seen it several times..."

"That means, you will feel adoration only when you feel the "wow" factor. Adoration won't come from fear. Anybody would want to run away from the fear. Nobody can worship fear. A human being won't even want to remember something fearful. Adoration will lead to worship or devotion, not fear."

"Hmm. I understood when you started itself. You mean to say nobody should fear God."

"Yes, until and unless God is a brutal tyrannical mafia king or inhuman terrorist."

"I don't understand."

"There are many concepts about God. Broadly it can be divided into two - (1) God is kind hearted and loving personality or (2) God is like a warlord, mafia king, dacoit chief etc.

He is angry, revengeful, wrathful etc. Which one do you want to follow?"

"Of course, the first one..."

"Swami Vivekananda said devotion motivated by fear is the lowest kind of devotion. Fear is death, fear is sin, fear is hell, fear is unrighteousness, fear is wrong life, he said.

Fear has to be the opposite of God because it is the opposite of love.

If a God wants you to live in fear of Him, that means such God is always afraid you will stop worshipping him. Do you really want to worship such an insecure God?"

How can you love somebody who threatens you that if you don't follow his commandments, you will be roasted in the hell? The God, if really exists, would not want us to fear him or her.

A necessity to instill fear in others is due to one's own feelings of insecurity, inferiority, and fear of losing influence. Unless one admits that God exhibits these feelings then he cannot logically say that God wants us to fear him.

God Fearing people are scared of punishments, bad luck, poverty, fear of future... the list is endless.

They approach God out of fear. They do not pray because of devotion instead fear is forcing them to pray.

If God created Man, why did he give the man the freedom to sin or not? Is it some sort of game for him that the sinner can be sent for ever to Hell?

Is he deriving pleasure from sending his creation to hell and heaven? Why does he behave like wrathful prison guards waiting to pounce on errant wards.

"Then how come most number of people is God-fearing?" Raj asked.

"How do the street rowdies make a living? They instill fear among people and collect money from neighborhoods and shops as 'protection' money. The priesthood is no way different from them. They threaten you showing a story of a wrathful God.

The religion has the necessity for 'God fearing' since instilment of fear was a major aspect of the culture that such religions grew out of. Fear of God is the only way the idea of organized religion can be propagated. It is obviously their business model."

Fear is the root of religions. When man did not understand, the cause of natural occurrences and calamities, he assumed that there must be more powerful individuals behind them and started doing all kinds of rituals to please them. This was the first God.

"So, you don't fear God"

"The followers of Sanatan Dharma NEVER EVER fear God, instead when they are afraid of something, they remember God." I said.

Our prayer is: Tvame va mAtA cha pitA tvameva, Tvameva bandhus cha sakhAtvamev, Tvameva vidyA draviNam tvameva, Tvamev sarvam mama deva deva

(You Truly are my Mother and You Truly are my Father, You Truly are my Relative And You Truly are my Friend, You Truly are my Knowledge and You Truly are my Wealth, You Truly are my All, My God of Gods.)

God is your friend, philosopher, guide, lover, child… God is available in any form but not in the form of oppressor or punisher.

Religions teach you to fear God. Dharma teaches you God is Love and compassion. It teaches you that you are integral part of the God or existence.

If you are a Sanatan Dharmi and you fear God, then it is time to go back to basics. For him, there is no God who rules by fear.

God does not reside in the heaven and decide on punishments. God does not distribute good luck and bad luck. God does not sit up and distribute poverty and wealth.

"It is not God (male) that created us in His image. It is we humans, who created God in our image (enhanced as super persons in some religions).

The concept of depended upon the mind-set of the creator. An insecure warlord has fear. Such concept of God has fear in it.

Only such people can make God an autocrat, who wields the whip for every minor misdemeanor."

"Hmmm. Uday, at least you should agree that there is one good thing about God-fearing. People tend to remain morally and ethically on the right side."

"On the contrary, there is a huge psychological and theoretical flaw in that. Those who propagate "God-fearing" concept also provide a solution - you can repent or bribe the God!

Why Am I a Hindu?

They say you can do all sorts of 'sins" (another concept) with the assurance that you can repent in the end and all will be forgiven..."

"Ah, yes. I never thought it that way. In fact, you can repent either by giving money to religious abodes, performing some rituals or funding terrorism..."he said. "You said God doesn't punish us. He is loving, caring and with you all the time. Then who gives you punishments?"

"It's our deed or karma that punishes us...The good and bad is relative, but I am using those words to explain this. If you do well, then you will receive well only. It includes thoughts, speech and any act we do."

"So, God is not responsible at all?"

"You should take up responsibility of his action (Karma). It is said the memories in the consciousness keeps the record of all actions (both good and bad) done during that life. This is added to any balance karma from previous births.

Ultimately one has to settle all accounts by one (or many) rebirth(s). The good does not cancel the bad. In a rebirth one may enjoy comfortable life (reward for previous good) and have miseries and hardship (punishment for sins). It is a simple theory that has universal appeal."

All things - animate and inanimate - are manifestation of God. There is nothing but God. So what are you afraid of?

Even when you lock the door and sit inside the room, you will pray to God - that means you believe that no barriers, concrete walls or lock can stop him.

That means the God represents absolute freedom.

You have freedom to behave as is with the God. For, God is the best friend at the time of sorrow. God is the light during the fearful darkness. God is something with motherly love. God cannot be a terror."

In Hindu mythology, the Gods have all the weaknesses of ordinary mortals, along with superhuman strengths and powers. Those Gods get angry, jealous, they cheat, they leech, they get headstrong, etc.

That is how one is initiated into the religion - fantasy stories packaged as mythologies, with a common denominator of human qualities thrown in.

Mythologies are entry level to the Sanatan Dharma - the primers for the pious first. From piety one graduates to philosophy.

From philosophy one gets Phd of enlightenment. There is no looking back from there, nor a reversion to books, rituals, spiritual practices necessary. One has become one with the One - Brahmam.

Primitive religions created the fear of God in their followers to keep them intact in their fold. For them God is all fearful and punishes those who err HIS rules (which actually is written by a self-styled prophet or messenger).

Fear of God is a common thing in Semitic monotheism.

That's why the Semitic and western culture is grounded on terror, and through terror the minds of people are manipulated to be used by empowered money holders and governments.

But civilized men understand God as love and peace.!

Chapter - 32
Offshore Spiritual Harvesting Industry

A message from a UK born Desi (person of Indian origin) who is my reader:"Why don't you write about forceful religious conversion happening in India by Vishwa Hindu Parishad and others?"

I asked her: "Have you ever heard of the "Coonan Cross Oath"?"

"No. But you are trying to change the subject"

"The oath, known as "Koonan Kurishu Satyam", was taken by Saint THomams Christian community of Kerala state in India on 3rd January 1653. It was against forceful conversion by barbarian Portuguese missionaries and to maintain the real secular life in India. The oath resulted in declaration of the sovereignty of Malankara Church in 1665 AD, denying the Pope." It was not Hindus, but Christians who had revolted against forceful conversion to Christianity! They raised voice even against Pope!

Many good Christians are distressed seeing misuse of the name of Jesus Christ for business of conversion. Religious conversion is an offshore MLM (multi-level marketing) business for these traders.

"You mean to say conversion is business and trade?"

"Yes, of course. Spirituality is the biggest industry in the world. The fights between religions are just about the market share.

Religion marketing can be defined as the art of separating the rich from their money and the poor from their traditions, under the pretext of saving the former from their guilt and the later from their poverty."

I am not talking about the true religious followers. Here the discussion is about the industry run in the name of religions. First, let us take Christianity for instance. For, this industry has mastered a business model better than others.

It has become heavily institutionalized involving giant multinational religious enterprises. They run huge offshore MLM business. If business is bad, who will pay for the luxurious life in palatial bungalows for those priests?

The various denominations (sects, cults, castes - now nearly 40,000) inside the industry (religion) can be termed as corporate (companies or firms). All of these firms are involved in the trade of conversion.

With corporate headquarters in the West, these firms did excellent offshore business to make it to No.1 in the world with huge size of staff and revenues. Currently, many firms in that industry make sure that the pastors go get degree (MBA) in marketing too.

They make good salesmen. Their potential customers are (1) innocent, naive people or (2) corrupt people who have guilt.

Those people may end-up in buying their services/products. What will they offer you? You will get a confirmed seat in the heaven or money.

If you take Indian market, you would find at least 25,000 retail outlets and more than 5 million salesmen for these firms.

Just take a look at any major city in India and do a little bit research on the land owned by various companies in this religion. The asset base of each firm is beyond one's imagination.

(Did you know that this global industry has a strong public relations department - there are more than 4,000 TV and radio stations? Every year 30,000 new book titles of literature are published. And there are 36,500 periodicals and magazines!)

Now, what's the revenue model for the corporate? To make it simple, I shall explain a personal experience.

Once a salesman (pastor) came to my house with "good news" - that there is a vacant seat in the heaven and I can get it, if I get converted or join his company.

Since I neither believe in heaven and nor want to go there, he couldn't sell his product/service to me. But I was very hospitable and we became friendly with each other.

I asked him: "Sir, no business can run without a strong revenue model...You are offering up to Rs 1 lakh per person to get converted. But how does your company make money? How would it pay your salary and commission?"

The firm invests Rs 1 lakh (Hundred thousand) on one person and converts him. Naturally, all other members of his family will be compelled to convert. Thus, suppose a five-member-family joined this firm.

All ceremonies of the family's- including birth, marriage and death - are now linked to the firm's local branch (Church). The branch and office staffs (clergy) get huge fees and commission.

The Church can get up to (at least) Rs 5 lakh per person from ceremonies connected from birth to death. 5x5 = 25 lakhs. Simple mathematics!

What investment will give you 25 times return? There are bonuses - the management (priesthood) of the firm can negotiate with the local and national political parties by showing the power of vote bank!

There are auxiliary revenues from other buildings they build for education and healthcare.

When all these things are done in the name of religion, nobody can question them too.

So, the conversion is NOT to Christianity or Jesus Christ's teachings. It's all about business and how to make money out of it.

Good Christians always fought against such firms. But these corporate are more powerful and influential so the religion will become a puppet.

Harvesting souls reaps great benefits for the evangelists who have made it a fine art and are funded by external powers.

Evangelists have made huge sums of money and always reap their corn from poverty illness depression by brainwashing and showing the carrot or at times the stick too.

Now, take Islam. Its business model is different. What happens to most of the converts? His/her worldview alters.

His holy places are now in Arab lands. His sacred language becomes Arabic. His idea of history alters. He rejects his own history. Then he becomes (whether he likes it or not) a part of the Arab story.

That's why brutal religious invaders could destroy the past of the conquered people, their religious places, temples, books and centers of learning. And even forcefully convert their identity into becoming as Arabic as possible.

Hence Arabic culture becomes centre of attraction and those economies will flourish.

And those oil-rich nations know very well how to intimidate peaceful countries by pumping in monies to nourish terrorists in those countries. Terrorism was a spin-off or diversification of spiritual trade. But it has the status of a separate industry now.

So, in Islam too - the conversion is not the real issue. There is nothing wrong in believing Allah and following Islam and converting people to Islam. But turning normal people into Arabs and then dying and killing for Arabs makes this industry unholy.

Why Am I a Hindu?

The irony is that the original Arabs won't accept the converts as Arabs, even if they dress-up like them or follow their culture.

At the best, Arabs can accept you as slaves.

Good Muslims know these facts. They know that Islam is not about being converted to Arab.

Now, take Hinduism - it doesn't believe in conversion. Still many firms, claiming Hindu background, are in the business of conversion, but in different forms. The Godmen of Hinduism too are part of the nexus of profiteers.

Hinduism is also now an emerging industry and there are lots of proprietary firms run by businessmen in the name of bhagavan, guru, master, baba, matha, etc (God men and God women). Some business owners accumulate enormous wealth.

Here investment is very less - the businessman (Godman) should know a bit of magic (initially), few Sanskrit mantras or words and should have a very good marketing team. He/she should appear in public in fancy dresses (Saffron or white attire).

Here, conversion happens not directly in the name of religion, but they use ethos of religion very well. It's kind of cult-formation.

Hinduism is a diverse system of thought with beliefs spanning monotheism, polytheism, panantheism, pantheism, panders, monism and atheism among others.

Hinduism has no ecclesiastical order, no centralised authorities, no binding holy book.

You really cannot convert people to Hinduism. One can self-declare that I am Sanatan Dharmi and follow Dharmic life, that's all.

Good Hindus should understand this and defend our Dharma.

I don't know if any religious conversion happened in India on merit basis. I personally know few instances abroad were people read and understood Buddhism and Sanatan Dharma and got converted themselves.

But I hardly met anybody who got converted to Abrahamic religions without any external pressure.

All conversions happened by force, cheating, trapping, exploiting etc. Poverty was the main reason behind most of the conversions.

A large chunk of Hindus got converted to Christianity in the South because they were given Bulgur wheat that was provided to India by USA during the famine in early 1900s.

"Not only economy, there were social issues too. History says that people got converted to Islam and Christianity in India to escape from the clutches of Brahmin domination..."

"Who has written Indian history? Indian Historians were majorly sponsored by evangelists, the British and communists.

So it is natural for them to create a history to make average educated Indian feel ashamed of their past and convert to 'modern' religions or follow communist ideologies.

Caste system in the present form was unknown to India before invaders after 1000AD. India never had Brahmin domination.

If the conversion happened to oppose Brahmamism, how come people like Sheik Abdulla and prominent personalities in Kashmir proudly claim that they had Brahmin ancestors!

Almost all Syrian Christians in Kerala claim that they are descendants of Namboodiri Brahmins!

Why do all elite class Christians and Muslims desperately try to establish their Brahmin ancestry? Such claims themselves are contradictory and baseless"

What's more there are millions of newly-convert Christians in India. They are being told by the converting companies that: "You change your faith and be loyal to the Church. But do not change your names, caste or religion in official records - so that you can avail benefits given to Dalits." Isn't this plain cheating? So how can you raise social issue here?

The UK born Desi girl didn't talk for a moment. Then asked me: "Hmm...Uday Sir, now I understand that all religious institutions are commercialized and make money out of their ignorant followers.

I understand that like any corporate, they need to increase market share by conversion. But how to stop this conversion issues..."

"Why should we stop it? We know today religions have nothing to do with divinity and humanism. It is cut-throat business, nothing else.

The government should encourage this conversion industry but make it accountable.

Let more and more entrepreneurs come to the field. But, like any other industry, the companies and employees MUST pay income tax and sales tax. Government should allow conversion, but fix registration fee for conversions"

Everyone in the biz of conversion keeps talking about humanity but no one wants to follow or practice it personally.

Our culture, Indian culture, is an inclusive one - so we need all religions here.

But all religions should be treated equally. There should be a common law for all citizens of a country, irrespective of the religion he/she follows.

Hindu Dharma does not hold any socio-political or financial agenda at its very heart.

In North America (the headquarters of various sects of one of the most prominent religion that converts people is there) there are original residents of that place who are now called aboriginals or native Indians.

When white immigrants went to North America, they subdued and sidelined these people.

Now the government realized the injustice done to the natives and nature, so funds are in place to bring them up.

But most of these aboriginals keep going on and off welfare and mostly don't come into mainstream as they become complacent because of this welfare system.

Otherwise, centuries ago these tribal were smart people in tune with nature and leading a simple life.

Now the country has made this culture as a heritage thing and seemingly they invest to bring up these people and nurture their culture. Essentially, the original culture of North America has become a museum piece.

Now, the attempt is somewhat the same to make a prominent Indian religion as a heritage piece in museum with seeming efforts to revive it.

So some of those Semitic cults now-a-days operates in India (especially in certain educational institutions) in so called "scientific" manner researching into ancient Indian culture, even supporting it at times and modifying adapting original Indian spiritual practices with fancy titles into their systems.

Tomorrow, (a century or two later) it will be no wonder if these people come to be known as revivers of Hindu culture (which at that time will be a museum piece).

A true human being will make the best of whatever religion he is born in because every birth is part of a divine plan.

Chapter - 33
Konkani Lullaby and a Tragic Goan History

"Dear Crow, have you been to Goa? Have you seen my beloved Grandpa there? What did he tell you? Did he tell about coming here for the next auspicious day?"

This is the first stanza of a melodious lullaby in Konkani that I heard during my childhood. My grandmother heard it sung by an old woman while caring and feeding her grandchild.

There is a hope in this lullaby. Even at this old age, she expects her Grandpa to come to see her - for, she came down to Kerala coast along with her father and remaining family members at very young tender age after a long tough, horrible journey through ocean from Konkan Goa.

There is deep disturbing sadness in this lullaby. She consciously knows that her Grandpa will never come. If alive her grandpa would have been 200 years old.

She understands that her Grandpa along with her relatives was brutally tortured and murdered by religious lunatics. But her heart is not capable of accepting the bitter truth.

She still aspires to see him once before her death! She loved her Grandpa so much.

She remembers her small beautiful thatched house that was built in tandem with the nature, the vegetable and fruits organic farm, the nice village and serene temple were brutally ransacked and destroyed by foreign barbarians.

The head of those barbarians was a venom spewing missionary.

And her Grandpa was one among 40,000-odd Goans who were murdered, massacred and tortured by them.

She still remembers those nightmarish and deadly escapes from Goa with her parents and few other family members.

She was deeply wounded by the distressing and disturbing experience- the sightings of suffering that she saw in her childhood. The frightening torture she saw included:

- Her forefather's eyelids were sliced off and extremities were amputated carefully so a person could remain conscious
- Daughters raped and sons killed in front of their parents who couldn't even close eyes since eyelids were sliced.
- Elders had to see those barbarians tear their women's breast from her body.
- The most devilish terrors inflicted on pregnant women made them abort.
- Water torture (where prisoner was laid across iron bar and made to ingest water non-stop. This would create pressure on stomach and sometimes they would beat stomach with stick till it would burst)
- Cutting off ears of one's head.
- No honor even in death: Those who died in the jail were buried inside the building, the bodies were exhumed.

Who did commit such brutal slaughter? Who were those inhuman butchers?

Who was the cold-blooded leader of the massacre that happened in the name of religion?

Well, before asking such questions, we should know the background of her ancestor.

Goan Hindus were a peaceful, lovable and graceful community whose prayer was "Lokah Samastah Sukhino BHavantu"(May eternal peace and goodwill prevail in the whole world).

They believed in non-violence and Vasudhaiva Kutumbakam (the world is one family).

Among them was a Brahmin community - Goud Saraswat Brahmins (GSBs) - pure vegetarians and propagators of Sanatan Dharma.

They have developed a sophisticated culture based on a profound spiritual connection to the cosmos. Her Grandpa was from that community.

They believed in "Manava seva Madhava seva" (Service to man is service to God) - their duty was to serve society and it was considered as the greatest virtue...

They upheld the unique traditions that has universal base and lived their life in accordance with the "Shodasha Samskaras" (sixteen sacraments).

They organized dwellings (known as "Keri" in Konkani = settlements or agraharas) and helped the Sanatan Dharma society to preserve its unique culture and customs.

In the Keris they learned in all branches of learning, and these were also specialized in Ayurveda, Pashuvaidya, Gajashastra, Ashwashastra, Astronomy, Astrology, Metallurgy, Botany etc in those days. The GSBs guided men of all professions in all areas.

They followed a simple, down-to-earth lifestyle and saved all the material wealth for the future generations to sustain the culture.

They have converted wealth of generations into idols and precious gems and built temples around Goa. There were nearly 4,000 such temples in Goa. Everything about them was environmental friendly.

It was a peaceful and joyous heaven in the earth - till the messengers of death came in the form of Portugese in the sixteenth century.

They followed the tradition of Atithi Devo Bhavah (The guest is God') and heartily welcomed Portuguese. Instead of God, they were welcoming the most devilish exploitators and non-involved human beings.

The world history says, the Goa Inquisition by the Portuguese was most merciless and cruel in the world. The notorious, murderous chieftain was Francis Xavier, a mercenary of death.

The Goan inquisition is regarded by all contemporary portrayals as the most violent inquisition ever executed by the Catholic Church.

Francis Xavier was a Portuguese Christian fanatic who exported the Inquisition to Goa The inquisitors came and started installing their barbaric law to dissuade Hindus from their faith.

Many Hindus were tortured and burnt at the stake for continuing to practice their religion by his team.

Still, a large number of Hindus refused to get converted. So, Portuguese persecuted them - it continued from 1560 all the way to 1812!

Over that period of 252 years, any man, woman, or child living in Goa could be arrested and tortured for simply whispering a prayer or keeping a small idol at home.

An order was issued in June 1684 eliminating Konkani language and making it compulsory to speak Portuguese language.

The first act was to forbid any open practice of Hindu faith like marriage, worship.

In the laws and prohibitions of the inquisition in 1736, over 42 Hindu practices were prohibited, including the wearing of the Brahminical shendi (ponytail), wearing of sacred thread, greeting people with 'Namaste', wearing sandals and growing of the sacred basil or Tulsi plant in front of the house.

Bathing before cooking, forcibly stopped and wearing Dhoti by men and Choli by women was not possible.

Women were put into jail and burnt alive as heretics after raping them in jail.

The idols and other valuables from temples were looted and then converted to churches leaving the hapless Hindus in dire straits.

More than 2000 temples were destroyed!

Francis Xavier landed in Goa on 6 May 1542, with a resolve of 'uprooting paganism' from the soil of India and planting Christianity in its place.

He was not just a religious lunatic, but derived pleasure from torturing and killing.

In his own words: " I KNOW NOT HOW TO DESCRIBE IN WORDS THE JOY THAT I FEEL BEFORE THE SPECTACLE OF PULLING DOWN AND DESTROYING THE IDOLS BY THE VERY PEOPLE WHO FORMERLY WORSHIPED THEM."

He celebrated and enjoyed the killing of innocent GSBs and other Hindus in Goa. His racial hatred was evident from his words: "Hindus believe that their Gods are black.

On this account the great majority of their idols are as black as black can be, and moreover are generally so rubbed over with oil as to smell detestably, and seem to be as dirty as they are ugly and horrible to look at."

Francis could not live to see the fruits of his request to King for "Goa Inquisition".

In order to increase the converts count, his followers and the bishops used force to feed beef to the Hindus which would leave the person with the only option to convert into Christianity.

But Sanatan Dharma was deep-rooted. Some of the descendants of the Vedic Indian civilization that flourished on the banks of river Saraswati from 9000 BC to 4000 BC ran away from Portuguese tyranny.

They ran away from Goa, leaving their rich land behind. Some of them unwillingly converted into Christianity. They lost everything they saved for centuries and migrated to Mangalore and Kerala coast.

What happened to Francis? If you thought that Vatican had rendered apology like it did to Galileo for the agony inflicted on him, you are mistaken.

Instead, they anointed him as "Saint". Now he is known as St. Francis Xavier. Some people consider Francis as "Vatican Poster boy"!

The descendants of GSBs lived in reduced circumstances in the coastal areas. A huge section of them inter-mingled with fishermen community and started eating dead animals and fish.

GSB was the only community in the world whose food-culture itself was healthy natural medicines. If their food-habit was preserved the entire world would have been lived a healthy life.

Konkani is the only language which is prohibited from speaking. At that time all the books and writing were burnt by the Portuguese. That is why for a long period people thought Konkani was a dialect of Marathi and it had no script.

In fact Konkani is older than Marathi. The Konkani certificate appearing in Hortus Indicus Malabaricus(1687-92) has proved this.

The Goan GSBs spread all over India - the Indian government has done nothing to reclaim their homeland.

Slowly the community lost their rich heritage, tradition and culture.

However, a small section in the community still continue the tradition that is 5000 years old - few of GSBs are still vegetarians and follow great Brahminical traditions.

The great writer Voltaire said:"Goa is sadly famous for its inquisition, equally contrary to humanity and commerce. The Portuguese missionaries made us believe that the people worshiped the devil, and it is they who have served him."

All the historical references given in this article are from Portuguese and Vatican records- you can check their libraries or search in Google - some documents are available online too.

I am not blaming any religion, community, race or creed - there are good people and bad people everywhere.

Hinduism is the only religion which faced several forceful conversions and brutally exploited from centuries. But this is the saddest among all the brutalities on Hindus in history, still even after independence; Hindus are still facing similar situations in India.

Majority of Hindus in neighbouring countries - Pakistan and Bangladesh - are wiped out. The Saraswats, original inhabitants in Kashmir, was driven away from the valley.

As long as the "Past is past, let's move on" attitude persists, more such tragic stories would be sent to the oblivion.

We are still seeing that the real victims in India are made to look like villains and the real tyrants are made to look like victims. The fate of the Kashmiri Pandits is another such story...

The courage is to admit the truth that, "yes, there are bad people in my community and my religion too and just becasue he/she happened to born (accidental) in my community, I am not going to support wrong doings" lacks in the hostile religions.

Unfortunately, people feel hurt and insecure when somebody brings out bitter truth.

No community should protect criminals and fanatics by supporting them. Let's be humane by not accepting inhumanity.

Chapter - 34

Global Warming - The Curse of Indian Pagans?

This incident happened in my childhood. During summer vacation, we went to a relative's house. There was a river - not a big one, a stream - near to his house. The uncle allowed us to take bath in the river.

I was so excited. I was about to take bath in the river for the first time in life. I ran towards the river along with other kids.

I saw an unknown old man standing on the banks of the river. He should be in his late 60s. He had long beard and was very dark complexioned. As he was chewing betel leaf with lime and arecanut, a reddish coloured liquid was oozing out of his mouth.

He might have guessed that I was a new boy in the pack. He looked at me sharply and said: "Son, go piss in the coconut tree root before jumping into the river. If you piss in the river, the Goddess would be angry. She would send a special fish to chop off your peeing organ..."

You may call him superstitious. Pagan. Animist. Barbarian.

The ordinary old man in that incident was a follower of a life-style that was founded upon the man's inseparable bondage with nature.

Today I can easily place him higher than any nature lovers, environmentalists, green leaders or self-styled gurus.

Our way of life (Sanatan Dharma) was sustained by those simple and illiterate human beings, not by philosophers and thinkers.

He told me to piss on the coconut tree roots, so God would bless me. The content of urine is a good organic fertilizer for the coconut tree. When you get into water, you normally piss. The water in the flowing river was used for drinking.

You should not contaminate drinking river. So, our ancestors tried to put scare of God in us. The modern man would tell you that the old man is spreading lies and superstitions.

The river has disappeared now. What our ancestors preserved for future generations for the last 5000 years by sacrificing their lives, was destroyed by our modern, progressive thinkers in 50 years!

- I recently saw the United States President's accusing India's role in Global warming.

Let's first consider who's responsible for the global warming that the world is currently experiencing and will continue to experience in the future.

The US and West do not have moral right to advise us. World Resources Institute says that from the US, a single country produced 27% of the total carbon dioxide emissions of the world.

No other single country was close — indeed, the U.S. even outdistanced all the nations of the European Union (25%) combined. This is not a justification for India to pollute. I am talking about a different reason to question the West's pointing finger towards India.

Who killed India's greenery? Our ancestors - followers of Sanatan Dharma - regarded everything around us as pervaded by a subtle divine presence, may it be rivers, mountains, lakes, animals, flora, the mineral world, as well as the stars and planets.

Western philosophy that founded upon Semitic beliefs, on the other hand, treats man and nature as separate entities believing that the former has the prerogative to exploit the latter.

This concept has distanced humanity from Nature.

As people came to perceive God as a singular supremacy detached from the physical world, they lost their reverence for nature. In other words, the tradition of maintaining sacred groves and sacred trees vanished, due mainly to the rise of dogmatic Semitic religions, which advocated faith in one God and were explicitly for the eradication of 'pagan' practices.

"God gave us the earth. We have dominion over the plants, the animals, the trees. God said: Earth is yours. Take it. Rape it. It's yours." This is the nutshell of all Western and Semitic beliefs.

The bloodthirsty fanaticism that characterizes the Semitic creeds was unknown to the 'Pagans' or the followers of Santan Dharma who had lived for long and in peace with their environment and every variety of plant and animal worship. In our ancient stories, birds and animals have always been identified with Gods and Goddesses.

Animism (a term used by the colonial British in India to describe our ancestors) used to denote the worship of forces of nature as opposed to a 'true' (Monotheistic) God.

Till then, our ancestors considered Earth as our mother. Protecting the environment was an important expression of Dharma.

We believed that God is present in all nature, in all creatures, and in every human being regardless of their faith or lack of it. We had a strong tradition of non-violence (ahimsa) that is UNKNOWN for the West and Semitics.

Trees were regarded as symbols of eternal life. So, cut those downs would invite the wrath of the Gods.

Groves in forests were looked upon as habitations of the Gods They have worshiped trees, have tied sacred threads around them, have taken shelter under them, have held social ceremonies around these, offered them water, milk and sometimes even cow dung.

India's sacred text, Rig Veda is a celebration of nature, its hero the God of Rain.

Our scriptures caution: "Oh wicked persons! If you roast a bird, then your bathing in sacred rivers, pilgrimage, worship and yagnas are useless."

The PadmaPurana (Bhoomikhanda 96.7-8) warns: "A person, who is engaged in killing creatures, polluting wells, and ponds and tanks, and destroying gardens, certainly goes to hell."

Typically, our social thought had always included an ecological dimension.

The man is forbidden from exploiting nature. He is taught to live in harmony with nature and recognize that divinity prevails in all elements, including plants and animals.

And Rishi Markandeya (in Mahabharata) warned us about forthcoming global warming.

Terrible wars and demonic diseases will decimate the human race, and savage cold and scathing heat, scorching droughts and sweeping floods will terrorize the people....

Atharva Veda - Prithvi Sukta states: "Earth is my mother, I am her son". Our ancestors saw Mother India as part of Mother Earth. India is the land of sacred geography (Punya Bhoomi) — but to those who followed the Dharma alone.

With the arrival of European pirates and looters (British, Portuguese, French, Dutch etc.), Middle East barbaric invaders, Evangelists, all our natural beliefs and Dharmic concepts were touted as superstitions.

The Sanatan Dharma was paganism or animism for them.

To foreigners, India has been a real estate, not a Punya Bhoomi (sacred land) as considered by our ancestors. The invaders have possessed India; our ancestors have belonged to it.

The invaders and pirates have thus distanced humanity from Nature.

As people of Indian sub-continent came to perceive God as a singular supremacy detached from the physical world, (naturally) they lost their reverence for nature.

Their concept of morality is based on taking into consideration only man, and leaving the entire animal world without rights.

Our tradition (that men submit to nature so the nature preserves its sacredness) lost in the Semitic West influence since the Industrial Revolution. They said: Man, should conquer nature. Anything that gets in the way should be brushed aside.

The modernist obviously is a worshipper of today's western culture which gives most priority to luxury.

We have forgotten the basic difference between "Needs" and "Wants" and if one is able to analyze things the right way, most of us have more things which we really "need".

But do we utilize those things that we always wanted? 90% of the times, the answer remains a big NO.

Then why did we run behind it like mad? Because, we have been conditioned and trained to do so.

The Semitic West's idea of industrialization and development destroyed trees, these are often chopped mercilessly, and the eternal search for firewood threatens their limbs.

And those wily thinkers have created a new breed of Indians conditioned with wrong concepts of life based on shallow philosophy of Semitics (They even created a religion that imitates Semitic concepts and called Hinduism).

They taught us: your job is drilling, mining and stripping.

Your life aim should be big gas-guzzling cars, flashy smartphones, smelly perfumes and wet bars. Life is all about comforts, pleasure and luxury.

The modernists taught us to be arrogant and ignorant. To live like them, we have destroyed the environment of this planet. Let's enjoy!

We forgot that the resources of nature belong to all including the future generations.

We have polluted the oceans, we have made the air unbreathable, and we have desecrated nature and decimated wildlife. This wrong, unessential thirst for lop-sided developments made India the world's third largest emitter of greenhouse gases.

The modern environmentalism can be summed up in a single sentence. 'Humans cut down trees; turn them into paper and write on it: "Save Trees".

But my ancestors said, tree is divine ("May plants, the water and the sky, Preserve us and woods and mountains, with their trees for tresses" -Rig Veda, V-14.11).

So, if at all you need to cut a tree, it has to be done with such a reverence that we have to pray, offer Pooja and seek the permission to cut it. We have to plant ten trees if we have to cut one.

Brihatsamhita says, before cutting a tree for food, fuel, shelter etc people from all four Varnas should join together and invoke those trees after the worship at night with a prayer: "O tree! I salute you.

Please accept my humble worship offered according to Vedic injunctions.

May those beings who reside here arrange for their residence elsewhere after accepting the injunctions! Let them forgive me!"

Ask your grandparents. It was a ritual to lay a child in the rock stage of the banyan tree near traditional temples to seek blessings of the grandpa tree. Their belief: "When the tree sees the new born, it feels extremely happy and the movement of banyan tree leaves will increase like when it happens during the wind blows."

Did you know newborn asphyxia happens in alarming rate? Did you know Banyan tree is the best resource of pure oxygen?

Ancient people believe that a child exposed to Banyan tree will never have any hearing problems.

I can hear you saying: "Uday, this is baseless superstition." Why don't the parents of kids with hearing problems try this? You have nothing to lose.

How does the gentle soothing sound of rustling leaves in the trees creates vibrations in the skin, nervous system, acoustic organs and improves Neuro-linguistic system should be a subject for research...

A child who had such exposure to the Banyan tree will never allow cutting it off. Why? The child would naturally develop bondage with the tree. This cannot be explained to a modernist.

Yes - for the modern guys these are superstitions.

They won't have any problems with cutting of a tree. (Remember the English movie Avatar?).

The tree also symbolizes life and fertility in our culture. It was under a banyan tree that our sages sat in a trance seeking enlightenment and held discourses and conducted holy rituals.

Superstitions, eh? You don't see exploiting, killing and dying for the imaginary wrathful God sitting beyond the clouds as superstition.

But some non-exploitative and harmless beliefs to protect life in the planet are superstitions!

Don't our ancestors deserve at least "We are sorry" from this generation?

Will I see such old man who takes protecting the environment and our trees and creatures as personal responsibility? Will I see the old man who prohibits kids from pissing in the water again?

Chapter - 35
The Gurudom - Easy way to make money?

Few years ago, an aide of a female religious Guru came to me with an assignment to write fiction about the latter's miracles and to boast her in the media. I refused.

He asked me" Why are you not accepting it? It would be a plum job for you"

I told him that a huge number of India's enlightened "God-men or women" are fake and end up in jail for financial irregularities, sexual abuse and, sometimes, even murder.

Many of these Godmen in India are simply savvy marketers with the ability to manipulate. I don't want to be a part to cheat innocent public.

"As a journalist, don't you know such allegations are conspiracy against gurus by anti-Hindus and media?" he said.

"Most of them, yes. Long ago, Alain Danielou (French historian) said in his book 'Histoire de l'Inde', that the British missionaries and the English media kept on floating rumours in British controlled newspapers about Hindu gurus performing black magic, of financial fraud, of sexual scandals, etc. This trend continues even today with a section of media..."

"There were umpteen arrest warrants against the Imam of Delhi. Did Indian police have courage to touch him? Because Indian police do not have courage to touch a Muslim." he said.

Why Am I a Hindu?

"Your logic would appear appealing to fundamentalists in other religions. But that's an idiotic logic. It's like saying: because all are corrupt what's wrong in me being corrupt!

Hindus do not have the responsibility to support fraud-Godman-turn-Hindu gurus. A fake is a fake despite any religion he/she belongs to.

I know that there are good Gurus with great love to humanity. But they are not as popular as fake Godmen who create cult and make money."

Religious gurus are among the big money-earners in India, so it is hardly surprising that they can buy police, media and politicians. These Gurus and Godmen appear in many names - messiah, prophet, mulla, moulavi, Holy Father, priest, apostle, saint, bishop, imam, ayatollah, bhagavan, guru, master, baba, matha etc are part of livelihood.

As Sankaracharya said centuries ago: "udara-nimittam bahu-krita vesham" (For the sake of the stomach, many disguises are assumed.)

He began flattering his "living God". Any fanatic follower would do the same; he also started equating his guru to God.

"During Tsunami, Earthquakes and Jharkhand calamity, our Guru had donated millions of rupees...She is so good and does many social services and donates lot to poor..."

I said: "Even Potassium cyanide (KCN) has good properties, so can you eat it? What's so special about donating some money? Many businessmen and industrialists also do such social services."

"What rubbish.... how dare you compare businessman with a pious spiritual guru?"

"Since I am not a fan of any of those spiritual traders, I can't see any difference between them and businessmen, except one - businessmen make their donation after paying all taxes.

But so-called God men are spending a small fraction (less than one percent?) of what they earn without any sort of hard work...

So, I appreciate social services done by normal businessmen much more than that of spiritual traders..."

The process of making a Godman usually begins with showing some magic. His/her public relation employees will publicize those magic as miracles. This will attract crowd. After a stage, Godmen turn gurus and would disown the magic.

Next stage is talking philosophy and morality (They hire people to get quotes and insights).

As part of publicity stunt, they would even donate a small portion of their wealth to poor. They preach against vice simultaneously taking advantage of people, especially women.

These anti-social gurus will promote themselves as self-fashioned spiritual leader, television lifestyle guru or self-styled crusader against corruption.

They sell millions of devotees the empty promise of "liberation" (who knows from what?). The common factor is that they are all large-scale landowner.

"Are you negating the need of a guru?" he asked.

"You might need a guru if you plan to learn a skill like archery, martial arts, sacred scriptures, religious theology, carpentry or programming. Or you might need one if you feel insecure and seeking a psychological safety...."I said, "But we don't need a guru to learn life and get enlightened.

When we learn something from someone, he or she automatically becomes our guru by default - I have hundreds of such Gurus in my life time.

But today's concept of a single "super-man" guru (or all-in-one guru), who will teach us about life and lead us to God or enlightenment, is ridiculous and indigestible.

We have a deep-rooted conditioning - you may call it concepts or perceptions - of a guru derived from our long tradition of Guru-Sikshya Sambradaya.

Though we know that today's Kaliyug gurus are epicenter of desires, perversions and money-hunger, we refuse to acknowledge it as it would hurt our age-old perception (read ego). And we are seriously confused with Acharyas and Gurus.

1. Acharya is a person whose primary Dharma is to see that the tradition is maintained. There are many Acharyas in India.

They have established mutts like Sharada Mutt, Shringeri Mutt, Pejavar Mutt, Kashi Mutt, Gokarna Mutt etc.

The head of the mutt considered to be the Acharya who is not necessarily a Guru. They have a lineage to keep up, so can't be big frauds, though the assets of Mutt create conflicts sometime.

2. We have philosophical schools for Sanatan Dharma like Sriramakrishna mission, Chinmaya mission etc. The Swamis from those missions won't show any magic. They won't advise you to follow superstitions.

3. Enlightened people (like sages or Zen masters) - They are truth-seekers and reached a stage of "athato brahma jijnasa" (means NOW one should inquire about Brahmam or now is the time to inquire about the absolute truth).

They need divine blessings to move ahead from that stage, as it is the final stage that can be reached by human efforts. They don't want anything from anybody. They don't entertain you to touch their feet. They see equal divine presence everywhere.

4. Gurus - anybody or anything that transforms you from illusion (conditioning) to truth is Guru. And a Guru will never let anybody follow him or her. A guru's duty is transformation, not creating the gurudom.

At the best, a guru can tell you that there is a state of being known as "athato brahma jijnasa" the highest state that a human being can reach. Guru can't take you there.

They all are human beings like us. They also have indigestion and gastric disorders like us. They also take painkillers for ache. So any guru who offers a magic pill, book, session, etc. for instant enlightenment is a charlatan.

Ancient scriptures say: "Guru-sakshat Para-Brahma" = means, Parabrahma (divine/cosmic) is your guru. Not the other way around.

If you observe and be aware, this force will teach the lessons you need. When you surrender to the Param Atman and do good karma, every other thing will be taken care of. Experience is the best teacher! Life is our Guru.

Our Dharma believes in individual self-realization and not borrowed or rented or bought self-realization.

Always remember the Brahmam (God or Supreme Truth) that resides in the most respected guru or spiritual leader also resides in us. The only difference is that we have not bothered to realize it.

Then, why do fake gurus thrive in Hinduism despite the scriptures and traditions do not support such people? That's because, the society has not understood the true teachings of Sanatan Dharma.

Ignorant, miracle and fortune-seeking followers are the ones who help such fake swamis to prosper in Hindu society.

Hindus never bother to read any scriptures. I have suggested many, before going to a Guru, read at least the Bhagavad Gita. A book of Gita will cost you less than 100 rupees.

But majority of the Hindus have no time to read the 700 verses but spend thousands of rupees, hard earned money, energy and time visiting ashrams and spiritual centers of such fake gurus.

"But Bhagavad Gita is hard to digest for common people like us" he said.

Gita, the greatest guru, is very simple. If one has time and patience reading and understanding the Bhagavad Gita is not the real issue. But I am sure that people won't read it. Why?

Gita does not talk about the ways to become billionaire overnight. Gita do not have mantras to find treasures hidden underground. It does not provide miracle cure to diseases. What's more, Gita does not predict the future.

Gita only teaches to you to attain Moksha and how to live a life of bliss. Or pick any of Sanatan Dharma scriptures (not stories) and read a few pages daily. Soon we will realize the futility of going to such fake gurus.

Suddenly he said: "I am following her because I get immense solace and peace..."

"If your solace is dependent upon her, what will you do after her death? The peace and relaxation should come from within. It can't come from anywhere. It's extremely futile to search for happiness and peace outside."

There are always some true spiritual persons silently living around us. But we fail to see them.

Our hurriedness to solve the problems or material greed draw us towards fake gurus just to deluge on them wealth and power, good for nothing.

There are genuine masters who can teach you the 'Art of Dying'.

He will not attract people by showing some magic or giving some mantra for a fee. People dont want to accept genuine guru because he is uncompromising in following the rules and regulation.

But people don't want to follow any rules and regulations which obstruct the sense enjoyment.

Whoever teaches us selflessly to lead a good life is our Guru. It can even be a child, a peer, an elderly person, nature, life itself is a Guru.

Once, an Englishman asked Sri Ramana: "I want peace". Sri Ramana instantly replied, "Drop 'I' and 'Want' from it!" (Only 'peace' is left) You can see such pure at heart saints with Godlike qualities in India. A true sage will never advertise and long for publicity.

A Zen master said: "My miracle is that when I'm hungry, I eat, and when I am tired, I sleep." How true!

We are all human, we all share the same range of emotions we are capable of feeling. What makes us different is how we react to these emotions.

Enlightenment is not about becoming divine or showing miracles. Instead, it's about becoming more fully human. It is the end of ignorance.

Being a guru has become a conman's first resort and guruhood became a money-spinning industry, built on the credulity, gullibility and naivete of the common and the uncommon folk.

Its commercialization, and even corporatization, soon developed political links and connections just as the priestly class came to be an influence-wielding power in the corridors of power such as the king's court in ancient times.

The religious institutions and the ashrams became dens of secret or dishonest activity and secret wheeling-dealings, and even storehouses of black money and sexual abuses and promiscuity.

However, the veneration of and submission to false gurus continues unabated, because there is still demand from the frustrated, miserable, confused and broken souls for these gurus.

Chapter - 36

Hindutva Politics

Recently, Shyam Sunder, one of my distant relatives, came to my house. He is a Swayam Sevak. He is a hardcore RSS worker. (For friends in other countries: Rashtriya Swayamsevak Sangh (RSS) is the largest volunteer organization of patriotic Hindu nationalists). He is very angry with Muslims in India.

"In India, Hindus are penalized. All governments and political parties support Muslims. There are government-aided Mosques. The government pays salary to Imams. Muslims get quota and reservations in schools, colleges, professional educational institutions and for jobs..." he was getting agitated while talking: "So, it is like Jizyah tax now. Tax paid by Hindus and money looted from temples used for welfare of Muslims. Their population is fast increasing in India due to child marriage and multiple marriages..."

"Hmm..."

"The government declared a holiday on Mohammed Nabi's birthday - but our own Rama's birthday is not a holiday..." he was raging with anger.

"Shyam, how many kids you have?"

"You know, right? Two kids. Seven and five-year-old..."

"If your uncle feeds them with daily alcoholic drinks to your seven-year-old kid, the kid may get addicted to that, right? Whom would you blame then? Your kid or uncle?"

"Uncle, of course, yes, what is that to do with Muslims?"

"Shyam, holiday for the birth day of Prophet Mohammed is not according to Islamic principles. No sane Muslim has asked for this Holiday as Quran does not agree worshiping a human being. So, is it the mistake of a Muslim that former Prime Minister VP Singh declared a holiday for them? Who is the real culprit here?"

"VP Singh. But anybody who reads real Indian history will have hatred and rage towards the brutal invaders who destroyed out peaceful culture and civilization, destroyed more than hundred thousand temples and killed nearly 75 million Hindus..." he said.

"That must be true. But look at present times. How come today's Muslims are responsible for that? Do you agree that the historians and politicians manipulated Indian history so that invaders are glorified?

Do you know that the Brahmins and some sections of Hindus who gave their lives for the sake of Dharma and welfare of the society are persecuted in modern India?"

"That's true...that's what is happening..."

Why Am I a Hindu?

"Yes - what had happened in Brahmins' case, the same thing is happening for Muslims...They are being isolated by cunning crooked politicians..."

"How?"

"Indian Muslims are not descendants of those invaders They are our own brothers and sisters who adopted Islam faith (I agree initially they used brute force and unholy methods for conversions).

For instance, those Muslims in Kashmir are descendants of Kashmiri Saraswat Pundits - they carry our same DNA.

There are other followers of Hindu Dharma who were also forcefully converted to Islam during Mughals period. But not even single person came from outside...."

"So?"

"True Indian Muslims never asked for any favour, though exploitative crooks with Muslim names must have asked. Just like your uncle provided alcoholic drink to your kid, the DEMO-CRAZY, SICKU-LAR Hindu politician controlled governments lavishly provides them more than they ask to create anger, jealousy and enmity in Hindus.

Hindus cannot be fundamentalists or fanatics, as religion or belief is not important for them. But the demonic "Hindu Secular Politicians" (all political parties included) want this separation as vote bank..." I said.

"But Muslims don't think so. They are all religious fanatics..."

"That's not right. I have many friends who follow Islam - they are patriots. What about people like Abdul Kalam or Maulana Abul Kalam Mohiuddin Ahmad Al-Azad?

Educated Muslims know that India is the only country in the world where Muslims enjoy full freedom. They don't have such freedom even in Islamic countries.

"Such people are very few..." he said.

"I just wanted to show that we cannot generalize. Muslims have their own set of problems. They are made to follow convenient interpretation of Islamic principle.

Most of them do not understand Quran so they follow wily priesthood just like any other religions. How many Hindus follow Sanatan Dharma? Have your read the Gita?"

"You mean to say Islamic principles are good?" he raised his eye brows.

"I didn't say good or bad. It's just different. All Semitic religions are based on beliefs. Beliefs may not be the truth. So, it will have its own strengths and weaknesses...."

I had read the Quran. For me, it was just like any other religious books. It never fascinated me. But when a majority population of the world considers it as a Holy-book, we should respect their beliefs.

I had read "Bunch of Thoughts" by M.S.Golwalkar and a bundle of literature related to RSS.

My understanding is that the RSS was established as a patriotic and nationalist welfare organization.

They believed that India's foundation is Hindutva. The real purpose of RSS was to uphold Hindu Dharma and patriotism.

"If a few people in the RSS have extremist views, won't it damage the real intention of RSS?"

"I understand. You mean to say that we cannot generalize with people's deeds based on their interpretation of religion or ideology. I too agree that a section of Hindus are tainting India's name more than Muslims... "

"That's the real problem. Not all Hindus are following Sanatan Dharma. Same goes for Muslims. Not all Muslims follow Islam. The invaders carried Muslims names. They used Islam."

"But brother Uday, Muslims do have problem- like, population growth among illiterate, blind faith, considering religion most important than anything else..."

"Then, we must address those issues, rather than fighting with our own brothers.

If your elder son becomes addicted to alcohol, what you would have done? You will treat him and counsel him, right?"

"Yes. Hmm...I understand your view points. But, what do we do about terrorists? I am not saying all Muslims are terrorists. But most of the terrorists are Muslims..." he said.

"Hmmm...Have you heard about the Security Industry?

Since wars between countries are reduced, the US corporates are tapping the security market. Who is sponsoring terrorism? The marketing or sales department of the corporates involved in the security business...."

"What's that to do with terrorism?"

"There are good and bad guys in every religion. You can't convert a good guy in Islam into a terrorist. The company marketing chief recruits terrorists through brokers. It's like campus placement.

The brokers (mostly priests in Pakistan) target just hatched out brainwashed zombie kid from any religious institution (easy target is Madrasah) through brokers. Brokers may use ethics, principles, ideology, religion or spirituality - any such ALL TIME saleable commodity - to trap teen-agers."

"Then?"

"The broker offers the zombie kid around Rs 1 lakh. The broker would come up with a holy statement: 'You are selected for Jihad. If you die, you will go directly to the paradise. There will be a seat near to God reserved for you (mann mein laddu futa!). You will get 7 beautiful virgins (mann mein 7 laddu futa!) to enjoy.' The deal doesn't end there - next day morning when you get up all the 7 girls would be intact virgins again! (Praise the lord - mann mein 7 million laddu futa!).

Don't ask rubbish questions like if your 'physical things' would be workable after your death.

But Rs 1 lakh and promised God-aisle seat plus virgins are ok for an upcoming terrorist. Our zombie kid, for instance, goes and fixes a bomb in Indian train. Boom! Bomb blast! We blame the poor Muslims just because a zombie Muslim-named kid does a heinous crime."

"I didn't know this..."

"Next day the government sets up umpteen security measures and spends 100 billion for railway security - like buying metal detectors or such equipment. (As usual 80% goes to the political brokers. If anybody from the opposition parties creates problems, this amount will be shared with them).

And for a few days, the front entrance of the railway station will be scrutinized by Jai Jawans!

This scrutiny is not applicable for beggars, lechers, thieves, anti-social elements who get into the train from all other entrance or through all other minor stations.

Inside the train, even the TTE ignores that ticket-less travelers even in the reserved compartments! So, this is just an eye-wash..."

"Really?"

"Nobody can even question them - the country's security can't be compromised, right?

After some days, all these metal detectors will turn into show-pieces in front of railway station entrance. Later, everything will be sold as scrap to rag-pickers. (With a cut back commission, of course). This is known as international security business. Our tax money thus goes to thin air..."

"Is it true?"

"Open your eyes and look around...Religion and politics are big business. We are just emotional donkeys..."

"So, what's the way out? You were telling about counseling and all."

"Invite a few Muslims to 'come and watch' your RSS Sakha and OTC camps...Let them see and experience that you are not doing anything against them...

Let them follow their faith, but not Arabian culture. They are Hindu-Muslims, you are Hindu-Hindu. And there are Hindu-Christians and Hindu-Sikhs...

Hinduism can be a religion in a narrow sense like that of Semitic religions. But the real Hinduism mean universal humanity, it shouldn't represent any religion. That was the wish and prayer of our ancestors.

That's why they prayed 'May all beings in the world be happy" (Loka Samastha Sukhino Bhavanthu) and that's why they said 'the world is one family' (Vasudhaiva Kutumbakam)" I said.

"Yes, the beauty of Hinduism was freedom and universality."

"Let's not let it change. Those wily politicians destroy the beauty of Hinduism by pushing them more towards caste and religion. So, don't fall prey to pimpish politicians' game..." I said.

Talk to Indian Christians and Muslims who are working outside India (non-resident Indians) - they will tell you that how much do they identify with Hindu culture.

Chapter - 37

Is the Word "Hindu" of Foreign Origin?

"The word Hindu has foreign origin...Europeans scholars state that the name 'Hindu' is a Persian corruption of 'Sindhu', resulting from the Persian practice of replacing 'S' with 'H'...Persians could not pronounce the name of the Sindhu River properly. So, they called it Hindu"..."

"The term "Hinduism" came into common use only in the 19th century, by the British...The British writers in 1830 gave the word 'Hinduism' to be used as the common name for all the beliefs of the people of India excluding the converted Muslims and converted Christians...."

(The New Encyclopedia Britannica 20:581, 'Hinduism' was a name given in English language in the Nineteenth Century by the English people to the multiplicity of the beliefs and faiths of the people of the Indus land.)

This is what scholars and historians teach us. And the convent-educated, well-cultured Indians swallow all these hard theories without even adding little water.

Ironically, there is no concrete evidence for any of these theories, whatsoever!!!!

If the word Hindu is a corrupted version of Sindhu - then why the Sindhu River or the people who live in the valley of this river did not acquire the name "Hindu"?

This river is called Sindh and the people are called Punjabis and Sindhis. Nobody calls the state of Sindh as Hind or Sindhis as Hindis!

Let's think rationally and logically....

Were our ancestors' unknown aborigines waiting to be discovered, identified and Christened by foreigners???

How can anybody even imagine, a country (and its people) which was enviably ranked highest in the world in terms of civilization and wealth would not have been without even a name???

Was this land (which was marked by extensive inventions and discoveries in science, technology, engineering, art, dialectic, literature, logic, mathematics, astronomy, religion, and philosophy while the cavemen in rest of the world is crawling in all fours) waiting to be named?

What's the major world history other than destination to this country? Most of the history texts starts with the Macedonian king Alexander the Great (326 BC) wanting to invade the wealthiest and most civilized land in the world - this country.

All great voyages in the world were undertaken to reach this country.

Christopher Columbus accidentally discovered USA while on his voyage to this country and named the natives there as Indians (Later to be known as Red Indians) because he thought he reached India!

Why Am I a Hindu?

It's so naive, ridiculous and idiotic to think that the highly civilized, wealthiest and most glorious land was waiting for the arrival of missionaries and invaders to be named!

"Himalayam Samarabhya Yavabindu Sarovaram Tham Devanirmitham Desam Hindusthanam Prachakshathi" Meaning: The holy land, between Himalayas and Bindu Sarovar (Cape Commorin Sea), created by the Gods themselves is called Hindustan.

The word Hindu was thus derived by combining the first letter 'Hi' of Himalayas and the last compound letter 'ndu' of the word Bindu.

If you cannot take that, here comes the next one:

"Aaasindo sindhu paryantham yasyabharatha bhoomikah, Mathrubhuh pithrubhoochaiva sah vai hindurithismrithaah"

Meaning: Whoever considers the land of Bharatha Bhoomi between Saptha Sindhu and the Indian Ocean as his motherland and fatherland is known as Hindu. Hence for all Indians this is Punya Bhoomi (Holy land)

So, the words Hindu and Hindustan were very much here from time immemorial!

These verses are not in English and hence the English-educated intellectuals (sic) cannot approve it.

We can also say authors of those verses are unknown sages. Okay. Then, how will you explain the term, "Hindu-Kush" (Slayer of Hindus) mountain range in Eastern Afghanistan?

Who were the people, who named this mountain range as Hindu Kush during ancient times? Afghanistan's original name was 'Gandhara' (King of Hastinapur Dhritarashtra married the princess of Gandhara)

The Asokan inscriptions (3rd century BCE), repeatedly use expressions like 'Hida' for 'India' and 'Hida loka' for 'Indian nation'. 'Hida' and its derivative forms are used more than 70 times in the Ashokan inscriptions. How can you explain that?

If these proofs are not enough for you, here are more:

- Hiuen Tsang who visited this country between AD 630 and 645 says that while the word "Shin-tu" (Chine-se for "Hindu"). To Huen Tsang India was a "sacred land."

- Persian monarch Darius (520-485 BCE) mention a people 'Hidu' as to be included in his empire in his inscriptions. Xerexes, successor of Darius, in his inscriptions at Persepolis, also mentions 'Hidu'.

- Shahpur II (310 CE) the king has the titles shakanshah hind shakastan u tuxaristan dabiran dabir, "king of Shakastan, minister of ministers of Hind Shakastan and Tukharistan".

- The inhabitants of the Indian peninsula were called as 'Indos' by the Greeks, evident from the works of Herodotus and Megasthenes.

- The 2nd century B.C. Chinese traveller Zhang Qian referred to India as Shen-Du.

- In the world's wealthiest and most civilized Kingdom Vijayanagara Empire (our history doesn't teach about this Kingdom for political reasons) the word "Hindu" used with pride by Bukkal who described himself as "Hinduraya suratrana".

- The patriotic symbol of India, Chhatrapati Shivaji used to call himself "Hindu".

- Padmanabha in his Epic Kanhadade Prabandha (India's Greatest Patriotic Saga of Medieval Times, composed in AD 1455) uses the word "Hindu" for glorification of the Chauhana heroes of Jalor.

Obviously, nobody named this country Hindustan and its people Hindu.

Now, what was and what should be the name of our great country? This land had a name "Bharata-varsha" (the land of Bharata) or Bharata.

In numerous references in the Puranas, Mahabharata and Vedic texts, the area of India is referred to as Bharata-varsha.

The main Sanskrit texts, and even the rituals that have been performed in the temples from millennia ago, used the word "Bharata" in reference to the area of present-day India.

Thus, it is traditionally and technically more accurate to refer to the land of India as "Bharata" or "Bharat varsha". In the Rig Veda, Bharata is referred to as the country of Sapta Sindhu, i.e. the country of seven great rivers.

When I read Indian history texts, I used to wonder - were these texts written for India or enemy country?

Those studies do not sync with any of Sanskrit or Indian language literature. The Indian history as we teach today is not backed by any evidence. Their statements were not verified. Still we study it without questioning.

Aryan Invasion Theory (AIT) or Aryan Migration Theory is classical example. The founder of this theory, Max Muller, himself denied it at later stage.

He remained an opponent of his AIT theory for the remaining 30 years of his life. Unfortunately, our 'desi scholars' still hold onto Muller's previous wrong views.

Whom did the paid-historians and their political masters want to please and appease?

I wish if our so-called intellectuals and historians, instead of making generalized sweeping statements about Hinduism, could read at least one ancient text among thousands that are still available even after brutal invaders burned and destroyed the scientific work of our ancestors.

Chapter - 38
Yoga is Not Secular. It's Part of Hindu Dharma

My ex-colleague Ananda Krishnan called me Last month. He wanted me to write an article about Yoga in his life-style in-house magazine for International Yoga Day, June 21.

"I don't understand why a section of Muslims and Christians oppose Yoga? I know you can beautifully defend yoga, Uday," he said.

"Nobody needs to defend Yoga. Do you have to defend Sun? However, I feel, this is for the first time, the fears of hardcore Muslims and Christians are not unfounded. Only Hindus can practice Yoga. For others, it is totally useless..." I said.

"You mean to say Yoga is NOT secular?"

"Yoga is NOT secular. Only those who follow Sanatan Dharma can practice it..."I said.

"What? Shocking! What kind of opinion is that?" Anand asked, thought for a while, smiled and continued: "Of course, you have a master's degree in confusing people. All your articles confuse people with completely unknown facts before ending up with crystal clear answer...So, I am excited to publish your article on Yoga..."

"Anandu, I am not going to write for you. It has been long since I wrote for others. I would write only in my website..." before finishing my sentence, he interrupted:

"Oh, you are trying to avoid your old friend. I have seen your articles in many publications and translated in Hindi and other South Indian languages...Don't lie to me Uday..."

"I write only for my website. It's a fact that people share, publish, translate and upload my articles - I also post the same article in social media. However, I am not writing about yoga right now, as the world would be flooded with yoga-related articles..."

"But why did you say yoga is not secular and only for Hindus?"

I told him about an incident. I was travelling from Cochin to Singapore in 2006. There was a person sitting in the next seat. He smiled at me and asked: "Sir, Are you Malayalam?"

"You mean to ask, do I speak Malayalam? Yes, I do." I said.

He talked to me in Malayalam: "I need your help Sir. From Singapore I must catch flight to KL and then to Langkawi. I know English. But I don't understand the announcements and can't talk to Airline staff as they won't know my English."

I nodded. He introduced himself. First name was Babu. He was from a remote village in Idukki district. He was going for his first job with great expectations and excitement.

"What job?" I asked.

"I am a yoga guru. Master Yoga Instructor. I have got appointment in a luxury resort in Langkawi..."

I wondered how he will communicate with a foreign tourist.

"Where did you learn Yoga from?" I asked.

He told me the name of an institution in his village. Something like 'Saint (Alibaba - some name) International Yoga Institute'.

He said he passed the course with distinction. I asked about the duration of the course.

"It was a three weeks course..."he said.

"What?" I was shocked. My yoga guru is 74 years old. He has been researching, practising, and teaching yoga for the last 60 years. He has learnt it from Vivekananda Kendra, then some highly reputed institutes and Gurus in India.

And he still says he is not yet touched the tip of the iceberg. He refused to be called a Yoga guru as he thinks he is not yet reached here. And this kid, Babu has addressed himself as Yoga guru!

While talking, I understood that the institute shares the room with a Barbershop. It is run by somebody who has learned few steps of yoga from somewhere. The total course fee is Rs1000/-.

After three weeks they would provide you a printed certificate (He cannot pronounce the word certificate. He said 'Certeet') stating Yoga Instructor Course passed. (A console -they provide two books on Yoga in Malayalam.)

"In fact, due to heavy rains, I couldn't go for two weeks. I have by hearted names of yoga postures from those books. That was very useful during the interview. They selected me immediately," he was proud.

The man-power agency in Ernakulam which recruited him as Yoga Instructor had taken away Rs 1 lakh as its fee. But his salary would be around Rs 50,000 per month!

Since nobody involved in this trade knew anything about yoga, this was a bright opportunity then.

All international resorts needed yoga instructors that time as yoga was becoming popular. But nobody knows about approvals or certifications. (I don't know if the situation has changed now)

I was really stunned. "Thank you Babu, but for people like you what would have been the future of Yoga?" I told him. He was beamed and even thanked me for the 'compliment'. I shouldn't have teased his ignorance, but my sudden arrogance that time was the culprit.

I have been visiting foreign countries for more than a decade- I have come across wide varieties of Yoga - Supermarket yoga, Instant yoga, Fast yoga, Dancing yoga, Sex yoga, Erotic yoga, Yoga for eternity etc.

Many people promote yoga as a miraculous cure for diseases ranging from cancer to aids! Hatha yoga is practiced in its various denominations, Christian Yoga, Kabbala Yoga or even Doggy Yoga.

"But you didn't say why only Hindus can practice it..."Anandu asked.

"I am coming to that. Born in India, almost 10,000 years ago, Yoga was practiced even in Satya Yuga, as per Ramayana.

Excavations give evidence of yoga's existence during Indus- valley civilization period. The people living on the banks of India's largest river, the Saraswati, were practicing yoga. The Yoga Sutras of Patanjali date from the first half of the 1st millennium."

"Okay. I know that."

"The word Yoga is derived from the Sanskrit word 'Yuj' which essentially means to join or unite. The union referred to is that of the individual self-uniting with Cosmic Consciousness or the Universal existence. Yoga is a means to achieving this goal...

The authentic and traditional Yoga seeks to provide plausible answers to such profound questions as, "Who am I?", "Whence do I come?", "Whither do I go?"

"What's the purpose of life" and "What must I do Yoga is only for truth seekers."

"Yeah, I know, but what are you driving me to?" he asked.

"In Semitic religions, 'the truth' (means, their concept of truth) is already given - There is one single God or creator of everything. He has given moral codes or commandments. He is sitting somewhere behind the clouds and watching you if you are following His commandments.

If you follow his Laws you will be rewarded with heaven, otherwise, you will be roasted in the hell. Hence, answers to all questions, according to them, are given clearly in the Holybooks. There is nothing else to learn. There is no other truth as far as they are concerned...

But yoga is all about finding and realizing the truth.

Every posture in Yoga is 'Sthira sukham asanam' (Sthira= steady, stable, motionless; Sukham = comfortable, ease filled; Asanam = meditation posture) leads to meditation with inner query to find out cosmic truth for himself/herself...How is it useful for the Semitic religions, where truth is already revealed? "

"Oh, yeah...yeah...I didn't think that way..."

(For beginners: Yoga is main core of Hindu philosophy. It is way to liberation (Moksha).

It has eight-fold steps: Yama (Universal morality - it conflicts with Semitic thoughts on exclusiveness). Niyama (Personal observances), Asanas (Body postures), Pranayama (Breathing exercises), Pratyahara (Observing Senses), Dharana (inner perceptual awareness) Dhyana (Meditation) and Samadhi (Union with Brahmam) - without these 8 steps yoga is not complete.)

"And what would be the final stage of Yoga? Samadhi! It is the awareness. It's about experiencing Brahmam.

The entire cosmos is just the manifestation of the divine, there is no creator different from the created. Everything is divine in which you are included. There is nothing else other than Brahmam.

Experiencing the blissful state of Brahmam and being one with it ('yuj') is the final stage of yoga. This concept contradicts 100% with Semitic fundamental beliefs.

For them, God is a separate person. So, their basic principle is challenged here."

"Oh, you are right, they can't believe in anything other than what's told as truth in their Holybooks.

The purpose of Yoga is to radiate peace, humanity and tranquility. But a religion can't take the entire humanity as ONE - it is exclusively for believers and not for infidels.

How can the true follower of a Semitic religion wish peace and happiness to infidels? But, what about those moderate and good people among them? Can't they practice it?" Anand asked.

"All religions, including Hinduism, have three segments. (1) Human: They know this is just belief, they keep it strictly personal and they can adjust with other beliefs too.

70 percent of Indian population fall under this segment, ofcourse with varying degree (2) Marketing - it consists of priests, evangelists and religious institutions. This is the only earning for them (3) Fanatic- blind believers and fundamentalists. The first segment in all religions can practice yoga."

"Now I understand. Hardcore followers of Semitic religions - the second and third segments claim they are THE real representative of the respective religions. The first segment NEVER questions them.

The 2nd and 3rd segments may feel insecure to anything that questions their fundamental beliefs.

As far as they are concerned, Yoga is relevant only for Hindus...because it has a cultural aspect. Yoga samskaras reflect only Hindu base. Now I understood it. But even they can practice it as an exercise, right?" Anand asked.

"That's a huge mistake. As per learnt Gurus, it is not an exercise. If you want to teach like that (example Babu) yes, yoga is for all. But such branded yoga would just be like a parody of the original Yoga.

That too is a pathetic, humorless parody. The authentic yoga can only be learned from genuine Gurus. Naturally, it can be practiced by the people who follow Dharma."

"Yes - I understand your points now. Semitic religions feel insecure about yoga like they do with many things. Their fear is not unfounded - A true practitioner of yoga will eventually leave their religion or cult. If their market is down, how can those priests and institutions survive?

Now I understand why you said Yoga is not secular..."Anand continued: "Those who pray for entire humanity are non-secular. Those who practice exclusive religion or cult are secular. That's why you said Yoga is non-secular, right?"

"Oh no. I go by facts only. The constitution of India doesn't define the word secular. Only the politicians and media have defined it. And Yoga doesn't fall under their definition of secularism. That's why I said it is not secular."

"Uday, I am telling the same thing but in a different way. If I talk in favour of our own ancestors, I am branded as non-secular.

The practical meaning of the word 'Secular' in Indian context is anti-Hindu.

A person earnestly practicing Yoga is or becomes a Hindu as the basic root of yoga is founded upon Vedic wisdom. When you talk about the Hindu Dharma or Hindutva, you become non-secular, right?" Anand asked.

"In that case Zero, Numeral System, Value of Pi, Earth orbiting Sun, law of gravity, baudhayana Sulbasutra (pythagorus theorm), trignometry, metullergy, ayurveda, plastic surgery, Button, Carbon pigment, Chaturanga (Chess), Kabaddi, Ruler, Snakes and ladders, Stupa, Cashmere wool, Cataract surgery, Cure for Leprosy, Diamond mining, Zinc mining etc are either discovered or founded by our Hindu ancestors, so those things are non-secular and should be banned, right?" I asked him.

Anand laughed.

"There is a chance that the priesthood of organized religions is insisting ban on those things. And our political parties would happily yield to such pressures for vote bank politics…" he said.

"I am sure that situation will change. In this age of information, majority of the youngsters might want to come out of conditioned concepts. We are seeing this trend in developed countries where people practice Yoga in a very authentic way with dedication and devotion.

Without any compulsion or fear they would realise the importance of Dharma. I can clearly see this trend everywhere in the world. You cannot always suppress people by brutal fanatic force and superstitions. The exposure to information will set them free. The ordinary people like me around the world want peace and happiness prevailing all over the world.

But the real problem I see is with the authenticity of Yoga. We have to create awareness about the authentic yoga rather than blindly supporting the hip-hop Yoga practiced in many places"

Chapter - 39
Does Hinduism Prohibit Love Marriage?

A Brazilian participant asked me a question while I was attending a conference in Washington DC.

"I have heard that there is a unique system of marriage in your country. Can you please explain it to me?"

She had read something about arranged marriages with ugly display of wealth, dowry system and filled with superstitious rituals.

It is quite normal that the media highlights only the negative factors in Indian culture. "Is it true that Hinduism prohibits love marriages and the society would outcast such couple?" she asked.

I told her: "There have been different kinds of marriages in traditional Indian culture. My ancestors considered the sole purpose of marriage as procreation.

The traditional Hindu marriage is a religious sacrament and not a civil contract. It is a sort of holy performance based on religious rites, with conspicuous utterance of Vedic hymns in the presence of the members of the family and society."

"But I heard a woman had no choice in Indian tradition," she said.

"On the contrary, girls had decided whom to marry. It was known as 'Swayamvara'.

Boys never had a choice. Sanatan Dharma is the only culture in the world that gives prominence to females."

"Uday, am I missing something here? I don't understand and getting more confused. What's an arranged marriage and how is it different from love marriage?"

"The original idea of love (self-arranged) or arranged (family) marriages have nothing to do with the drama that's happening now."

"How come?"

"Contrary to popular misconception, in love marriage, you don't have a choice. But in an arranged marriage you do have."

"Why?"

"You fall in love with a person. You do not see anything else other than the individual you're in love with. You don't see or think about the past generations or future generation. You don't know about genetic issues of that person. You don't know his/her background or mental condition.

You don't know the traditional diseases running in the family. You just fell in love blindly.

So, naturally in your mind, the self-interest and selfishness comes first. You don't have any other choices here. You will be totally brainwashed here."

"So, do you think arranged marriages are better?" she asked.

"No. In today's world, arranged marriages are equally or bit riskier than love marriages..."

"Uday, I really, really don't understand.

The number of divorces was very less compared to our country. Is it because of arranged marriages?"

"It is misinformation, again. Yes, there was less number of divorces in the past - probably because females were silently bearing the male chauvinism. Today, girls are educated and realize that they have equal human rights."

"I am still confused. Can you explain the concept of Indian arranged marriages? "

"The original principle of arranged marriage was to make sure that the next generation is healthy, prosperous and follow Dharma.

The parambara (rich family tradition) should continue. So, they have focused on family, Gotra (clan) and desam (place).

It has a scientific base. They start loving each other only after marriage and this love grows into devotion as they grow together to an old age. So, there is no scope for any sort of insecurity in any family. This has been continuing for thousands of years in India then things changed..."

"Okay. What happened?"

"Today's arrange marriages in India are the worst form of marriage in the world. The importance of Gotra, family, community, desam etc disappeared. Today's big and fat arranged marriages are all about money and superstitious rituals - nothing to do with humans.

The principle of arranged marriages envisaged by our ancestors has nothing to do with today's so-called human-trade in the name of arranged marriage.

Parents are ignorant about their Dharma so, they are blindly following current market trends..."

"So, there is no rationale or logic in today's arranged marriage..."

"You are right. The arranged marriage has become a horrible thing today. Instead of scientific tradition, they follow superstitions like horoscope matching which is against the science and essence of Sanatan Dharma.

Earlier, priests are supposed to do the rituals on behalf of the yajamAna (person paying the cost of a sacrifice or master).

Now greedy priests became masters of ceremony. So, the marriage has become a market event, rather than a pious, divine ritual..."

"Hmmm...I have read that till recently Indian family bondage was stronger but after liberalization of economy, Indian families are in chaos..."

"Yes. As I said, during the last 500 years, a great deal of changes happened in India. Not only the importance of women (as per Vedic tradition) disappeared, but male-chauvinism became trendy due to influx of alien culture. Indian females were silently tolerating and accepting the atrocities of male domination in families. But not anymore..."

"Hence more love marriages are happening too..."

"Yes. The tragedy is that, love remains as a cinematic concept. Hence the so-called love marriage is just living together of two egos with different concepts.

Why Am I a Hindu?

The real love marriage is a lost art.... I have seen only few in my life who live with love."

"So, you mean to say, today's love marriage as well as arranged marriages have lost its meaning and values..."

"Almost. We could have learned from our ancient history about different types of marriages. For instance, Krishna and Rukmini had a love marriage - a successful one.

But today's practical love marriages can be labeled under "Gandharva" marriage. The man and woman meet, mate, then what? Some people may live together, some may be separate.

No one cares for what happens to a child they produce. Parent's separation is NOT healthy for the next generation.

If parents separate in future, how can you call it love marriage? Is love time-bound, conditional affair? I would label it under sudden gush of hormones, rather than a marriage."

We had examples of such "love" marriages - Dushyantha and Sakuntala. We know how much did both suffer. They mated and separated. Another example of sudden gush of hormone is that Kunti's falling in love with a charioteer.

Mahabharata tells us how much she suffered in the future when she came to know Karna was her illegal son.

How much misery did she face? But the marriage of Dhristarashtra and Gandhari was arranged one with a catch.

Both faced miseries. So, our historical stories are full of all sorts of marriages. The epics and Puranas give you very clear messages on life, love and marriages."

"What's that?"

"There should be an element of everlasting love in any sort of marriage. If you don't understand this, irrespective of self-arranged or family arranged, sufferings and miseries would follow...Hence the only way out would be Dharmic marriages."

"What's Dharmic Marriage?"

"The third chapter of Bhagavatham talks about the FIRST EVER MARRIAGE that happened in the earth. It was between Kardama and Devahuti! Vishnu told Kardama Muni: "I am pleased with you. I shall arrange a suitable girl for you.

King Svayambhuva Manu is the emperor who rules the earth. He has a very a beautiful daughter of marriageable age by the name Devahuti. She is suitable for you.

From you she will beget nine daughters and those nice daughters will marry other sages thus will increase the population"

Sri Bhagavatham Kanta 3-Chapter twenty-three, text 2 then talks about the marriage compatibility and married life.

This is written by our ancestors thousands of years ago! And those who follow the advice will never have a failed marriage. The advice for couples (married or before marriage) is as follows:

"VisrambhenAtma-saucena gauravena damena cha, Susrusaya sauhrdena vaca madhuraya cha bhoh (Meaning: The couple should live with intimacy, with purity of mind and body (not only in your mind and your body but also around you and in all your actions), with great respect but like an intimate friend, giving up all lust, pride, envy, greed, non-righteous activities and vanity, with a passion for service for each other, with love and with sweet words.

Atharva Veda, which is written about 7000 years ago, lists the duties of husband: (Chapters: 1/34/5 to 6/89/1) "The sweet and loving behavior of husband should make the wife to inculcate love and affection towards him.

The husband should not hide anything from the wife. In this way, he shall win over her heart. He should lead a disciplined, pious life.

The husband should always try to win over his wife with his love. The husband should lead a disciplined life and should earn money to sustain his married life.

The husband should respect his wife and consider his duty to protect the honor of her life."

It also talks about successful married life: "Husband and wife should share everything in common. This sharing leads to their long life.

Wife should possess serene/calm nature and husband should be hard working, possessing strong body. This leads to generation of brave children. Husband and wife should be completely devoid of anger and should work together to accomplish house hold tasks."

So, the type or sort of marriage is not important. Are you Dharmic? Are you fulfilling the first purpose of marriage (procreation)? Do you really love your spouse?

If any of the above answer is "NO", your children and grandchildren are likely to have problems.

If you become selfish, your future generations will suffer because of you. And you are doing total injustice to the past generations.

Male chauvinism is at its best now in India, thanks to political and religious leaders. Go through any matrimonial sites. Most grooms would say: "I want a girl who will live according to MY whims and fancy and take care of MY family". Don't girls also have whims and fancy? Don't they have parents?

Manu Smriti asks a husband to worship his wife as a form of Shakti, the mother of all creation. It was after the invasion and modern life-style, that women being regarded as just objects of pleasure.

The husband then becomes Pati Dev (God) and wife becomes Patni Devi (Goddess).

Marriages happen, here in the earth and not in fictitious heaven - it is not between soul mates. Soul is a false notion.

A Dharmic marriage joins two individuals for life, so that they can pursue Dharma (duty), artha (possessions), Kama (physical desires), and moksha (contentment) together.

Simply put, the couple works hard in a righteous way to make money (Dharma and artha), use that money for fulfilling desires and reach to the state of contentment.

Chapter - 40

Marriage Compatibility

Nandini Raj from Palakkad asked me a question: "How come there is no story in any Puranas about ideal husband? No wonder, many men don't know how to be a husband, let alone an ideal one!!!"

Vineeth Sharma from San Jose: "In Indian culture there is no pre-marriage and post marriage counseling. Such counseling is now compulsory in many developed countries and in many other religions and cultures. Uday, see the alarming rate of increasing divorces in India."

Neethu Thomas from Delhi: "India still is far behind when it comes to women empowerment and supporting prestige of women. From ancient times, Indian husbands think wives are just slaves to serve them and their families."

I get much more such questions - mostly related to marriage and family life - the problems and challenges they face. I am not a professional counselor - but let me share what I have learned from my ancestors.

Ask your grandparents - probably they would know. People were reading Srimad Bhagavatam at home. It is a very simple story telling book.

The third chapter of Bhagavatham talks about the FIRST MARRIAGE that happened in the earth. It was between Kardama and Devahuti. (See above)

It says: The couple should live with intimacy, with purity of mind and body (not only in your mind and your body but also around you and in all your actions), with great respect but like an intimate friend, giving up all lust, pride, envy, greed, non-righteous activities and vanity, with a passion for service for each other, with love and with sweet words.

Chanakya says: "When there are no fights between husband and wife, the Goddess of fortune automatically comes to the home"

India is the only country in the world that respected women for the last thousands of years! We call out country "Bharat Mata" (Mother India) not Bharat Pita (Father).

The place of God is fourth in the order, the first being mother (Mata, Pita, Guru, God).

We consider our earth as "Punya Bhoomi" or "Bhoomi devi" (divine earth Goddess). As per tradition, the first thing that we should do in the morning when we get up, is touch the floor and seek forgiveness of mother earth because we are touching her with our feet. (Vishnu patni namastubhyam, padasparsham kshamasvame)

And the nature itself is seen as female power- the Prakṛiti or Prakṛuti!

For any auspicious ritual, a man is not allowed to sit without his wife. Even Ram, in the absence of his wife Sita, had to create Kanchana Sita (golden sita) to perform a Yaga (haven).

No serious temples allow a head priest to perform any rituals if he is not married.

The Manusmriti says the society that provides respect and dignity to women flourishes with nobility and prosperity hence the society needs to be more considerate towards ladies.

If women are taken care properly, if they are devoid of any worries, you are promised healthy and intelligent children, who will live in harmony with the nature.

That is why women should be taken care of properly, by father, husband and son.

It gives more responsibility for man than woman and hence woman should have self-discipline ("Na sthree swathanthram arhati") with a caution that freedom can be extremely dangerous, if not handled properly. Nowhere has it said man should control woman.

A ritual of touching wife's feet - when the husband do sashtaang namaskar (a type of prostrating in which all body parts touch the ground) - during 'Pumsavana Simantonayana' (The 16 rituals or sacraments during the lifetime of a person are called Shodasa Sanskar.

This is the third one) was followed in most of the Vedic culture (I do not know how it disappeared from the rituals, giving room for total male chauvinism).

"You are carrying me in your womb." husband would say. Then the wife will look at him in mathrubhava (motherly). With this the love between the couple goes to a different divine dimension.

During Vedic times, women were wearing sacred thread (jenoi).

Why Am I a Hindu?

All these rituals were developed to imbibe society's respect to the mother in the woman. It had great Neurolinguistic effect too.

But we stopped following all those rituals and termed it as "Superstitions". And you blame it on to Indian culture.

Now, let's see what are the reasons for the divorces and unhappy married life in our country? In olden days, our ancestors checked only two things before marriage: Varna and Gotra.

If you marry from the same Varna, then the compatibility will be more as both (boy and girl) follow the same culture.

For instance, it would be better for a boy carpenter to marry a girl from a carpenter family.

Today, people marry from different Varnas (Varna has nothing to do with caste) - if a vegetarian (Sattvik) marry from non-vegetarian (tamasic or asuric) family - though both families may carry the same caste tag - what will happen?

For instance, when a vegetarian Brahmin girl marry a non-vegetarian Brahmin boy- the genetic codes that developed from 1000s of years of memory get confused with the deadbody you eat - and in a couple of generations, you will see disastrous results.

(Krishna warns that the Kaliyuga - current age - would be marked by the mixing of various Varnas creating aDharmic generations).

And one should not marry from the same Gotra - The marriages under same Gotra are forbidden due to the close connection of DNA among a boy and a girl if they belong to the same clan.

If two docile genes, one from mother and the other from father, happen to join then the manifestation of single gene-specific disease is sure. So far more than 1,000 such diseases have been identified.

Another emerging reason for divorce is blind superstitions. Instead of following our sacred scriptures and our ancestral wisdom, we follow a fraud astrologer; check horoscope matching and get marry.

There is NO single authentic scripture that support horoscope matching - You can check Brahmasutra, Vedanta, Vedas, Gita or Upanishads. No sacred scriptures support such superstitions.

(Jyotish or Jyotisavedānga is one among six Vedangas - limbs of the Vedas - it is neither Veda nor deal with today's concept of astrology)

Our ancestors advised us to trust in God. Since we cannot trust GOD, we go the other way - follow superstitions like horror-scope matching.

What a way to insult our great astronomers and ancient advanced Indian astronomy! Divorce and unhappiness in life could be the punishment for insulting our divine wisdom.

However, the major reason for unhappiness in married life remains the serious brain damage (or brain-washing) due to market-media.

You are being deeply conditioned by market and you don't even know about it. They dictate what culture, life-style and concepts you should follow in your life.

And you just follow their concepts. You think you have freedom of thought - but the inputs by market media controls your thoughts and you are not aware about it. Still you think you can think therefore you are!

According to Hindu Dharma Shastra there were eight types of marriages - Gandharva Vivaha (fall in love, but don't follow the ceremonies), Brahma Vivah (ideal family arranged marriage), Prajapatya Vivaha (fall in love and then follow the rules) ,Arsha Vivaha (man pays gifts), Daiva Vivaha (marriage during the ceremonial Yajna), Asura Vivaha (marriage where the bride pays dowry), Rakshasha Vivaha (forced marriage) and Pisacha Vivaha (intoxicated marriage).

Chapter - 41

Is Horoscope Match Necessary for Marriages

Few years ago, a young boy and girl contacted me: "Sir - is horoscope matching a MUST for the marriage?"

"Why?" I asked.

"We are in love. We want to marry and live together..."

"Good. Did your parents approve your marriage?"

"Our parents are not allowing us to marry only because our horoscope is not matching. My friends suggested us to contact you for a genuine advice..."

"Hmm...If you believe in horoscope, you MUST check and marry accordingly. If you don't believe in it, there is no problem at all..."

"Sir, we wanted a concrete opinion. We really want to marry. But as per our Vedic scriptures and Gita we can't marry without horoscope match, right?"

"That's strange... Horoscope matching was not even heard in Vedic times. No authentic scriptures like Veda, Upanishads, Gitas, Brahma Sutra, and Dharma Sastra talk about Horoscope Matching marriage. It has NOTHING to do with any original sacred texts. "

"Really? Then why do they insist on Vedic Horoscope Matching?"

Why Am I a Hindu?

"There could be Vedic Pizza, Vedic Street Dance, Vedic Yo-yo, Vedic Inner wear too...

It's all marketing gimmicks! Our great sages who wrote Veda didn't say such things."

"But our family astrologer vouches that astrology is part of Veda. That's why he practices Vedic astrology," he said.

"Jyotisha is one among six auxiliary disciplines related to Veda, known as Vedanga (limbs of the Veda). It is primarily concerned with the preparation of a calendar to fix the date of sacrificial rituals. It also deals with time measurement, forecasting movement of Sun, Moon and planetary movements.

In Vedic times, Jyotish meant astronomy in all its aspects. It's science. Today, the word 'Jyotish' is used for predictive astrology. Predictive and horoscopic astrology came to Indian subcontinent from Greece during third century (AD).

The first ever text in the Sanskrit on astrology is "Yavanajātaka"(Sayings of the Greeks) written by Yavaneśvara in AD270 - that is 1745 years ago. Veda dates back to 5000-7000 years! Astrology has nothing to do with Veda. Clear?"

"Yes...but sir, even Christians and Muslims believe in horoscope matching!"

"My humble understanding is that horoscope matching is not logical, scientific and rational and absolutely nothing to do with human life. If you look at Philosophical angle, it is insulting the very basic foundation of Hinduism - the karmic theory.

In devotion, horoscope questions the very concept of God and making a statement of NO trust in God. It is neither Sastra nor science.

Great Hindu philosophers like Swami Vivekananda made it very clear that only mentally sick person would practice or follow horoscope."

"Then why do millions of people follow it?"

"It's a belief...It remains a belief, till science (Vedic or modern) explains and proves it. But I mostly support belief as it has some placebo effect. Beliefs are good as long as it doesn't create hurt in others.

Ordinary people like us have many fears and insecurities in life. So we are pinning our hopes on some irrational beliefs that will help at mind level. Beliefs can sometime come true for some people as it instigates your deeds. That's why I said, if you believe in it, you should follow it."

"Sir, is there any other scientific base for today's Jyothisha?"

"My base is what Swami Vivekananda said: Anything that is western origin, first you verify it, then accept it. Anything that is Indian origin, first accept it, then verify it if necessary. This belief doesn't have Indian origin.

When a person seeks scientific explanation for irrational beliefs, it just shows the insecurity of the believer.

Science has a different methodology based on empirical evidence and systematic methodological experiments, hence such beliefs cannot be proved.

A famous astrologer once told me during an Interview: 'There are many things that science cannot prove'.

I replied to him: 'Yes, of course. Does that mean whatever you are telling is proven and correct?' What lousy logic? Why are you desperate and frantic to prove your beliefs?"

"If there was no horoscope matching in Vedic times, what did they check for matching or compatibility?" the girl asked.

"Good question. Marriage, according to Sanatan Dharma, is part of Dharmic life in tune with the nature. The sole purpose of marriage was purely creation. Marriage was never an individual thing in our Dharma.

Since they had a concept "the world is one family" (Vasudhaiva Kutumbakam) mental, physical and community health were most important for them. Hence, they developed very advanced matching system based upon Gotra, Varna and Guna..."

- The Gotra is about a parambara - ancestry, line of descent, genealogy and heritage - is synonymous with DNA.

To get a problem less child, they gave more importance to Gotra. As you know, diseases (mental and physical) can pass through generations. They wanted to rule out such things.

- Varna means profession - parents preferred families in the same Varna.

For instance, if a bride belongs to teacher's family goes to a family of warriors, the ambience and attitude would be totally different hence it may create conflicts and mental tensions.

But if she get married in a family of teachers, she can feel home. And the new born will have genetic character and wisdom (acquired through generations) who can make a good teacher in the future.

- Gunas are subtle qualities - there are three major Gunas - tamas (darkness, dullness or inertia), rajas (activity, passion), and sattva (beingness or purity). A girl with Tamasic guna won't be a match for a boy with Sattvik guna and vice versa.

- The idea behind the institution of marriage in Sanatan Dharma is to foster not self-interest, but love for the entire family and the society.

During the nuptial ceremony in a marriage, both the bride and the bridegroom take an oath for the practice of self-restraint, to work together for the welfare of the family and Dharma and to help each other attain peace.

- During the marriage ceremony, the couple goes around the Holy Fire (Agni) with the male taking an oath: 'After crossing seven steps with me thus, you become my friend.

I too have become your friend now. I will never discord this friendship and you should not also do that. Let us be together always.'

"Oh! That's very romantic! We didn't know all those things..." both of them said.

"Unfortunately, we don't understand the meaning of such rich tradition. We blindly follow imported Semitic and silly beliefs and life style. Instead of actual Sanatan Dharma marriages, a pathetic mimicry of it came into being.

Todays' traditional arranged marriage is not fully according to Dharma, though there are some elements from the latter."

"What are the major differences then?"

"In today's arranged marriages, we have adopted few rituals from the Dharmic marriage, though we don't understand its meaning. The malpractices like horoscope matching, dowry, caste, show business, ugly display of wealth, dominance of priests etc. came into being and the sole idea of Dharmic marriage disappeared. The threat for Hinduism is really not external, but evil practices like this."

"In today's life, is the actual Dharmic marriage practical, Sir?" the girl asked.

"Not much. Gotra has lost its validity. The chastity concept disappeared so you cannot guarantee that bride or bridegroom is from the same Gotra that the family claims to be. Children may be by-product of affairs.

Our ancestors wanted to avoid such situations hence insisted upon the purity of Gotra and Varna. The West mimicking modern man thought (or was taught) that those Varna and Gotra are unscientific.

For the modern man, ancient Vedic science is superstition. And outside-induced horoscope matching is scientific! What an Irony!"

"So, what can we do if somebody wants a Dharmic marriage?"

"Hmm. At the best, you can trace at least known past 3-4 generation of the spouse's family to make sure that he/she doesn't carry any genetic mental disorder. If they were following a Sattvik life, many miseries and hardships in married life can be avoided..."

"It's pathetic that we lost such a great tradition" the boy said.

"Uday sir, how will we convince our parents about the horoscope matching?" the girl asked.

"You cannot convince them. They already have assumed that their belief is true. People with irrational beliefs will be more fanatic, like ISIS.

Beliefs have the power to deeply condition the mind and convert into huge ego. If you question their beliefs, ego will be hurt and they would get angry at you. Blind believers always show dangerous level of insecurity."

"Is there any other way to convince them?"

"Hmm... How much is one plus one?"

"Two"

"1+1=2 is same everywhere. It won't change. Why? It's a universally acceptable theory of mathematics or science.

Horoscope matching doesn't have such a single authentic text, theory or methodology for the matching. So, it varies from place to place. You ask your parents to show horoscope to ten astrologers. Your parents will get ten different opinions.

When they are confused, you can politely request them to go through our authentic scriptures to acquire real Vedic wisdom.

Those who understand Sanatan Dharma cannot be superstitious," I said.

"Sir, a personal question - have you checked your horoscope before marriage?"

"I didn't have one to check. Its 24 years since we married. So far, so good. My father married my mother without checking horoscope.

They lived together till my mother passed away at the age of 76. My father believed that horoscope is insulting the God, so he didn't prepare our (children) horoscopes too.

Ask your grandparents - Horoscope checking is a very recent phenomenon developed by insecure modern man.

However, people may have different viewpoints, so it is personal choice and I still suggest that those who believe in it should go for it. I am not saying it is right or wrong. All I am saying is it is not scientific and Dharmic."

"What will you do in your daughter's case?" the girl asked.

"I would not hurt anybody's belief. I would politely tell them that I don't believe in it, but if you want to check, please go ahead, I am all for it."

"Sir, what about the experiences of others? Like, your relatives, friends etc. Did the horoscope matching marriage work for them?" the girl asked again.

"I have seen 10 such horoscope matched marriages during the past 10 years and 8 among them were flop. The typical one was that five experts said the boy and girl had 90% match.

The boy passed away in just 7 months. You may look around and collect actual data of those who married after perfectly matching horoscope. You will get your answer."

They went happily. As I suggested they had shown their horoscopes to various astrologers in the country.

As I expected they had got totally conflicting opinions. They married. They are blessed with a son. They are living happily.

Once I met a famous astrologer in Kerala and within no time he had to admit to me that all these things are bullshit.

I asked him: "Don't you feel guilty to exploit innocent, naive people? Isn't it Adharma?"

His reply: "If I tell the public that astrology is humbug, they would say I am gone nuts and they will go to another astrologer. For me, this is a profession like magic, public speech and counselling. I learned all the tricks of the trade."

What he said it true, if you tell the truth, public will kill you. If you approve their beliefs, they will adore you.

Chapter - 42

Hinduism and Child Marriage

While I was travelling to Fort Lauderdale from Seattle, an old lady sitting near me talked about India. She has been a social worker.

She said she has collected donation to send to various charity organizations and NGOs in India to save girl children. "Recently, I read a newspaper report saying that child marriages still happen in many parts of your country. It is so pathetic..."

"Yes, I have also read reports that such deplorable things happen once in a blue moon in India."

"The article says that your religion advocates child marriage and as per Hindu Holy scriptures it is mandatory that one should marry during childhood. All Hindu sacred texts promote child marriage. Had it not been for strict legal system, all Hindus would have married at tender age itself."

"You are absolutely wrong. Vedic society knew nothing of child-marriages, nor is it mentioned anywhere in the epics. On the contrary, all the marriages mentioned in our historical epics are between men and women who had attained puberty."

"That article, I don't remember the author's name - she is an activist in India - clearly quotes your sacred texts and epics that advocates and promote child marriages..."

"That's a regular unfortunate practice to manipulate Indian ancestry. I know most of the activists write such things to please their masters.

As I said, Vedic literature does not say about child marriage.

Indian Dharma satraps (treatises) mention eight forms of marriage (brahma, diva, area, papaya, aura, Gadara, rakshasa and piassava) but not about child marriage.

An authoritative text, Yajnavalkya Smriti, doesn't give a particular age difference in marriage. It only says it is preferable to marry a girl who is younger than the boy. Of course, you know the physiological reasons for that..."

"Yes. I agree, physically it is better if the girl is younger than boy. But I remember the author was quoting something like maanu cemetery, your Holy Law Book"

"I don't know about maanu cemetery. It must be Manu Smriti. Yes, if you take a verse from that text out of context, it does prescribe a very young age of marriage, especially for girls," I said.

"Ah, that's what! It clearly shows your Holy books promoted child marriage..." she was kind of excited. People are so much fed with wrong information about our scriptures that they believe they are right.

"Let me explain this way. Number one, Manu Smriti is not a Holy Book. There are thousands of texts in Hinduism. And Hindus need not follow any Holy books or commandments.

Two: Manu Smriti is suited for Krita yuga. Not for today's world which, per us, is Kali yuga.

Three: you should read the remaining part of Manu Smriti - a girl who has come of age must wait for three years for a groom to come seeking her hand. If no such groom turns up, she may herself go looking for a groom." Here too it is post-puberty marriage that is indicated.

Not only that. So, Manu's code of conduct is "modern" in that it permits a girl to look for a husband herself without any need for her elders to do so.

And finally, there is a cultural difference too - marriage does not mean a license for sex in Hindu tradition."

"Oh, is it so? It was a mis-communication..."

"Indian history is written by anti-Indians. Indian media run by people who want to spread wrong information about ancient Indian tradition. So, I am not surprised that you have wrong information on India."

"If it was not part of Indian tradition how come such draconic practices came into being?"

"The tradition got reversed when Invaders came on the scene. The lecherous tyrants demanded that every virgin who attains puberty must be submitted to officials for examination.

If she was beautiful, she'd be sent to their Harem.

If she was simply attractive, then she'd get gang-raped and then no Honorable Hindu family would accept her as a bride.

Therefore, the practice of Child-marriage was started in the Rajputana, Maratha region, etc. to make sure that the girl was 'defiled' before she could be turned into a sex slave for invaders."

"Oh, I didn't know that..."

"Unfortunately, the real history is not politically useful today. Women were worshipped in India. However, the fear of inhuman invaders was the reason why women were treated like burden in India since the Medieval Age.

Even after the Invaders were vanquished, ignorant villagers continued this practice without knowing its origins and purpose."

"Are you sure that the child marriage was not in practice before the attack of invaders?" she asked again.

"The only believable historical records of India are epics. All other history books are written for political reasons.

According to Ramayana, the first historical epic, Rama was around 23 when she married Sita who was around 17 years old. That, of course, was not child marriage. "

"But Ramayana is not a historical record," She said.

"Right, but for me, it is more believable than the present day manipulated history. And if we look at the other epic Mahabharata, the heroine Draupadi was 30 years of age when she married Pandavas."

"I don't know about these characters and didn't read any of those epics, though I have visited India. So, those invaders were ancestors of Islamic State (ISIS) who use girl children as sex slaves..."

"Yes. However, I can't blame the invaders for everything. Things could have been changed by social reformers after Independence. But that didn't happen.

The social reforms didn't happen in India as our leaders were busy appeasing vote banks. Also, fear of scandal was a strong impetus in marrying off girls as quickly as possible, so that some later scriptures insisted that it is best if a girl is married even before menstruation."

"Oh. It is very sad to see that all your traditions and culture are manipulated and presented in a wrong way..." she said, "I am curious to know. What do those scriptures say about the suitable age for marriages?"

"I have not read all the scriptures. That will require few hundred years. I can tell you only from my memory. Gautama Dharma Shastra says a householder shall take a wife of equal Varna (profession, not caste as manipulated), who has not belonged to another man and is younger than himself"

"Oh great that is acceptable for modern age too..."

"Yajnavalkya Smriti says a Youngman should marry only after his student stage. He shall marry a girl endowed with good characteristics.

She shall be younger in age, not sickly, not of the same rishi, lineage or Gotra"

"That's also acceptable. In fact, today's college grads should read it," she said.

"There is one more thing. As per our tradition, the Marriage or Vivaha is known as "saha-Dharma-karini-samprayoga".

That could be translated like this: union with a wife together with whom a man practices Dharma. The clear implication is that carnal pleasure is not its chief purpose, but the pursuit of Dharma."

"Okay, I understand now. Child marriage is not advocated in your scriptures. Your country needs to take strong action against such atrocities..."she said.

"Yes. I agree. Ours is a developing country. But what about a developed country like USA?"

"No... Such things won't happen here in US," she said.

"Have you heard about Tahirih Justice Center?"

"Yes, it is an NGO"

"Few years ago, I have read about a survey by Tahirih found that 3,000 known or suspected forced-marriage cases during 2011, many child marriages. Tactics used against the victims included threats of ostracism, beatings or death.

The report is not an opinionated piece like that you have read about India. It's based on facts and research by your own agency..."

"Oh, really? I didn't read that. I will search and find"

Chapter - 43

Gotra System in Hinduism

The seniors and elders in the family and the old family priest used to tell me that we should go for our KulaDevatha (Kuladev and Kuladaivat = family or Gotra deity, that is either a God or a Goddess) darshan.

In performing any religious rituals Hindu devotees must mention their Gotra/Sub-Gotra.

We have a tradition of village (community) deity -that's Lakshmi Narasimha - and Gotra deity - that's Mahalasa Narayani.

Our Kuladevta temple is in Mardol, Goa hence we decided to go for a quick visit and reached temple on November 1, 2014.

The temple of Mahalsa Narayani is located at the small village of Mardol, about 22 kms from Panaji, the capital city of Goa.

The Goddess Mahalsa is an incarnation of Vishnu, hence the name Mahalsa Narayani (Mohini, a a beautiful damsel representing the form of an enchantress).

There are several legends associated with the deity and how she came into being.

For starters, the Sanatan Dharma followers (or Hindus) were living happily and peacefully from Gandhara Desa (today's Afghanistan) to Philippines (including Tibet and China's Yunnan Province) centuries ago.

My ancestors were believed lived somewhere in Kashmir to Nepal belt five thousand years back. Mahalsa Narayani temple was somewhere in Nepal.

The Goddess deity was moved from Nepal to Aurangabad in Maharashtra.

During the Mugal invasion in Aurangabad the idol was moved to a secret location in Goa. Later, the deity was housed in a temple at a shrine in village of Verna which is now the site of an industrial estate.

Along with other 4000 Goan temples, this beautiful temple at Verna was also marked for destruction by the Portuguese missionaries around 1543 as a part of inquisition.

However, before the actual demolition could take place the idol of the deity was smuggled away across the river by faithful devotees, to the safer locale of Mardol, where it is located today.

Mahalasa is KulaDevatha for my Gotra. My Gotra is Vishwamitra- Aghamarshana- Kamsi.

"What's a Gotra?"

Gotra = lineage (Sanskrit). Many lines of descent from the major Rishis (Sages or Saints or Seers) were later grouped separately.

The sages were probably the source of the gene pool in ancient India.

The Gotra is a system that associates a person with his most ancient or root ancestor in an unbroken lineage.

Why Am I a Hindu?

For instance, if a person says that he belongs to the Vaashishtha Gotra then it means that he traces back his ancestry to the ancient Rishi Vashishtha. So Gotra refers to the root person in a person's lineage.

There are approximately 49 Gotras. The major Gotras were divided into ganas (subdivisions) and each gana was further divided into groups of families.

People belonging to various castes may have same Gotra Hindu social system. Even Gods have Gotra - Sri Rama is considered to be of Vaashishtha Gotra and Sita is of Vatsa Gotra. Venkateswara belongs to Bharadwaja Gotra.

For thousands of years, people maintained the genetic track in their own way – never mixing it up or doing anything which will disturb the track – so that their progeny come out well - remember, those sages perfected life-style to attain 'Ayur, Arogya and Saukhyam'(longevity, health and happiness).

The system was founded upon yoga, meditation, pranayama (In many forms like Sandhya Vandana, Surya Namaskar, Shodasa Karma etc) and perfect food habit based upon pure vegetarianism.

It was known as "Sattvik" life style. The life-expectancy of an average human being was 126 years then - that too with good health.

"Is Gotra scientific and relevant today?" You might ask.

I am not an expert to comment on that.

Our ancestors considered the best method to verify the genetic feasibility of a marriage is to prevent same Gotra marriage.

Based on the knowledge and traditions inherited from our forefathers, people who fall under the same Gothra have brotherly and sisterly relationship.

Hence our ancestors do not agree for the marriage of a boy and girl of the same Gotra as the Bride and a Bridegroom belonging to the same Gotra are considered to be siblings. Hence it is prohibited for them to marry even if they belong to distant families.

Such marriages may cause genetic disorders in their offspring. It's a fact that we all inherit the DNA of our ancestors.

If both are from the same lineage, they will carry more or less the same type of DNA. So, Gotra system may have had some wisdom to avoid in breeding.

Today, we can conduct a DNA test of little bone of someone who died a hundred years ago and compare it with your DNA and find if he was your grandfather. You can do this even for someone who died ten thousand years ago.

Modern science is researching more on this. They can find something that works for your DNA, and all the people who have that type of DNA will get benefit. Reflect this on Sattvik life-style.

If marriages take place within the same Gotra then the risk of Recessive Gene Disorder (RGD) becomes higher.

But it does not mean every such couple will give birth to a baby with the RGD.

If two recessive genes, one from mother and the other from father, happen to join then the manifestation of single gene-specific disease is sure.

According to medical science, an inbred man or women may suffer from as many as 6000 ailments, arising out of genetic disorder.

The Gotra System might have had its benefits in its initial days - so Gotra was the single criteria for marriage. But thousands of years later today Gotra is replaced by superstitious horoscope matching and material gains in matrimonial alliances.

The Hindu Marriage Act of 1955 legalizes marriage between members of the same Gotra. So, it doesn't have any legal or traditional sanctity today.

Very few people (especially those who belong to Brahmin community) know about their Gotra. Even they are not following the life-style perfected by those Sages.

We don't know how many of our grandparents maintained the lineage. There have been plenty of cross-breeding, inter-connections, mutations and conversions happened during the last few centuries.

There are cases of artificial insemination too. So the chances of having the same recessive gene or perfect gene are very scarce ... (around 0.000001%). So, we cannot prove anything in a laboratory.

Still, why should one take such risk? I am seeing and listening to hundreds of miseries in life - diseases, infertility, stress, depression, failures etc. It could have come from RGD too. And we have fools-proof system to fight it out.

Hence, I advocate the Sattvik life style to all. Even if we do not know our Gotra and even if Gotra is irrelevant today, our DNA would quickly heal itself by being Sattvik.

Hence it is worth your life. As you go ahead in your life you will understand this truth.

Chapter - 44

Brahmins - Victims are penalized!

They say:
1. Indian Brahmins have been oppressing the lower caste population in India.
2. Brahmins introduced the inhuman "untouchability"
3. Brahmins are cunning, parasitic exploiters and creators of the iniquitous caste system.
4. Indian sub-continent's biggest problem was 5000 years of Brahmin oppression!
5. Brahmins never allowed others to read and write or to learn Sanskrit!
6. Brahmins are arrogant, dis-respective, communal and abusive extremists who whip the dalits (lower caste Hindus) till they die.
7. Brahmins exploited and continue to exploit everyone else.
8. Brahmins authored the Hindu scriptures just to ensure their own highest position in the social hierarchy.

The list is endless! And any educated person believes this as 100% truth. Even those who born in today's Brahmin caste are apologetic about their birth due to these "truths"!

However, these 'truth' arguments clearly lack historical validity and logical consistency. It is merely a case of "repeat a lie a hundred times and it will become the truth".

(Joseph Goebbels' theory). It is amazing to see that how fiction can become truth in course of time!

Let's examine truth based on facts and real history.

To start with, there is no SINGLE Brahmin God in Hinduism! All Gods are from backward castes, dalits and tribals. Brahmins never created the concept of Gods in Hinduism.

There was no even SINGLE Brahmin King that ruled India. To be able to oppress others requires positions of power.

The Brahmin's traditional occupation was that of temple priest (purohit) officiating religious functions. Their sole income was Biksha (alms) given by the land-lords (non-Brahmins). And another section of Brahmins were teachers, that too without salary.

Vedic literature was mostly written by non-Brahmins! The most powerful of the Dharma shaastra, that gives Brahmins a high status, is the Manusmriti written by Manu, a non-Brahmin. Brahmin means a profession (Varna) then, not a caste.

If the reading and writing of Sanskrit was confined to Brahmins, then how do you have the tribal Valmiki composing Ramayana? Ved Vyas, who classified four vedas and wrote Mahabharata, was born to a fisher-woman.

Sanskrit was used mostly by non-Brahmin writers - there are very few scriptures in Sanskrit authored by Brahmins.

We consider the teachings of Ved Vyas, Vashishtha, Valmiki, Krishna, Rama, Agasthya, Vishwamitra, Shrunga, Gowthama, Buddha, Mahavira, Tulsidas, Thiruvalluvar, Kabir, Vivekananda, Gandhi, Narayana guru etc as most valuable.

If none of them were Brahmins, why cry so much about Brahmin didn't allow you to learn?

There are numerous works on bhakti by non-Brahmin bhakti saints. Brahmins never prevented others from learning.

Brahmins were neither rich nor powerful at any point of time in history. Pick up any old Indian story book, you will see 'Garib Brahmin' (Poor Brahmin) quoted as a virtue. (Remember Kuchela-Krishna story?)

Though their profession was considered as highest stature of the society, the Brahmin ascetics' only way of survival was alms given by people.

The biggest contribution of Brahmins is sustaining the best language ever spoken in the earth - Sanskrit. If you learn English or Arab, you have commercial benefits.

Nobody ever promoted Sanskrit. Without any benefits, Brahmins took up voluntary task of learning Sanskrit. Then, now you accuse them of monopoly in Sanskrit!

Dr.B.R. Ambedkar, the father of Indian constitution, stated that "untouchability" began in Indian sub-continent after 400 AD, when beef-eaters shunned as "untouchables."

When people of India were forced to embrace Islam by invaders, many Hindus, including those in the professions of Brahmin and Kshatriya among others decided they would not accept Islam at any cost – even if they die.

To destroy their Dharmabhiman (religious pride), swabhiman (self-respect) and rashtraabhiman (pride in nationality), they were forced into carrying the night soil and engage in leather-work.

This is how Scheduled Castes were created. They were forced to eat cow-meat. Then they have marked them as lower caste.

Peace-loving people were pushed into "unclean occupations" because they refused to bow before invaders and convert to invader's religions during the medieval times, thus making them "untouchables", as per many historians.

Whatever, it is obvious that caste system and evil practices like Sati were introduced after around AD 500, thanks to insecurity created among Indians by invaders! Slavery was unheard in India till then.

All ancient literature gives highest position to Brahmins, because of the virtue and ethics they upheld.

Can you quote a single incident of violence by those "merciless Brahmins" ever happened anywhere?

Historical evidences show that poor hapless Brahmins were beheaded by Arabian invaders, crucified in Goa by the Portuguese Inquisition, vilified by British missionaries, and morally crucified today by their own brothers and sisters.

Aurangzeb massacred 150,000 Brahmins and their families in Benares, Ganga gnat, Haridwar, etc... He wouldn't eat his everyday breakfast without seeing a bunch of "janeoos" (holy thread) soaked in the blood of Brahmins after killing them!

The brutal and fanatic barbarians from Portugese mercilessly persecuted and killed lakhs of Konkani Brahmins who refused to get converted, in Konkan-Goa.

The brutal barbarian Francis Xavier, who led the massacre, later canonized as Saint.

Sarawat Brahmins were living peacefully in Kashmir and Gandhara desa-regions-(part of today's Afghan-Pakistan included) area. You can't see them there now.

The foreign invaders killed thousands of Saraswats. Pundits, the original inhabitants of Kashmir were tortured and driven out of their dwellings in Kashmir.

Genocide of Kashmiri Pundits has reached its climax with terrorism succeeding in 'CLEANSING' the valley of this ancient ethno-religious community.

Dr. Ambedkar quoting Muslim historians says the first act of religious zeal by Mohammad bin Qasim, the first Arab invader, was circumcision of Brahmins.

"But, after they objected, he put all above the age of seventeen to death."

In early 19th century, Tipu Sultan's army descended in Melkote on a Deepavali day and massacred 800 citizens, mostly of a sect known as Mandyam Iyengars. He was a fanatic killer.

Brahmins, who historically dedicated their lives for the sake of Dharma and the welfare of the society, are still persecuted in modern India for their falsely alleged sins of the past!!!

The anti-Brahmin theory was planned and successfully planted by hostile religious invaders, colonialist and missionaries of conversion and by politicians to keep the public blind and at the same time rob Indians off everything.

This baseless theory was propagated by Leftists, priests and religious leaders from hostile aggressive religions, separatists and casteists, die-hard fans of invaders, the British etc.

And modern literate believe in this utter non-sense!

When they attack Brahmins, their target is unmistakably Hinduism!

The prayer of a Brahmin was: "Loka Samastha Sukino BHavantu" (May all the beings in all the worlds be happy).

In turn, the world is trying to crucify them, for no fault of them. Brahmins are never involved in any caste-based violence in India TILL this day!

People ask me: "Uday, was everything about Brahmin all good?"

Why Am I a Hindu?

"No - Some Brahmins certainly would have manipulated caste system - just as they do in political parties or religious groups.

Insecure Brahmin communities may have later developed into closely held groups or castes for survival.

There were also few exceptions among Brahmins as a community - like Peshwa Chitpawan Brahmins, Namboodiri chieftains of Kerala, Bhumihar chieftains of Bihar, few short lived minor kingdoms like Anangpal, Jaipal and Bhamini - who were either rich or powerful.

There were Brahmins who exploited others using there status in the society making use of situations, just like corrupt Bureaucrats.

They are few, not even one percent of the Brahmin. Should we generalize the whole community for the mistakes done by a small section among them?"

During feudal times, the land-owning class (Zamindars) oppressed dalits. Even today, OBCs also oppressed the dalits. But Brahmins became the scapegoat.

There is so much of vicious propaganda against Brahmins that the modern Brahmin always felt apologetic, for the oppression allegedly committed by the Brahmin class on the lower class.

Brahmins have been torch bearers of spiritual knowledge, upheld the spiritual and cultural legacy, kept the sanctified rituals alive and gave a distinct identity to sanatan Dharma.

Brahmin-bashing is reverse discrimination, another form of discrimination nonetheless!

It's very unfair to marginalize such an important community from Indian political relevance and discourse. Caste was always just a political tool of rulers.

Brahmins were pushed to bottom in level of importance and treated as villains (scape goat) in the caste based politics since elections/democracy meant use of populist methods which was easy to sell.

For many past centuries, mostly Christians and Muslims were ruling India. Do we have to blame Brahmins for everything that went wrong in India? Brahmins have never ruled India.

Even after Independence, if Castiesm exists in India, who are to blame other than rulers?

Modern Brahmins having abandoned their traditional way of life and being cut off from their traditions, suffer from an unjustified guilt complex and have swallowed this suppression propaganda uncritically.

Caught between the greed of the masses, the unscrupulousness of the politicians and the malice of the real exploiters, they are persecuted mercilessly in modern India.

There have always been deliberate attempts to confuse the concept of Brahmamism with the caste of Brahmins in India.

Caste system, introduced during medieval period because of invaders, is absolutely wrong. It's against Sanatan Dharma.

According to our ancestors, everybody should thrive to become a real Brahmin.

For the sake of a beautiful green world, let's support Brahmamism that propagates non-violence and peace.

The intended or actual meaning of Brahmin is one who has knowledge about Brahmam, the ultimate and impersonal divine reality of the universe from which all being originates and to which it returns.

Let's fight against evil caste system. You don't have to compensate poor Brahmins for the utmost cruelty shown to them. At least, give them equal opportunity in terms of merit.

Chapter - 45

What's Brahmam? Is it scientific?

Many readers ask these questions. Answer to the second question first. The answer is NO! Now, the first question - the honest answer must be: "I really don't know".

How can anybody define something that cannot be scientifically explained?

To make things simple, I am reproducing part of a discussion between me and my old walk friend and philosopher Gopikrishna (who is no more now) about Brahmam. This happened nearly 20 years ago.

This is what he said: "Uday, Brahman means the absolute reality - it is eternal, and not subject to death, decay, or decomposition.

Brahman is Nishkriya (means not active or undynamic. It is Nirguna (means no attributes or without qualities). ONLY Brahman is real; the material world is unreal or illusionary (Brahma satyam jagat mithya). "

"Could you please explain?" I asked him.

"What's in your finger? You would say, "Its ring". But I would say it is "gold". The ring is an illusion, but gold is reality"

"Ji, I would call it a "gold ring". So it contains all. You just said material world is unreal and illusionary. How can you use unreal thing to prove real? So your example doesn't make any sense to me." I said.

Why Am I a Hindu?

"Uday, you won't understand. It is like you are seeing a rope in the dark; it is mistaken for a snake. We mistakenly superimpose the image of an illusory snake onto the real rope.

In just such a way we superimpose the illusion of objects etc. upon the Brahmam"

"Ji, there is a huge logical fallacy in your example. For me, snake and rope are real. You say those are part of material world (Jagat), hence unreal. Now, mistaking rope for a snake is just mind-coined confusion in the absence of light. It is just an error in judgment.

You cannot use a silly error to explain or prove existence of Brahmam. The fundamental fallacy in this much-hyped example is that, according to you both snake and rope are unreal (mithya). How can you use unreal (mithya) to prove the real (Satya) exists. It doesn't prove anything about Brahmam," I said.

"Hmm. You are a tough-nut to crack Uday. Let me quote a more scientific example," he pointed towards a table in his room: "This is a table. But is it a real table? No. It is made up of molecules. The molecule is made up of atom..."

"Yeah, Ji, I got it. Atoms are made up of sub-atomic particles, then comes nucleus, neutrons, protons and if we go further you can reach quantum..." I said.

"You said it. Table is unreal but the quantum energy is real. We can call this quantum energy or cosmic energy that is inside each and everything as Brahmam..."

"Again, it is another invalid argument. Ji, table exists, so is molecules, atoms etc. How can one's existence disprove existence of the other?

I know you will now quote another much-hyped example of clay pot and tell me that pot is unreal and clay is real...As far as I am concerned, all are reality. I can see it and feel it."

"Oh Uday, that's atheist's argument (nasthik tharka). But you are not one, as you believe in Vishnu and Shiva...all gods..."

"Ji, I am not nasthik. I am a rational thinker. I follow something that can be explained scientifically and logically. Sanatan Dharma is pure science. I can explain the concepts of Vishnu and Shiva. But how can you define or explain Brahmam?"

"Brahmam is unexplainable. It is beyond our mind. You can experience Brahmam only when you cross over towards liberation (Moksha, Nirvana or Mukti). For which you have to shed your "ego" (ahankara) or the feeling of "I" from you. That's the final stage a human being can reach - before he experience Brahmam and be a Brahmam..."

"Ji, haha...Beautiful escape route. But there is a huge blunder in your philosophy..."

"Aha...this is the ultimate philosophy. Advaita Vedanta...millions follow it...And you silly human being call it escape route and blunder?" Gopikrishna got bit angry.

"Ji, yes. There is an inherent blunder in this philosophy. Do you know about species reality?"

"What's that?"

"Cows are red/green colorblind, which means they see every shade of red and green as a version of gray or black. If you tell a cow that there is something known as colour, it will laugh it off. But human can see seven colours of a rainbow.

We cannot see infra-red or ultraviolet. Similarly, the range of human hearing is between 20 to 20,000 decibels. But dogs can hear even 60,000 decibels. Each species have certain limitations."

"Great! You have put the ball in my court now!!!

That's exactly what I told; there are many things beyond human senses..."

"Hmmm. The limitation of senses is known as species reality"

"There ends your argument. Brahmam is beyond human senses..."

"In fact, my argument starts NOW. According to you, similar to a salt crystal dissolves in an ocean; we can experience Brahmam when our ego gets dissolved, right?"

"Yes, absolutely right. The person who understands Brahmam and experience it is called Brahmajnani...Proper profound meditation (dhyana) and disciplined and dedicated practice (sadhana) can make you Brahmajnani" he said.

"But there is a small issue, ji. The salt cannot experience the salty taste. To experience something an experiencer is needed.

If you want to experience something you are needed - that is without the "I", how you can experience something! When "I" dies, how can there be an experiencer to experience the experience?"

He didn't expect that question.

"You said one can become Brahmam when you lose ego. If there is no ego, then who can experience it? And, how a person can experience something beyond his/her species reality?

Otherwise, just like in the case of infra-red and ultra-violet, you should prove it scientifically. Science has tools, methodology, parameters etc. You cannot prove Brahmam that way too."

"But science has limitations..."

"Science is evolving and cannot explain many things. Does that mean all you people say are true?

This is the lame argument posed by all those god-men, fraudsters and soothsayers - 'we are telling truth because, science cannot explain'...What a silly argument is that?"

"But many sages and divine gurus said these things by their experiences..."

"A Schizophrenic sees things that we don't see. He hears voices. The experience is real for him. Can you accept that? What we see in the world is that, a mental patient, either he/she ends up in psychiatric treatment or become god-man (god's messenger or guru).

Ji, personal experience and anecdotal fallacies are not accepted as empirical evidence in science"

"Haha..You are telling all those Vedic sages were nuts?"

"No. Sanatan Dharma cannot have anything unscientific or superstitious. In fact, to best of my understanding, no Vedic literature (Vedas or Upanishads) say Jagat is unreal and only Brahmam is real."

The proponents of Brahmam quote four most popular Mahavakyas (The Great Sayings) (There are many Mahavakyas, but the interpreters select the most suitable ones for them)

1. Prajnanam Brahma = Consciousness is Brahman (Aitareya Upanishad/Rig Veda)
2. Aham Brahmasmi = I am Brahman (Brihadaranyaka Upanishad/Yajur Veda)
3. Tat Tvam Asi = that absolute reality is the essence of what you really are (Chandogya Upanishad/Sama Veda)
4. Ayam Atma Brahma = This Self is Brahman (Mandukya Upanishad/Atharva Veda)

People who are initiated into sannyasa in Advaita Vedanta are being taught the four mahavakyas as four mantras to attain this highest of states in which the individual self dissolves inseparably in Brahmam.

All these great sayings are acceptable. But it doesn't say world is unreal.

"Hmm."

"Ji, you also said Brahmam is Nirguna and Nishkriya, right?"

"Yes, it is"

"The three subtle basic 'gunas' (attributes, components or tendencies) are the very fabric of cosmos.

When these three gunans present, how can you call Brahmam as Nirguna (no gunas)?" I asked him: "According to Vedic literature and Hindu cosmology, the change of form of energy (transformation of energy) constantly happening in cosmos - this appears as cyclical creation and destruction.

Modern science also proved that constant energy change is happening in the entire universe. When this energy transformation happens, how can you call Brahmam as undynamic (Nishkriyam)?" I asked him.

"So, you don't believe in Brahmam, Uday?"

"Yes, I do. And I can prove Brahmam exists...The entire cosmos - that includes mass energy and vacuum - is named as Brahmam. There is no separation of Dwaita or Adwaita. It is like separating infinite and finite.

When you say infinite, it should include finite too. Hence, our Brahmam is something that includes everything. If Jagat is not real, Brahmam is also unreal. The reality depends upon species reality."

We cannot understand or know Brahmam. You need a mind to to understand or know something. Mind=ego. Mind has limitation based upon inputs.

Our mind can be compared to a small spoon.

Brahmam or cosmos is an ocean. We are trying to contain a vast ocean into a small spoon. Is it possible? No.

So there is no point in describing Brahmam. We cannot define that. Then why should we go for futile exercise - an egoistic intellectual overflow that leads to nothing. And even if Brahmam is there or not, what difference it can make in everyday life?

There is no absolute truth or reality. We cannot generalize any statement from any Vedic literature. Everything is questionable. In fact, that's the freedom and beauty of our ancestral teaching.

Everything would appear contradictory and confusing - until and unless you understand the vastness.

Our ancestors believed in freedom of thought and expression. They didn't want us to follow oneness path - there are millions of paths. We can choose according to our choice. But trying to claim "my path is the only path" is plain idiotic.

Just like your fingerprint, each and everything in this universe has separate identity, still it is part of the cosmos. Brahmam is real. So is Jagat.

Mundaka Upanishad says: That supreme Brahman is infinite, and this conditioned Brahman is infinite. The infinite proceeds from infinite. Then through consciousness, realizing the infinitude of the infinite, it remains as infinite alone."

Infinity is a mathematical fallacy. I don't know about the Brahman. But my ego would drag me into the belief. Frankly I don't know. I don't believe in belief.

IshaVasya Upanishad says:

Om poornamadah poornamidam poornaat poornamudachyate

Poornasya poornamaadaaya poornamevaavashishṣyate

(That is whole, this is whole; from wholeness emerges the whole and if you remove wholeness from wholeness, wholeness still remains)

Brahman is in every particle, every being, practically in the whole universe. If Brahman is in all, the whole thing becomes one.

Chapter - 46

Hinduism Vs. Sanatan Dharma

(This chapter may look like repeat as it sums up many points in this book)

"What is the difference between Hinduism and Sanatan Dharma (SD)? What's Hindu Dharma?" - Joseph Sebastian, a young reader, asked me. Seemingly simple question!

"Unfortunately, today's Hinduism has been designed, evaluated and advocated on the basis of Semitic thoughts..." I said." Hinduism as you see today is mostly the distorted version of Sanatan Dharma."

Let's see the difference between SD or Hindu Dharma that was founded upon Vedic traditions and where do today's Hinduism and its practices stand now.

Quick Facts:

1. Sanatan Dharma is strictly for the truth seekers. It doesn't promote any beliefs, though believers also can be a part of it (inclusiveness). The belief-based religions are introduced by Semitic cultures. The believer can not be a truth seeker.

If you question beliefs, you are an infidel and out of the religion.Because, according to them, the ultimate truth is already given in the Holy books and one shouldn't question it.

All you have to or can do is blindly following it. There is no scope for truth seeking in religions.

SD is about individually seeking and experiencing the cosmic truth and seeing divinity in each and everything.

2. Many Hindus today say: "I believe in creator". But the great sages in SD (our ancestors) had pooh-pooed the irrational belief in a creator God as a childish idea some 7000 years ago itself.

If there is a creator, then who created the creator?

Please do not compare the Semitic belief of a creator God with that of Brahma. Brahma is not creator; he is the mythological "ancestor" in Hindu Puranas.

3. Many Hindus apologetically say that "there is only single God, we call it in many names and worship in many forms" to compete with Semitics. What makes you so sure and how can you derive into such belief as long as nothing is proved?

"We have only one God, Brahmam - all Gods are many forms of it," even learned pundits would tell you the same. Brahmam is NOT God, though, like everything else, Gods also may be the manifestation of Brahmam.

The world should contain any sort of beliefs and atheism too. Single God theory has given rise to fanaticism and terrorism.

4. I hear many Hindus saying "I am spiritual" or he is "materialistic". What's the difference between "spiritual" and "material"?

Our ancestors taught us everything is divine. The difference in spirituality and materialism had come to India through 19th century evangelists, Europeans and the British.

They had a historical concept of Church Vs. State. Or Science Vs. Religion.

On the contrary, Indian Sages were scientists who were researching in astronomy to Healthcare (Ayurveda). Science was the foundation of Sanatan Dharma.

5. According to our tradition we had "Devalaya" (God's abode = temples) and NOT "prarthanalaya or aradhanalaya" (prayer halls = Churches and Mosques). Today most of the Hindu temples tend to be anti-Sanatan Dharmic.

A Hindu will not go to temple for at least 7 days if a birth or death happens at home. But in Semitic religions, birth and death are related to their prayer places.

Hindus were not conducting marriages in temples (except in some rare cases) as marriage has nothing to do with temple customs.

Today most of the temples have marriage halls and make it a huge business. The purpose of temple was entirely different from what it is doing now.

The basic rituals in Sanatan Dharma - Shodasha Samskara - have absolutely NOTHING to do with GOD.

6. Gita is NOT a Holy-book like Bible or Quran. Because Semitics believes in one God, one prophet and one book, many people propagate Gita as Holy book.

Krishna or Vyasa doesn't say Gita is the ultimate book. There are 39 Gitas among Vedic literature.

We have thousands of Vedic sacred texts like Gita. When you are in LKG one book is enough. You should learn or read lots of books when you reach at post-graduate level.

7. God fearing - real Hindus never ever fear God. For a Sanatani, God is everywhere and we are also integral part of God. God is rather a good friend than a scary thing. Even Puranic concept of Gods has a scientific base in that.

8. Caste system: SD doesn't advocate any sort of discriminatory Caste system. There was a social system based on Varna (profession) that was a horizontal division and not vertical.

Varna system is proved to be logical and rational. But today's Hindus follow a vulgar caste system.

9. Vedic Dharma (SD) doesn't support any superstitions. Today you can see Hindus follow many superstitions. The traditions as per Vedic literature have scientific basis.

You cannot find any ritual in Sanatan Dharma that you cannot explain logically and scientifically.

A true Hindu is a rational and logical thinker who believes that he/she is divine. The evils like Sati and Child marriage came in our culture with the influence of brutal invaders.

10. Santana Dharmi did not follow superstitions like horoscope matching.

Jyothisha (Astronomy) is Vedanga (limbs of the Veda) but today Hindus use the term Jyothisha with a different meaning – that is astrology.

Vedic Jyothisha (astronomy) has nothing to do with predictive astrology. Our ancestors never followed horoscope matching.

Instead they checked for Gotra and parambara that have scientific reasons. Today lots of Hindus believe in superstitious version of Vastu too.

11. Priesthood: Earlier, the sole income of priests was either Dakshina (donation or payment for the services of a priest).

Today (most of the) Hindu priests are no different from (most of the) Semitic priests - exploitative and greedy.

Traditionally a Brahmin made his living by the way of Bhiksha (begging for alms with the purpose of self-effacement or ego-conquering). Now you can even see many caste Brahmins among the priests.

12. The RIP culture. I have seen many Hindus write "May his/her soul Rest in Peace". Soul is a funny irrational and illogical concept.

We have JeevAtma but it is something else. It doesn't rest and wait in peace - it recycles. There is no "soul" concept in Sanatan Dharma. Jeeva and Atma have nothing to do with soul.

13. Inviting death and darkness on Birthdays: Ask your parents - how did we celebrate our birth days? By lighting lamps and praying "Thamasoma Jyothirgamaya" (From Darkness to Light).

Today, how do the modern Hindus celebrate birthday? By blowing off the lamps and insulting the Agni deva concept of SD

14. Falling prey to organized structure: Many Babas, Mathas, Gurus forms cult and spread their own version of Hinduism for making money. Anything organized will be commercialized, corrupt and perished.

We had Guru Concept only based on teaching of skills or a particular domain of knowledge. But today you can see Gurus who teaches you "how to live".

15. A Hindu is not a sinner. We only have Dharma and Adharma. I hear many people talk about sin. Papa is not sin, it is Adharma.

16. Fake science: This is the single biggest problem that educated Hindus going to face in the future. I would call it a conspiracy theory.

There are some people who connect ancient Sanatan Dharma with science and it is an informal fallacy based on giving the impression that it is scientific.

This is a Trojan horse that tomorrow they can utilize. They intentionally connect something that they can question tomorrow. We have to be careful about such pseudo-intellect Hindus.

Please don't fall into traps of setting western concepts as the 'benchmark' and standardization ignoring our ancestors' ideals.

Read history - the religions or cults do not bring peace; it always makes you piece-piece or piece meat. Our ancestors had a broader universal view. Let's follow that.

The most obvious misconception about Hinduism is that we tend to see it as a religious faith. To be precise, the real Hinduism is a way of life, a Dharma. Dharma does not mean religion.

It is the law that governs all action. Thus, contrary to popular perception, real Hinduism is not a religion. Out of this misinterpretation, most of the misconceptions about Hinduism have come out of these misinterpretations.

Karl Marx said: "Religion is the opium of the people". It's true - he was talking about religions known to him.

He was not aware of a Dharma where even atheists are considered as Sages. He didn't know about a Dharma in which there was no discrimination based on caste, creed, race and color.

Hinduism doesn't have missionaries, crusades and process of conversion. There is no official authority controlling Hindus. There are no Pope/Caliph/any living prophets/intermediaries.

Nobody offers anything (tangible or intangible) for a person to be a Hindu - still thousands of educated people and intellectual voluntarily want to be a Hindu - why?

Ask yourself - do you want to follow Sanatan Dharma or live like blind faith followers of fanatic religions by imitating them?

Chapter - 47

Hinduism = Humanity

There is present and clear danger in front of us. The situation is dangerous than you think. It will kill human race. It will kill humanity. It's a deadly virus.

These viruses have names - Blind faith, irrational beliefs, lopsided concepts and deceptive ideologies.

All we can do is: "Insulate yourself. Immunize yourself. Protect your family (not just individual family, but the whole world -Vasudeva Kudumbakam) from such viruses. We have to support all those who consider human first and religion last."

When people are ready to kill and die for such beliefs, how to stop it? Especially when they attack you from the dark?

How will you eliminate darkness? Put on light.

The only weapon against the belief is truth. Truth can be revealed by science. When we teach science to the generation next, they won't go behind beliefs. They will seek truth.

A truth seeker can immunize himself/herself from such conversions. One has to protect oneself. But you cannot do it alone, you will have to create light for others too.

"Na Abhisheko, Na Samskraha; Simhasya kriyate vanae, Vikramarjita satvasya svayameva mrugendrata"

There is no official coronation ceremony held to declare lion king of jungle. He becomes king by his own attributes and heroic actions.

Swayam Eva Mrigendrata - You can rise to prominence only through its own virtues, strengths, sacrifices and efforts. Nobody's approval is needed! Lion won't bitch about others.

Lion won't spread hate speech. It just acts. It does its karma.

If you don't act, these viruses will destroy your next generation. Politicians will exploit your helplessness. The only hope for humanity is Dharma.

"I really want to do something for Dharma. I am alone, I am an ordinary man - what can I do?" many people ask.

We have lot of other responsibilities or we have to take care of our family. You can also become a millionaire - and live a happy lavish life. But what did you do about the next generation?

Do you want your grandchildren kill or die for blind beliefs? The virus is spreading so fast that it will definitely infect them easily.

Let me tell my personal experience.

No - I am not a Lion. But I can do like a small squirrel. What's my strength and weakness? Looking at weakness, I have plenty. But I have a couple of moderate skillss - I can write.

I have learnt bit about Santan Dharma and modern science. So I decided to use it effectively to create awareness about it.

Many of my friends and relatives said - you are wasting your time, money, efforts, health and life for nothing.

Nobody will support you. I said: "I have always taken huge risks in my life but this is not one of them.

I am doing whatever I can for our Dharma". There is no other "all inclusive" solution for the humanity.

So I continued my Karma without any expectation. I am writing not for money, fame or name - so I don't have to worry whether somebody appreciate, criticize or tease me.

I do everything with a prayer: "Krishnarpanamastu" (Everything I offer to Krishna or the divine).

At least I can be catalyst for few people to think and creating awareness. I didn't want to compromise, so I have decided not to write in any publications, magazines, websites or newspapers.

I will write only in my website or share in my social media accounts. But I let all readers share it for the benefit of humanity.

The results are wonderful. The number of e-mails I am getting is overwhelming. I was expeting that I would be instrumental in bringing changes in few people's lives. But as a chain reaction it went to the multiples of 100s.

Once I start taking care of Dharma, some unknown unexplainable blessings happened to me.

Unknown people all around the world considering me as a brother or friend! Everything appeared brighter and happier! I am telling you from my own experience.

So let's do our little bit for creating awareness. That's what our ancestors taught us. They didn't patent sacred wisdom. They gave everything to humanity.

Everybody can do it. You don't need any organization, money or power to bring awareness among few people at least.

So, here is my request: "Please don't spend time on hate speech, finding fault of religions, beliefs, ideologies, concepts etc. It's of no use. The more you get angry with them, the more you are empowering them.

You are energizing them and falling in their trap. Don't be football of the virus-makers. They want you to get angry and react. Please respond without emotions. Be a Sthiraprajna. Look at a lion - how calm and elegant he is!"

Let's do our level best to spread awareness of Sanatan Dharma - it will show light in the darkness. You don't need certificate and validation from others. You are not trying for a job.

Every day before going to bed, ask yourself - "What I have done for our Dharma? Did I spend at least ten minutes a day for it? No avatar will come and save us - that's just a belief.

Rama and Krishna were historical character - they elevated to the level of Vishnu's (Cosmic) avatar because they tried to sustain the natural Dharma. So don't wait for avatars.

Who knows, maybe you can be an avatar. Bean avatar yourself - do your the best for our Dharma.

We have seen bigger powers - the Greek or Romans ruling the world. Where are they now? We have withstood attacks of Huns, Ghoris, Khans, Gaznis, and Portugese.

Religious terrorists can kill all other cultures, they can rule the world, but how-much-ever they try, they can't touch Sanatan Dharma.

Why? Sanatana Dharma is the only ideal theory and practical philosophy in this universe for the humanity to survive - it is ordained by nature itself. It doesn't need prophets, gods, armies to sustain.

There will be silent followers whom the Dharma will appoint - they are not here to make money in the name of religion like Swamis, Gurus or political parties.

Look around - only philosophers, intellectuals, real scientists, authors are getting themselves associated or converted to Sanatan Dharma - nobody asks or prompts them to get converted. But they feel that this is the only way for humanity to survive.

Believe me - you can't fight blind beliefs with violence or power. The only weapons with which you can destroy blind faith are truth and science.

Otherwise how could Hindu dharma still survive despite attack from all corners for the last few centuries?

The cosmic intelligence will choose some people like you to work silently for the sake of humanity.

Sanatan Dharma has been preserved through such people - not by warlords, chieftains or angry hate-speech.

Nobody will offer you heaven for your good deed. For, the heaven is just a psychological space. Heaven is here on earth! Let's be human. Let's be Sanatan Dharmi. Let's be a real Hindu. Let's make the earth a heaven.

Dharma protects the protected. Remember - The word Hinduism needs to be replaced by Humanity.

(End)

The Secret of Krishna's Birth

Excerpts from my forthcoming book: The Secret of Krishna's Birth

INTERVIEWING KRISHNA!!!

A full length interview with Krishna.

Excerpts from the Interview:

Q: "Krishnaji, I have a doubt...The Gita has at least 745 verses. Even if it takes one minute to read one verse, it will take 745 minutes = 12.41 hours. The situation was the war-field in Kuruksetra All those in the battlefield stood still till then?"

Krishna: "No...I had sent Gita as ZIP file to Arjuna's conscious. It's beyond your knowledge and logic. Your science is yet to evolve and will take few more hundred years to reach that stage. You can now talk to somebody in USA over wireless connections. If you tell this to people who lived 100 years ago, would they believe it?"

Q: "Krishnaji, you gods crack jokes?"

"Why not? We Gods have jokes on astrologers and some doctors. When they open their mouth about your future or if somebody plans (as if they can) the future, our (God's) comedy time begins"

Forthcoming books by Udaylal Pai

1. **You Don't Eat a Lion Doesn't Men Lion Won't Eat You!** *(Why Do Bad Things Happen to Good People?)*
2. **The Secret of Krishna's Birth** *(Interview with Krishna)*
3. **Bye-bye Positive Thinking** *(Positive Thinking: Pseudo Scientific Con!)*
4. **Mind Your Mind** *(Does the Human Mind Possess Any "Super Powers"?)*
5. **Happiness Unlimited** *(The ancient secrets of instant happinessin life)*
6. **Tidbits of Life** *(Destiny or Free Will)*
7. **The Book of Hindu Gods** *(A compendium of Hindu Gods and Mythological Characters)*
8. **Is Rebirth for Real?** *(The science and rationale behind Rebirth)*
9. **Art of Dying** *(Ancient secrets of fear and stress management)*
10. **Hindu Economics** *(The theory and practice for prosperity)*
11. **Astrology, Vastu, Reiki, Faith healing – Hoax or Real?** *(Can anybody predict your future? About pseudoscience)*

Website: *http://udaypai.in/*
Facebook: *https://www.facebook.com/udaylal.pai*
Twitter: https://twitter.com/udaylalpai

E-mail: udaylalpai1@gmail.com

WhatsApp: +91-9447533409

Printed in Great Britain
by Amazon